WASTING THE DAWN

San Diego, CA

AG
HUR

Published by IDW Publishing
4411 Morena Blvd., Ste 106, San Diego, CA 92117
www.idwpublishing.com

Softcover ISBN 1-933239-35-2
Hardcover ISBN 1-933239-50-6
Hardcover S&N ISBN 1-933239-51-4

Printed in Canada

Written by **David Hurwitz** for AFC Studio
Artwork by **Breed** for AFC Studio
Cover Artwork by **Ben Templesmith**
Designed by **Robbie Robbins**
Compiled and Enabled by **Robert Scott** & AFC Studio
Edited by **Kris Oprisko**

Originally presented in 10 limited edition signed and numbered
chap books. Each volume was limited to 250 copies.

First Edition

08 07 06 05   1 2 3 4 5

Visit AFC Studio online at **www.afcstudio.com**

WASTING THE DAWN

Written by
David Hurwitz

Art by
Breed

"Everyone knows what they are just by the word: bloodsucking"

VAMPIRES

Everyone knows what they are just by the word: bloodsucking, undead creatures of the night. But what do we really know about them? Are they the ugly and vicious creatures depicted silently by F. W. Murnau, or more the romantic and gothic loners penned by Anne Rice? Do they fear garlic and crosses as the wise Edward Van Sloan told us? Was Peter Cushing right when he said they couldn't traverse moving water? What about not being able to enter Bernard Hughes's house since the vampire hadn't been invited in? Must they rush back to their coffins at night or will the soil from their homeland keep them safe? What about sunblock SPF 5000? Are there day-walkers? Even the whole sucking of human blood comes into question thanks to Robert Sean Leonard and his little mini-fridge of pig's blood.

The bottom line is that there are no set rules for vampires. Every time a writer sits down to tell a story, whether it be a George Hamilton comedy, the life of a heavy metal band, or a horror tale about a small town in Alaska, the writer has to set his own rules for the undead. Like going down a supernatural checklist, the writer gets to play Dr. Frankenstein and create his own monster. A little of this, a pinch of that, and he's created his own version of Nosferatu. And there are no wrong answers. It's the writer's job to set forth these rules as the story goes along and stick with them; to tell the reader what the vampires can do, what they are afraid of, and what will end their eternal life.

So as you sit down to read this or any other vampire story, you need to remember that the only rules that apply are those set forth by the author's imagination. As the reader, it's your job to immerse yourself into the strange new world laid out in front of you. So close your eyes, take a deep breath, and then turn the page and see what the amazing world of Randall Springfield has to offer.

Dan Wickline
April 6, 2005

No eternal reward will forgive
us now for wasting the dawn.

-James Douglas Morrison

Randall Springfield awoke in the sand. He did not open his eyes. He knew better than to do that. Sensation drifted gradually back. The dry pressure all around him. The tickle of sand in the cracks and crevices of his skin. Grains between his fingers and toes. In the creases of his knees. Pressing almost into his breathless lips and nostrils. Caking in the corners of his sightless eyes. His body felt warm but not hot. Early evening, he decided.

He thrust an arm upward, away from his chest. It had taken him a moment to remember how to move, and a moment longer to make his arm obey. Wind stirred the hairs on his outstretched limb. The sand fell away, running down his skin in an arid stream. He thrust out his other arm, then lowered them both to the surface of the sand, palms downward. Slowly the muscles in his back and legs spasming into life, Randall Springfield sat up.

Sand ran off his body, pouring off his chest, leaking reluctantly from his hair. Eyes still closed, Randall gathered his feet under him and stood.

Once he felt sure of his balance he scrubbed his hands roughly through his hair. It felt longer than when he had buried himself, nearly to the shoulder. Sand pelted his chest and back, stung his face. Soon his head and hands were relatively clean. Very slowly, very carefully, he opened his eyes. Sand got in them anyway. He resisted the urge to rub at them, letting tears clear his vision.

The ruins were just as he remembered them, nothing changed. Brick walls the color of sand, big chinks showing. Sunlight slanting through the remains of a wooden roof that seemed just a little too low. Deep sand covered the floor, with a man-shaped depression in the middle. The light seemed to be fading.

Randall crouched in a corner of the room and dug up his pack. A good deal of sand had gotten into it, but no scorpions or other desert creatures. He straightened, stretching his arms towards the gaps in the roof. Six weeks, he thought. Maybe more. Next he scraped vigorously at his body, hard nails taking off layers of dead skin along with the sand. After fifteen minutes he felt almost clean, though there were a couple places he could not reach. He shook out his clothes and put them on. He would have to take a shower at the first hotel. There was no getting around it.

Swinging his long brown coat up over his shoulder, he walked slowly into the front room. A red sun sinking below distant mountains glared at him through the hollow doorway. The peaks themselves cast long shadows over the canyon below. Randall coughed at the taste of sand, and only then remembered to restart his lungs. The last time he slept he had forgotten for two whole days, only noticing when he tried to speak to someone.

Looking around the room, Randall saw the remains of a fire and a large number of crushed beer cans stacked in an irregular pyramid. Rose must be around somewhere, he thought. Very few people ever visited the Dolomite mine, let alone spent the night in the old ridge-fort above. The place was dull, even as historical sights went, and nearly three hours drive from genuine civilization. It was a good place to hide, to sleep and heal.

He walked outside, shrugging into his coat, up the path along the edge of the ridge. The ground looked nearly level, but Randall could feel the grade in the backs of his legs. Soon he could look down on the gaping roof of the fort below. He reached the ridge-top, smiling as he caught sight of the rock chair. Long ago, some clever miner had built himself a seat of adobe bricks and discarded stones hauled out of the shaft. It was big, more of a couch really. Fist size pieces of quartz glinted in the armrests. Thumbnail cactus sprouted from the unmortared chinks. Randall dusted the seat with the tail of his coat and sat. The most amazing thing about the rock chair, so far as he was concerned, was that it somehow managed to be comfortable. And the view from the ridge-top was truly vast.

The setting sun lanced over the mountains and across the canyon, burning fierce and red before its death below the peaks. In that last burst of light, the land below took on the aspect of an alien sea. The dunes became frozen swells of strange water, white as wind-cut bone. Scrub and cacti seemed to be aquatic plants, stilled momentarily in their dance with the tides. Small animals poked their heads above the surface, then disappeared through holes in the petrified waves. Randall had not set foot in the sea in decades. The view, the contrast, pleased him.

Just as the sun vanished from sight, Randall spotted Rose approaching the ridge-fort. He sported his old leather jacket and a new beard. He held a grocery bag under one arm. "Greetings, Renfield!" Randall called. "How nice to see you again." Rose made a show of shading his eyes and scanning the ridge-top. Then he gave a little laugh and stomped the rest of the way up the hill.

Reaching the plateau, he set the bag down with metallic thud and draped himself over one arm of the rock chair. "You would wake up an hour after I decide to go into town for supplies. Your timing has always been shit." He smiled, and reached down into the bag. "Beer?"

Randall accepted a can and popped the lid. "I should really stop drinking alcohol. Brain cells take forever to grow back, and I've only got so many of them. I just might run out some day." He took a long drink, then made a face. "Jesus, didn't they have a refrigerator?"

"Small though Ocotillo is, they do have most of the major appliances." Rose drained his can in one continuous series of swallows, crushed it, then popped another. "I, however, am short on cash as usual." His lopsided grin seemed to make the new beard bristle. "And if it's true what you said about brain cells, I'll be starting in the red."

"All in due time, my boy. All in due time." Randall arched his back. Several of his vertebrae cracked audibly. "I'm still not used to this shit myself sometimes, and I've been at it for years."

They drank in silence for a while. The sky deepened from blue to black. Stars hung in great unwinking clusters. A sliver moon glowed just above the horizon, turning the valley shadowless and grey. Rose polished off another can, then cleared his throat. "So, did you find her?"

Randall sighed. "No." He leaned back in the chair, hands behind his head. "You hear about that little town in Texas where they kept pulling people out of the river with their heads cut off?"

Rose rummaged through his bag, coming up with a strip of beef jerky. "Yeah, it's been pretty big news."

"Well that used to be one of Mother's bad habits. I thought it might be her, so I went to check it out. Turned out to be just some psycho asshole collecting human skulls."

"I heard they found the guy with his throat cut. Bled to death in his breakfast nook. Cops figured it must have been some vigilante thing, or maybe just an extreme suicide. They're not investigating too hard, I guess." He ripped off a piece of beef jerky with his teeth and chewed it vigorously. "You telling me you did that?"

Randall shrugged. "I didn't want anybody else getting hold of him."

"What do you mean?" Rose squinted at him curiously, his fuzzy brown eyebrows bunching.

Randall turned away from the view to look his friend in the face. "There are some of my... relations... that get their kicks by recruiting killers, psychotics, bad-ass criminals. You don't want to run into one of those boys. Immortality tends to erode the conscience anyway. Just imagine if you never had one to begin with."

Rose nodded slowly. "Sounds nasty." He extended a strip of salted flesh. "Beef jerky?"

"Thank you, no." Randall stood and walked slowly along the cliff's edge. "You been here long?"

Sliding down from the chair arm, Rose stretched himself out full length and stared up at the stars. His boots dangled over the far end of the stone seat. "Not long. A couple of weeks. When you didn't show up in Vegas, I figured I'd find you here. It's probably just as well."

Randall turned abruptly. "Why's that?'" He looked down at the sprawled figure, frowning in irritation.

"Well," said Rose, "Let's just say I'm wanted in Nevada now, too." He flinched at the expression on Randall's face, only partly visible in the fading light. He sat up quickly.

"What was it this time? Another drugstore?" Seen from the chair, Randall's eyes were pits of shadow lengthening into sharp spikes of darkness below his cheekbones. His tangled hair stirred in the wind.

Rose took a sip of beer, then looked away. "Seven Eleven, actually." Before Randall could say anything he continued. "I know, I know. It was stupid. But what else could I do? I had no money. I needed food and a drink, not to mention gas. And you hadn't showed." He shrugged helplessly.

Bending down, Randall gripped the other man's shoulders, digging his nails into the hard leather. "My dear Renfield, you know how much I hate it when you deliberately do something that impairs your usefulness. Once we find her I'll give you everything I promised, but until then you have to help me. So please, please, think before you do these things." He rose, turned away, and gazed out into the darkening gulf below.

"I'm sorry," Rose said quietly. He inched up until he was sitting on the back of the rock chair, boots resting on the seat.

"It's all right." Randall's voice seemed to float up out of the canyon. "I have business here in California anyway. And there's some people I'd like you to meet."

"Swell." Rose pulled another beer from his bag. "Here's to it." He drained the can, crushed it, and stuffed it back in the sack. "So," he asked lightly, "do I qualify as a bad-ass criminal?"

"You're going to make a beautiful immortal." Randall still faced away, standing on the very edge of the cliff. He hardly seemed to move at all, even when he spoke. "You're just crazy enough to survive."

Rose let that sink in, chin resting in his hands. After a while he ventured a new subject. "What delayed you, anyway? You still haven't told me."

Randall stood motionless, feeling the pull of the wind. He suppressed the fleeting desire to leap off the ridge-top into blackness and space. His skin still itched with sand. Shaking himself, he began to pace along the ridge once more. "I had to walk out of Texas. Nobody was picking up hitchhikers and I didn't dare steal a car, what with all the cops on the highway. I traveled at night, straight as I could out of the state, through fields and ranches and waste. You wouldn't believe how big that fucking state really is. You just don't see it driving.

"Anyway, one night I hop this fence, walk across what looks like a dead farm. There are plow furrows, but nothing's in them. The soil looks dried and cracked. I pass pretty close to this beat up shack and as I walk by a light comes on. There are no windows, but it shines out between the boards. A door opens and this bent old man levels a shotgun at me, barrels resting across one arm. He spits a wad of tobacco into the dirt. Doesn't say anything. I just keep walking, not even looking at him, not going any faster or slower than before. Without a word the old fucker shot me in the back."

Rose whistled in the darkness. "That's Texas for you."

"Indeed." Randall found another beer and popped it open. "I stood up pretty quick, blood coming out these big blast holes in my chest. You should have seen that bastard jump! He turned dead fucking white and ran backwards into the shack, slammed the door. I pounded on the walls for a bit, but the blood loss started to hit me and I staggered off. I dropped just short of another fence, had to sit for while.

"You can probably imagine the rest. I dragged along by night, never getting very far. Finally I made it to set of railroad tracks. I jumped the next cattle car that came along. Scared the shit out of a couple of winos. They actually leapt off in the middle of the wasteland. Took the train through Arizona, dropped off when I recognized the territory. Hiked the rest of the way here."

Rose belched tremendously, the sound echoing faintly off the distant mountains. "Does shit like this happen to you a lot?"

"Only when I'm in a hurry." Randall downed the remainder of his beer and tossed the can back into the sack. "I'd like to start out at dawn, if you don't mind." He stood, scratching his sandy scalp. "Why don't you get some sleep? I need to find food."

"A disgusting practice," Rose muttered, gathering loose beer cans and stuffing them into his bag. "Chewing on live animals. Revolting."

Randall laughed. "You're going to have to get used to the idea sooner or later."

"Are you sure you wouldn't rather have some nice beef jerky?" He pulled some out of the sack and waved it tantalizingly in Randall's direction. "This is teriyaki flavor, yum."

"Thanks all the same." Randall began to descend the ridge. "See you in the morning, Renfield," he called over his shoulder.

※

At dawn Randall kicked Rose awake. The man groaned in his sleeping bag. "Beer," he mumbled, "must have beer." He began to inch forward like a large worm.

"I think you've had enough for now," said Randall. "I'd like to get up into L.A. today, maybe even as far as Santa Barbara." Rose thrashed around on the sandy floor, knocking over his can pyramid. "Would you like some help getting out of there?"

Rose rolled over onto his back, his shaggy hair and bearded face protruding from the top of his bag. "Please." He smiled winningly, then peered curiously down the length of his cocooned body. "I seem to be having some trouble locating the zipper."

Kneeling down in the sand, Randall quickly unzipped the bag. "Thank you." Rose sprung to his feet, still fully clothed except for his boots and jacket. "Now if you'll excuse me…" He hurried out of the fort and up the ridge in his socks. Randall followed him outside and leaned against the adobe wall, watching curiously. At the top of the ridge Rose unbuttoned his fly and urinated off the edge of the cliff for a full four minutes. The stream of liquid scattered and gleamed in the sunlit air.

Rose returned slowly, more mindful of the rocks and burrs in his path. "All better now," he said, and began jamming on his boots. "My bike's at the bottom of the ridge. I've got enough gas to get to Ocotillo, but we'll need to fill up there." He dug into his crumpled grocery bag, removing a box of Pop-Tarts. "You want breakfast?"

Randall did not reply. He merely shrugged into his pack and slung his coat over one shoulder. "Clean up your shit and we'll go."

They descended the ridge in silence. The only sounds came from the faint breeze and the rustling of unseen animals. Even now the heat had begun to build. Randall noticed himself sweating, squinting against the glare of sun on sand. Warmth radiated from the ground, making his boots uncomfortable. He glanced over at Rose, but the other man did not seem to feel the temperature. Randall kept walking.

At the bottom of the ridge sat Rose's motorcycle, a giant horseshoe lock through the back wheel. Rose had rebuilt it from Army surplus, and it looked it. Every piece of metal in it was either dull black or a dark, ugly green. Even the pipes, forks, and fenders, parts that would normally be chrome, consisted of the same dead metal. The seat was patched with peeling layers of electrical tape. A thin film of brown dirt coated the bike. Only the gauges looked clean and new. Two helmets sat side by side on the gas tank.

"You brought me a hard hat?" Randall picked one up and turned it over in his hands.

"Why not?" said Rose, removing the lock. "You may be immortal, but you still wouldn't want to smear your precious brain cells all over the highway, not when you've got places to go and people to see."

"Can't object to that, I guess." Randall shoved the helmet down onto his head. "Ouch, shit!" He yanked it off again quickly.

"You better take your earring out first." Rose pulled his own helmet on and straddled the bike.

"Thanks for the warning." Randall removed the tiny hoop, dropped it into one of his pockets, then replaced the helmet. Foam padding surrounded him on all sides, reducing his vision to a narrow swath. "Much better." Sweat dripped down his neck as he clambered onto the back of the motorcycle. "This thing must turn into a furnace on the road."

"What?" Rose jump-started the bike and the engine coughed into life, vibrating the entire frame. The jackhammer sound of the glass-packed pipes bounced off the ridgeline and echoed through the wide valley.

"Never mind!" Randall yelled as they began to move.

They cruised slowly along a dry arroyo sluiced out of the soil by some long ago flash flood. Rose maneuvered nimbly around the larger rocks and ruts. They passed tall ocotillo, lank arms groping futilely in their dusty wake. A roadrunner darted across their path, a blur of legs and brown feathers. Randall recalled the one he had caught in the night. Very stringy, almost no blood.

The arroyo leveled out into a winding track, carved into the waste by jeep wheels. Soon the black ribbon of the highway came into view on the horizon, partially screened by a hedge of dry brush. Randall thought it looked ridiculous, running through the desert sands like the solidified extrusion of some ancient breed of monster snail, a fragile bridge that natural forces would shatter and grind and one day consume completely. As they drew closer he saw that the shoulders of the asphalt strip had already begun to crumble away and sink into the dust.

They topped the short rise leading to the road. Once the twin wheels hit the tarmac, the ride became much smoother. Rose shifted into high gear and the landscape began to blur. Roadside rocks and scrub flew by in brown haze while straight ahead the road remained unchanging. Randall concentrated on the double yellow line, watched it shrink and vanish in the distance. Reflectors flew towards them, accelerating suddenly before they disappeared. He closed his eyes, surrendering to the forward motion.

༄

Ocotillo is one of those communities that spring up around a strategically located gas station, squatting at the confluence of Interstate Eight and the state highway that leads into the Anza-Borrego Desert State Park. Its main street runs perpendicular to the larger freeway, passing under a low bridge. The only structure south of the overpass is a family diner with parking spaces for semi rigs. North lies the filling station with its adjacent general store, the office of the sheriff and coroner, and the trailer containing the public library. The Ocotillo Bible Church sits across the street from the Lazy Lizard Saloon. Residential streets branch off at regular intervals, named for gunslingers and precious gemstones. A few weathered homes huddle on lots that seem small compared to the vast emptiness surrounding them. Cactus gardens help conceal the satellite dishes.

Rose pulled up beside a rusty gas pump and killed the engine. The two men pulled off their helmets. Randall shook out his damp hair then scratched furiously at his scalp, growling between clenched teeth. "You all right?" asked Rose. "You seemed mighty quiet back there." Bits of his own brown hair stuck plastered to his forehead, but he seemed as cheerful as ever.

"I must have fallen into a road trance." Randall peeled off his coat and slung it over the seat. "This sand is driving me nuts. We'll stop in San Diego, get a room so I can clean up." He stifled the urge to scratch any further and dug through his pack instead, coming up with a large wad of money sealed in a waterproof container. "Pay first, right?"

Rose nodded. "Yeah. And would you look at these prices? Is America that hard up for fossil fuels, I ask you?"

"When you're the only gas station in a seventy mile radius you can pretty much afford to gouge." Randall unscrewed the lid of the container and pulled out a few bills at random. "Want any food?"

"Are you buying?" Rose smiled sweetly, an expression that was effectively ruined by his curly beard.

"I'd just as soon you didn't rip the place off."

"In that case I'll have bag of Doritos, a cold Coke, and a giant pickle." Rose waved him in the direction of the general store. "Go on, go on. Just ask at the counter, they'll know what you mean."

The inside of the store was air-conditioned. Randall savored the temperature drop, although it gave him an instant headache. He left a ten with the old man at the counter, then wandered slowly down the aisles. The place seemed entirely devoted to snack food and alcohol. One tiny shelf held both cat litter and tampons, horribly overpriced. He found Rose's chips and soda, plus a bottle of beer for himself. Back at the register, Randall studied the old man as he rang up the sale. He wore a plaid flannel shirt that looked as if it had a former life as a blanket. Blue veins stood out from his hands and neck. His battered cap might have once advertised something. His face looked etched by the wind. Rose burst through the door at a brisk walk, calling "Urination break!" as he swept towards the back of the store.

"Uh, those are with the gas," said Randall. The old man frowned, warping the lines of his face, and began poking at the register again. Randall yielded to temptation and scratched his scalp.

Shortly, Rose sidled up and leaned against the counter. "So," he asked, glancing from one man to the other, "did you get my giant pickle?" He stared pointedly at the counter. "I don't see a giant pickle. What's the matter Randall, too embarrassed to ask this fellow for a really big pickle?"

Randall rolled his eyes, looked pleadingly at the old man. "He wants a giant pickle."

They sat at a concrete table outside, Randall drinking his beer while Rose ate his pickle in tremendous bites. The heat felt brutal after the cool of the store. "You didn't happen to see the bathroom?" asked Rose.

"No, I think all the fluid in my body was sweated out of me." Randall took a long pull of beer. "Why do you ask?"

"They have the most amazing condom dispenser in there. It's got everything, things I never heard of even. Swedish dusters. Black Mambas. What the hell is a Black Mamba? Is it supposed to be self-evident? 'Cause it's not." He popped open his soda, shotgunned it, then lobbed the can into a wastebasket.

"I'm sure I have no concept."

"And why?" asked Rose, stuffing chips into his mouth. "Why? No one in a town this small could be that hip and happening. And who the hell would drive all the way out here to fuck?" He stared at Randall, hands raised in a classic gesture of confusion.

"Maybe they want to prevent inbreeding." Randall downed the last of his beer and stood up. "You ready to go?"

"I suppose." Rose pitched the remains of his meal in the general direction of the trashcan. "San Diego, you said?"

"Yeah." The inside of Randall's coat was damp, the helmet slick with sweat. "I want to clean up at the first civilized motel we come to."

Rose started up the bike. "Try not to blank out back there. This scenery gets pretty hypnotic."

"Hey, you're the one driving." Randall gripped his friend around the waist, took his boots off the ground.

"True enough." They pulled out of the station and onto the road.

�

Opening the door rang a bell which summoned a hugely fat woman from some back room. She lumbered up to the counter, cracking the knuckles of surprisingly delicate hands. "Just the two of you boys?" She looked beyond them, out the glass door. "You come in on that motorcycle?"

"Yeah," said Randall in a tired voice. He dropped his pack and fished out his container of waded bills. Pulling a few out, he stepped up to the counter. "Two beds, one night. And I need a room with a bath."

"They've all got showers," the woman replied. She talked as though she were chewing on something tough and unpleasant.

"That'll do," said Randall. "How much?"

"Twenty-seven fifty." Randall passed her a pair of bills. She made change, then presented him with the register. He scribbled a random assortment of loops and curls, ending in M.D. She handed him the key. "Room two forty, stairs are by the pool." Randall turned to leave. "There's no cooking allowed in the rooms, and no animals neither. And no loud noise after ten thirty."

Ironwork stairs clung to the back of the building near a battered Pepsi machine. Drowned insects and dead leaves floated in the pool. It was only a little past noon and there was nobody around. They climbed the stairs and found their room. It smelled of old cigarette smoke and weak disinfectant, but the beds were made and the sheets looked clean. "Why did you get a bed?" asked Rose. "You don't sleep, at least not like a person."

"So I would have some place to sit," said Randall, tossing his pack onto one of the beds. Rose looked quickly about. There was no other furniture. Randall peeled off his t-shirt, then sat down and pulled off his boots. Dirt crusted his grey socks, falling onto the carpet in crumbling flakes. "Should we try and find a laundry or should I just burn these?"

"I don't think that would improve the smell in here any." Rose sat down on his bed, back against the wall, boots still on. Randall took off the socks and then began to pace up and down the narrow swath of carpet between the beds and the far wall. "What are you doing?" asked Rose.

"Getting ready to take a shower." Randall stomped back and forth, fists clenching and unclenching.

"So what's the big deal?" Rose leaned forward inquisitively. "Did you suffer some childhood trauma involving bath water? Mommy didn't scald you, did she?"

"Water burns," said Randall. "I told you that."

"Oh, come off it. I saw you knock back a Heineken just this morning, and that's not exactly a hundred percent alcohol, you know." Rose glanced at his boots as if just noticing them, shrugged, and left them on.

"That's different. Diluted water doesn't count for some reason. Running water hurts the most. Rivers, rain, that sort of thing. Even a Jacuzzi with the jets going'll do it. Volume is factor too. I stuck a toe in the Atlantic once and nearly burned it off."

Rose frowned. "Then why don't you wash up in the pool? I mean really, that's about as stagnant as you can get."

"You misunderstand. Running water is the worst, but still water stings pretty nasty too. At least in the shower I'm not liable to drown." Randall yanked open the bathroom door. "Okay, enough screwing around." He turned on the light and shut the door behind him.

"Good luck!" Rose called from the other room.

Randall dropped his jeans and boxers, then stepped into the narrow stall. The tile felt like ice under his feet. He unwrapped a piece of motel soap and clutched it in one hand. Putting his other hand on the Cold faucet, he took a couple of deep breaths in and out. With a convulsive twist he turned the knob as far as it would go. Nothing happened. The pipes knocked and groaned. Randall stood there with his eyes shut tight, waiting for the spray to hit him. Nothing happened. Just as he opened an eye water shot out of the showerhead full force, searing his face. He choked back a scream, smacking his clenched fist into the tiled wall. The pain poured down his body. He waited for the crawling agony to dull his nerves. Slowly and deliberately, Randall Springfield began to wash.

chapter two

When Randall finally emerged from the bathroom, damp towel hanging from his hips, he found Rose watching the television bolted to the far wall. The sound was down. On the screen, a mangy looking leopard stalked a herd of sleek quadrupeds that he could not readily identify. "He returns at last!" Rose sat up in bed. His boots had left a series of horseshoe shaped smears on the white sheet. "In another ten minutes I was going phone a plumber to pry you out of there. As it was, I had to piss off the balcony." He looked Randall up and down. "Jesus shit, you're red as a street walker's lipstick. What did you wash with, ammonia and sand paper?"

"No, just soap and water." Randall sat down heavily on his own bed, lay back and stared up at the ceiling. Random spasms shook various portions of his anatomy. "Shit."

"Running water, you say. What a crock." Rose stood up to hover over Randall's prostrate form. "Next thing I suppose you'll have me inviting you across thresholds and defending you from garlic."

"Those two are myths."

"Glad to hear it. I don't think I could live without the occasional Caesar salad." Rose leaned into Randall's field of vision, ginning with cheerful insanity. "What about crosses? Holy ground, that sort of crap? You know, you haven't exactly gone out of your way to fill me in on this stuff." He sat down on the edge of the bed.

"Well, Randall propped himself up on one elbow, "so far as I know, religious artifacts only bother those of my kind who were believers in their natural lives. A couple centuries ago that meant practically everybody. Of course now it's a lot less prevalent. I've certainly never had any trouble in that direction. It's kind of funny, actually. The last priest who tried that hocus pocus on me shit his pants when it didn't work." He lay back down, laughing a little to himself. "That was quite a while ago. Anything else you want to know?"

Rose considered, scratching at the stubble around his adam's apple. "Okay, how are you killed?" He frowned. "Let me rephrase that. How are you destroyed? I guess that's what I mean."

"Well, Renfield, it isn't easy. I've had almost every kind of violence done to me over the years. Some shit you would not believe. I've been shot, practically blown in half a couple of times. I've been stabbed pretty severely. Some asshole nailed a railroad spike through my chest once. I've even been electrocuted. But I've found I can still function with none of my bodily processes going. Doing anything in that condition is a major drain. But enough sleep seems to heal it all. My guess would be that only total destruction of the brain would do it. Anything less than that just wouldn't be permanent." Randall stretched painfully, random twitches shooting through his inflamed skin. "You know, my boy, that this isn't going to be simple."

"I wasn't planning to knock you off just yet."

"Not me. Lisel. She is one very serious bitch. Even if we do catch up with her, the two of us will be hard put to fuck her up that meaningfully. She's quite old. Maybe even pre-Christ. Claims to be one of the seven daughters of the ancient one, though that's probably just bullshit. Taking her out may be beyond us."

On the television screen, the leopard had finally managed to pull down a straggling quadruped. Ivory jaws locked about the thick neck, crushing and tearing. Blood flowed and the horned creature collapsed, all without sound. "Listen," said Randall, "I'm going to be a little out of it for a few hours. Why don't you take a drive, find some food or something. We'll move on this evening."

"Sure." Rose stood up, found his jacket and helmet. "No sense my sitting around to watch your flesh change colors." He stuffed the room key into a pocket.

"Take some money if you like. I'd rather you weren't a wanted man in the entire Southwest."

Rose smiled happily. He poked through Randall's pack and took a couple of bills out of the plastic container. "Thanks pop, I'll be back from the sock-hop before curfew. You want me to bring you anything? Beer? Fresh rodents?" He held the door, looking questioningly back into the room.

"Can't think of anything, thanks." Randall rolled over onto his stomach, leaving a wet Rorschach blot on the mattress. "See you."

"Yeah." Rose left, then poked his shaggy head back through the door. "Just where are we headed, anyway? If you don't mind my asking, that is."

Randall closed his eyes. "U.C. Santa Cruz. I'm going to see about getting us some help in this little venture of ours."

"Cool deal," said Rose, and shut the door.

❧

Traffic came to a stop. Rose stuck out a boot, leaned over and halted the bike. He pulled off his helmet and looked over his shoulder at Randall. "Do you believe this?" He gestured fiercely at the five lanes of immobile cars that held them prisoner. "Do you? For Christ sake it isn't even four yet and look at this!" Children stared at them from the rear window of a Ford Taurus. The traffic inched forward. "I could walk faster than this! God damn, I hate L.A." He slumped down, defeated.

Randall flipped up his helmet visor. "Probably an accident up ahead. I'm sure it'll clear."

"Are you kidding? We're hardly past the city limits. Whatever it is might be miles ahead. We could be here for hours." The Fiat behind them honked its high pitch horn. "Okay!" Rose shouted. "I'll move! You can advance a whole fucking yard! Happy now?" The driver said nothing, merely stared. "Speak up man! I can't hear you over all this screaming rubber."

"Look," said Randall, "just try to calm down."

"This is all your fault, you know. If you weren't so paranoid about driving between cars we could bypass this crap." He blew a long breath into his sweat-soaked bangs. "What say we get off at the next exit, find a bar and sit this out. In a few hours we can cruise along north no problem. How about it?" He looked pleadingly over his shoulder. "Can we? Can we? Please. Please. Can we?"

Randall shrugged. "Just as long as you promise to be straight enough to drive by the time we head back out."

"A thousand blessings upon your home and livestock." Rose shoved his helmet back on and signaled for a lane change. It took him over ten minutes of shouted curses and evil eyes to maneuver the motorcycle to the edge of the freeway. Once there he drove along the shoulder to a chorus of car horns. Some punkers lounging in the back of a pick-up sprayed beer at them as they slid past. They took the next exit off the highway, traveling faster down the off-ramp then they had in the last half hour.

Rose negotiated the crowded streets, passing by several obvious nightclubs. At length, he drew up before a battered shack of a place sitting well back from the road. There was no name to it, just neon signs for American beers hanging in the dirty windows. A row of motorcycles sat out front, all big Harleys. Rose added his army surplus bike to the line up, not bothering to lock it. Helmets and coats off, they stepped inside.

Cigarette smoke hung in the air, almost drowning out the odors of stale beer and human sweat. Rose inhaled deeply, as if smelling a favorite flower. A score of people, very obviously the owners of the machines outside, stood talking in noisy clumps, their faces indistinct in the poor light. A middle-aged waitress waded through the knots of leather and denim, one hand holding aloft a gigantic, bottle-laden tray while the other fended off slaps at her ass. A jukebox sat in one corner, playing some nameless steel guitar blues.

Rose walked briskly up to the bar. "Two beers, if you please." He slapped the last of the money Randall had given him down on the counter. The bartender brought them their drinks without comment. He took the cash to the register without bringing any change. "Guess he figures we might run up a tab."

"He could be right." They leaned back against the bar, surveying the crowd. Randall sipped at his beer while Rose downed his first and motioned for another. "Remember, Renfield, you promised not to get too twisted."

Rose nodded, sipping noisily his second beer. He swished it around in his mouth, gargled, then swallowed. "A heady little number." Holding the bottle by the bottom, he swirled it under his nose. "Plenty of bouquet."

A large figure detached itself from the nearest clot of bikers. "Hey Wormwood, is that you?" The man lumbered forward on tree-trunk legs. He stood well over six feet tall, all six of them thick with muscle. The beer gut hanging at his abdomen hardly seemed to hinder him. "God damn if that ain't you, Wormwood."

A grin sprung up on Rose's face. He set down his beer and rushed forward. "Toad-Eater, you gigantic fuck!" The big man crushed him into a bear hug. Randall winced just watching it, reliving a memory of cracked ribs.

They separated, the huge man holding Rose out at arm's length. "I knew it was you. I'll be damned, Wormwood. What have you been up to since the Pen?"

"This and that, same as always." Rose hung an arm around the elephant shoulders and marched back to the bar. "I'd like you to meet my guru and benefactor, Randall Springfield." Randall nodded fractionally. "And this is Toad-Eater. We did some time together once."

"Hell," said Toad-Eater, "we rode together before that." He flagged down the bartender and secured another beer. Rose polished off his second and started in on a third. "I see you still drink like you had a great fucking hole in your stomach." He turned to Randall. "I once saw this puny bastard shotgun an entire case of beer inside of fifteen minutes. Next thing we knew he'd pissed the bonfire out." He laughed hugely, doubling over, elbowing Randall in the side. "Don't that beat everything you ever heard?" He sobered suddenly. "Say, I almost forgot my manners. Silverfish is throwing a party tonight. You remember Silverfish, don't you?"

Rose nodded. "Leo's old lady, right?"

"Yeah, you got the woman alright, but Leo's up in Chino now. A.D.W. on an officer."

"Leo shot a cop?" Rose arched an eyebrow dubiously.

"Nope, ran him over with his bike." Toad-Eater doubled over again, wheezing and laughing. "Don't that beat everything?" This time it took him a couple of minutes to recover. By then Rose was into his fourth beer. The bartender hovered nearby, frowning. Randall passed him a twenty and he drifted off.

"But like I was saying, Wormwood, Silverfish is having a bash tonight. You know, she got that house up in the Hollywood Hills when her daddy kicked. All the old crew'll be there, them that ain't in the slam anyway. I know Bad Bob would love to see you." He elbowed Randall once more. "And any friend of Wormwood's… Well, I'm sure they'd find you a bottle."

"Sounds great," said Rose. He looked nervously at Randall. "If you have no objections, that is." Randall said nothing, merely looked grim. "Aw come on, we have to do something to amuse ourselves–until the wee hours, anyway. I've been camped out in the sand for two weeks all by my lonesome. I want to wallow in depravity for an evening." He smiled slyly. "You might even find some likely candidates for our little plan."

Randall's expression of annoyance never changed. "Just remember your promise, Wormwood."

"Deal." Rose flashed his maniac grin. "Toad-Eater, my man, when does this shindig start?"

The huge biker glanced around the room, as if in search of an answer. "I guess we don't need to take off for a couple hours yet."

"In that case…" Rose pounded his empty bottle on the scarred wood of the bar. "Innkeeper! More ale!"

৵ঌ

They got up into the hills just after sunset. The air cooled as the orange haze to the west faded slowly into night. They drove along a winding road, trees thick on either side. Randall noticed that the pavement looked abnormally smooth and well maintained. Long steep driveways led up to large, vaguely cabin-like houses. Genuine mailboxes on tall wooden posts stood next to each drive. The further they climbed into the hills, the further apart the mailboxes became. The driveways became longer, the cabins larger. Altitude equals money, Randall thought. Must be the smog.

The road grew steeper. Randall could feel himself slipping off the back of the army surplus bike. He tightened his grip on Rose's leather jacket. Just ahead of them, Toad-Eater shifted his enormous Harley into low gear. A series of switchbacks took them farther and farther up. Here there were no mailboxes at all. Finally the road leveled out, simply vanishing into a gravel driveway packed with motorcycles.

They stopped, dismounted, and just stood looking at the house. Two stories of seasoned, unpainted wood dominated a wide lot atop the peak of some minor mountain. The gravel drive trailed off into a stand of trees that meandered down one side of the hill. A hardwood deck larger than most motel rooms jutted out over the opposite side, support beams imbedded in the slope. They could see a few people standing, watching the dregs of the sunset. A cobblestone path led to a set of double doors carved with scarabs and dragonflies. "Pretty swank, eh?" said Toad-Eater. "Silverfish owns the place outright. She comes from money, you know. But that don't mean she ain't good people." He laughed his huge wheezing laugh, bending down to slap both thighs. "Well come on boys, let's make ourselves known."

As they drew closer, they heard the unintelligible mutter of human voices coming through the shuttered windows. It sounded like quite a crowd. Dozens of carved eyes peered at them from the doors, insect feelers groping forward. "Should we knock?" asked Rose, eyeing the bugs with trepidation.

Before anyone could answer the doors swung open. A teenage girl wearing only chaps and a ten-gallon hat stood before them in the smokey light and increased noise. She grinned from ear to ear, a sassy, knowing smile. "Leave your keys and hardware at the door, boys, then come on in."

"Sure thing, darling," said Toad-Eater, stepping inside. He handed the girl the keys to his Harley along with the knife from his belt. "Your mother around, sweet thing?"

She jerked a thumb over her shoulder. "In there someplace."

"Much obliged." He pulled the brim of a nonexistent hat, then vanished into the crowd.

The girl turned to examine the remaining two, who still stood out on the mat. "Why sir, I do believe you're drooling."

"Result of an old bullfighting injury," Rose replied. "Can't be helped." His eyes leapt up to her face, only to glide slowly down again.

"Keys and weapons at the door, gents," she repeated. "Can't have you driving over the side of the mountain, crashing through some poor bastard's roof."

"What'll you give for 'em?" Rose stepped into the house, his smile insanely wide.

"Try me," said the girl, matching his grin.

He handed her the keys to his bike, then dropped his pack to the floor. "Everything dangerous is in there."

"So you say." The girl lunged forward, almost jumping on him, locking him in a lusty kiss. A roar of approval went up from the room behind. While her mouth worked, she padded down his torso with her hands, searched along his legs with her bare feet. Rose did not object. Finally, she sprung away. "You're clean."

"Marry me," said Rose. "Bear my children." She laughed and shoved him toward the crowd.

"I rode with him," said Randall, stepping through the door. He held out his arms to facilitate her search.

"That's okay." She waved a hand dismissively. "You're the first person to walk in here straight." Instead of kissing him, she handed him a half full bottle of white tequila. "Enjoy the show."

Randall found Rose on the fringes of the crowd, though Toad-Eater was nowhere to be seen in the mass of bodies. People filled the room, blocking any view of the furniture or even the walls. Everybody had at least one drink handy. Rose had somehow acquired a thirty-two ounce bottle of Colt. He drank it in huge swallows. Most of the men seemed to be in jeans and biker t-shirts, though quite a few stood around in loincloths. Some women were completely nude. Others wore just a piece or two of clothing. A leather jacket, hip boots, bikini bottoms. A woman brushed by Rose covered in dried gray mud. Cave paintings decorated her chest and back, stick figures on the hunt for buffalo.

"There's something that just occurred to me to ask you." Rose had to yell to make himself heard over the noise.

Randall took a hit of tequila. "Such as?"

"Well, are your kind... you know, sexually able? I mean in the movies guys like you seduce women but you don't really do much with them. Just nibble on them a bit then cast them aside. I'd like to be immortal and everything, but that's a long time to go without, if you get me." He took a long pull on his beer. "So do you?"

"Do I fuck?" asked Randall. "Is that what you want to know?"

"In a nutshell."

"Yeah, you can still have sex. But it's a little complicated. Such close contact usually triggers that nibbling you mentioned. Any sort of continued relationship with a normal woman is impossible. And we're all too paranoid to fuck each other. But don't worry, you'll still be able to get off." He took another snort of tequila. "Why this sudden interest in carnality? You have designs on that bit of fluff at the door?"

"That's got to be Silverfish's daughter. Didn't have tits the last time I saw her, but it's the same girl. Rule one of a clan party is don't try to fuck the host's children." His eyes lit from one female to the next. "No matter. It's not as if we're in a drought here." He tilted the Colt up, leaning back until the beer drained into him like water from an office cooler. When the bottle was empty he held it out into the crowd. A random hand grabbed it, passing it along somewhere. Another replaced it a second later with a cold can. "Which reminds me," he said, "did that nymph get your knives?"

"As a matter of fact, no, she didn't." Either the tequila was beginning to work itself on Randall or his head had adjusted to the noise. At any rate, Rose was no longer shouting and he could still hear.

"Just don't flash them at anybody. If these people find you wandering around armed and sober they're liable to get suspicious and beat the shit out of you."

"They'll try." Randall took another drink from his bottle.

A woman in gartered fishnet stockings and an unbuttoned Hawaiian shirt scooted past, bearing a case of beer. "You cool to go it alone for a while?" asked Rose. "I feel the irrepressible urge to mingle."

"Call it whatever you like," Randall replied.

"Jealous." Rose downed his can of beer. Then he was off, weaving through the crowd in hot pursuit.

Randall took one more swig of tequila. The presence of so many close-packed bodies was starting to get to him. His eyes followed the mix and motion of the crowd, focusing occasionally on a pale shoulder or exposed thigh. He could no longer ignore the combined funk of so much human sweat. It had been over a day since that bit of roadrunner, and that after a fair sleep too. There were just so many of them, brushing against him, breathing in his face. Naked and alive. He noticed himself salivating.

Control yourself Randall, he thought. The absolute last thing I want to do is start gnawing on one of these people. Immortality is not invulnerability. Besides, Rose was right. Any of them would make beautiful recruits. Just the right level of savagery to really enjoy the idea. Best slip out back and find a squirrel or something. No need to start trouble. Not just yet.

He took another big swallow from his bottle, then moved toward what he assumed was the far end of the room. People were slow to make way. Randall nudged, prodded, and squeezed through the noisy crowd, flinching away from each soft touch of human flesh. Feminine hands caressed him randomly as he went by, skimming lightly over his chest, legs, thighs. He began to hear heartbeats, and tried to convince himself they were merely his own.

Coming out of the press, he found himself in an open kitchen. Bottles covered every conceivable surface, including the stove burners. A mix of whiskeys sat on the open oven door. Beer cans filled the washing machine. There was a small keg in the sink. Randall scanned the contents of one counter, exchanging his tequila for an unopened bottle of whiskey. He removed the lid and took a large belt. Jesus, he thought. I've got to get some air. He recapped the bottle, stuck it in a coat pocket and waded back into the throng.

Eventually, he made his way to a connecting hall of some sort. A few people stood leaning against the walls, talking and drinking quietly, but there was room enough to move and breathe. Randall inhaled deeply, feeling instantly better. A toilet flushed somewhere nearby. Still hoping to find an exit, Randall walked to the end of the hall and opened the last door.

Naked men and women littered the room, grunting and moaning in various states of passion. One pair occupied an entire sofa, copulating furiously. Springs shrieked and dust flew from the cushions as the woman clawed at her partner's back. Another couple ground against each other in a rickety chair, her breasts in his face. A delicate blond rode atop a man who appeared to be asleep, buttocks pumping visibly beneath her longshoreman's coat. On the floor, an older woman sat with her legs wide apart, carefully explaining her hairless anatomy to an attentive teenage boy. Other couples and trios sprawled over the furniture and one another; kissing, grasping, pulling off clothing.

A hand reached up and hooked itself into Randall's jeans. The song of blood pounded furiously through his head. Tearing away from the inquisitive fingers, he staggered across the field of lovers and out the far door. He walked blindly down a few wooden steps, halting just before a sunken hot tub. Randall hissed, backing quickly away from the steaming water. Standing still, he took several deep breaths of night air. Bodies filled the tub, mostly naked, though none of them seemed to be mating. A man in a three-piece suit sat up to his shoulders in water, a naked Amazon in his lap, smiling whimsically. "She said this was going to be a cocktail party."

"No kidding." Randall staggered off into darkness, breathing heavily.

๛

He returned some time later. Game had been scarce on the steep slope of the mountain. As he walked around the outside of the big wooden house he pulled the bottle of whiskey from his coat pocket and swirled some around in his mouth. He swallowed, still tasting blood. Well, he thought, that should cover the stench, at any rate. He wiped his lips on his sleeve.

Rounding a corner, he came to the edge of the huge deck that overhung one side of the hill. He hoisted himself over the guardrail, spying both Rose and Toad-Eater sitting at picnic table. Across from them sat an nondescript fellow in standard biker garb. Further on, a man stood talking with two young women. He wore a loincloth and a gun belt which sported large water pistol. A patrolman's hat sat on his head and a badge hung from his pierced nipple. As Randall watched, he pulled the water pistol, twirled it around his trigger finger, then shot some of the contents into his mouth. The girls punched and wheedled him, and he gave them each a squirt.

"Is that guy for real?" Randall asked, hunkering down next to Rose and taking another drink. Rose nodded vaguely.

"He's a cop, all right," said the plain-looking fellow. "A couple years back he came to break up one of our little social events. Silverfish talked him out of it." Toad-Eater sniggered at this, elbowing Rose in the ribcage. He did not seem to notice. "Came back after he got off duty," the man continued. "Been coming back ever since. The gals love him. He's a total animal." Randall glanced at the cop again. He appeared to be negotiating the price of another squirt from his pistol.

"Randall!" Rose exclaimed, as if just discovering his presence. "So glad you caught up with us. This is Bob. Bad Bob." He flourished an arm in the nondescript man's direction. "Bob, this is Randall." Having made the introductions, Rose lapsed into silence once more, staring cheerfully at the night sky. Randall looked Bob over. Thin. Gaunt really, but with a bit of a paunch. Patchy black hair, receding. Face and hands starting to wrinkle. The basic biker jeans, Harley shirt, leather jacket. He looked like a used car salesman that had watched *Easy Rider* during some mid-life crisis and decided to run with the idea. And this guy was some sort of biker clan heavy?

As if sensing these doubts, Rose swung around toward Randall again. "Don't let his look fool you," he said conspiratorially. "Bob's a bad-ass criminal, aren't you, Bob?" The man just nodded, smiling very slightly.

"My pleasure," said Randall. He took a big hit from his bottle then thumped it down in front of Bob. The man put it to his lips and upended it, swilling down nearly a third of the amber liquid. He banged the bottle back down in front of Randall, not showing any loss of coordination.

"You know," Bob said seriously, "you don't look like much for a prince of the damned." His smile widened. "Wormwood has been telling me some fantastic stories about you. Making some very wild offers indeed. Now, they'd be great if they were true. But old Wormwood here farts sugar and burps bullshit even when he's not fucked up." He leaned forward, searching Randall with deep brown eyes. "So I'd like to see a little magic if you please, before I sign on for this half-assed crusade you two have in mind."

"What would you like?" asked Randall, spreading his hands. "Water into wine? Manna? Pennies from Heaven?"

Bob frowned while Toad-Eater wheezed uncontrollably, banging his head on the tabletop. "Had in mind something a little more... I don't know... visceral."

"Visceral, eh?" Randall stood, shrugging off his coat. Taking the whiskey, he poured the rest of the bottle out over his left hand. The alcohol ran down his skin, soaking the hairs of his forearm, dripping onto the wooden deck. "If I could trouble one of you for a light?" Toad-Eater stopped laughing abruptly. Bob looked at him for a long minute. Without a word, he handed over a heavy U.S.M.C. Zippo.

Randall snapped it open and held the flame to his dripping left hand. The alcohol ignited in a flash, blue fire shooting upward. The downy hair on his arm withered and died. Soon his skin turned red beneath the flames, blistering, sizzling with audible pops and hisses. His hand began to blacken, skin cracking and oozing clear liquid. All the while Randall stared directly at Bob, trying very hard to look completely casual.

"Okay," said Bob thinly. Randall's finger bones had appeared within the peeling, flaming mass of his hand. "Point proven. Go put that out, for Christ sake."

"So you're with us?" Randall persisted, not moving from where he stood.

"We're with you, boy," Bob repeated. Toad-Eater nodded rapidly, never taking his eyes of the smoking limb. "Now extinguish yourself, please." Bob stood up, looking around the deck. "Anybody drinking anything that ain't gonna catch fire?" The cop just stared at them, slack-jawed.

"That's all right," said Randall. He hopped down from the deck, arm still burning, and walked in the direction of the hot tub. He refused to hurry, even once he had rounded the corner out of sight. Reaching the steaming pool, he knelt down plunged his arm in to the shoulder. The water hissed and crackled. "Shit!" Randall yelled, yanking his blackened limb out of the tub. The water felt like napalm on his raw flesh, burning more painfully than fire. He swung his arm around in the air, flinging away as many of the clinging droplets as he could. "Mother fuck!"

The man in the three-piece suit gawked at him from within the haze of steam. Nobody else in the tub seemed to have noticed. "What happened?" he stammered.

"Careful what you say to these biker women," Randall replied. "They're vicious." He turned away and walked back to the deck. Hopping the rail, he found Bad Bob and Toad-Eater talking rapidly to each other. Rose sat as before, gaze lost in the stars. The cop and his groupies had gone.

The two men straightened when Randall approached the table, falling silent. Bob smiled widely now, though the larger man looked sick at the sight of the burnt, dripping arm. The limb twitched involuntarily, charred fingers clutching. Randall slung his coat back on. "It's agreed," said Bob. "We'll back your play. In return for the reward Wormwood mentioned, we are at your service. Or at least as many of us as really want the payoff. I'll bring it up tomorrow when folks are sober again." He cracked open a warm beer. "You two gentleman hanging around? Our casa is your casa. Though I don't think you'll land any of the girls with that crisp hook of yours."

"Actually, we're heading north." Randall slapped Rose on the shoulder with his good hand. "We should really be on our way. There are some people we need to see before we can make our move." He looked at Rose, who still sat staring blissfully up at the sky. "Come on Wormwood, we've got a lot of driving to do."

"I don't think so," said Rose, his voice distant and a bit slurred. "I don't think so, no."

"And why not?" Randall demanded, placing one boot on the bench beside his friend, eyeing him suspiciously.

"Well... you know... the acid has started to kick in." His voice trailed off; his gaze swung back to the heavens.

Randall grabbed him by the collar of his jacket and hauled him up off the bench. "What acid?" he yelled into his face.

"Oh, you know... the acid." Rose gestured loosely. "That nice woman with tropical tits gave it to me." His head drooped down to his chest, then sprung back up. "Maybe I shouldn't have taken it," he whispered loudly. "Right now your tongue is about twenty feet long and it's trying to pick my pockets." He slapped at his jeans. "Stop that! Come on now. Nice tongue."

"For Christ sake." Randall dragged Rose into the house, leaving Toad-Eater in hysterics. They emerged in the middle of the long hall. Randall made for the door, his good hand clamped around his friend's shirt front.

"Please don't put me in a box," Rose pleaded.

"What?" Randall pulled him into the crowd.

"A box. The last time I did acid some guy came up to me and said 'I am enclosing your head in a black box. You can't see anything. You can't hear anything. You can't even smell anything.'" Rose halted suddenly, jerking Randall back. "Oh God! Oh no! I've done it to myself! Shit! Shit! Shit! Are you still there? Let me out!"

"Only if you promise to behave."

"What? I can't hear anything. I'm trapped in a fucking box!" Rose's hands clawed at the empty air about his head.

"Oh, come on!" Randall dragged him toward the door, parting the crowd with his injured arm. In the center of the room two men sat face to face on bar stools staring at each other while a circle of stripping, cavorting, masturbating women tried their best to distract them. A voluptuous belly dancer caught sight of Randall's hand, gagging audibly. One of the men glanced in her direction, loosing the game. He pounded his head with both fists, cursing in several languages while the women fawned over his opponent.

They reached the entryway. The girl in chaps leaned back against the door, talking to a man in a toga. Randall barged between them, hiding his hand in his coat pocket. "Give me his keys," he said. "We're leaving."

The girl gave him a hard look. "You straight?" She glanced over his shoulder at Rose. "He sure as shit isn't." Randall just glared at her. "Okay, okay." She rummaged through a velvet Crown Royal bag by the door, coming up with Rose's dog-tag key-chain. "It's your funeral, mister."

"As always." Randall took the keys with his skeletal hand, hefted their packs, then walked out past the stunned girl. "Come on, you." He pulled his friend after him.

chapter **three**

Rose vomited into the surf. A sluggish wave smeared the brown stain towards the shore then sucked it back into the ocean. He staggered up the beach to the sea wall, sand caking to his wet boots. Groaning, he sat down heavily next to Randall. Water lapped at the fringes of the sand. Barnacled rocks dotted the strand, their shadowy bulks revealed by the receding tide. "So," said Rose, "how did you say we got here again?"

"I drove." Randall sat astride the retaining wall picking flakes of burnt skin off his left hand, trying not to look at the vast stretch of water. "You held on all right until Santa Monica. Lucky for you we were still on surface streets, and I'd stuck a helmet on you."

"Funny," said Rose, "I thought my head was in a box." He wiped at his lips with the bottom of his shirt, then scrubbed at his teeth.

"I know." Randall winced as he poked at the red wrinkled flesh near the top of the burn. "Anyway, when I dragged you up onto the sidewalk you were yelling something about gnomes and lizards and then you said you needed to hurl real bad. We weren't too far from the beach, so I parked the bike and walked you here." He scraped at a charred fingernail. It fell off into the sand. "Feel any better?"

"Some." Rose touched his head carefully, as if searching for fractures. "Things are pretty much back to normal. A little fluid still, if you know what I mean." He wove one hand through the air, twiddling his fingers. Randall nodded. "And either I'm still hallucinating or there are a bunch of people in tuxedoes and party dresses standing on the edge of that jetty over there."

Randall squinted, peering down the unlit shoreline. "I see them too."

"Good." Rose massaged the back of his neck gingerly. "Must be prom night or something." He blanched suddenly. "What happened to your hand?"

"Jesus, you missed that?" Randall held out the injured arm. "Let's just say I convinced Bob that I'm not just some random fuck-head. It's minor, should heal fairly quickly."

"I think I'm going to puke again."

Randall pulled his arm back into the sleeve of his coat. "Sorry." He swiveled toward the sidewalk and stood. "Ready to go?"

Rose hauled himself up and swung his legs over the retaining wall, banging his boot heels against the stone to knock the sand loose. "Have I got a choice?"

"No."

"In that case, I'm ready."

They stopped in Santa Barbara to fill the tank at an otherwise deserted station. In a few minutes they were back on the road. The remainder of the night passed in half-lit views of office blocks and shopping centers, gradually giving way to open land. Darkness transformed fields of withered grape vines into endless rows of crucifixes. Cows slept upright by roadside fences. Oil pumps glowed in the moonlight.

The eastern sky brightened, running through the shades of blue. An impossibly yellow sun rose to their right, cut off abruptly as they left the highway and drove into a forest. Light filtered through a thin, cool mist. The motorcycle climbed slowly up a steep two-lane road. To either side, redwood trees heaved their towering bulks into the sky, their ancient bark shaggy, wet with dew. The mist seemed to thicken around their far-off crowns, blotting out all sense of the world beyond.

Randall motored past a three-sided wooden shack plastered with layer after layer of multicolored flyers, the aluminum bus stop icon barely visible. Topping the rise, he eased the bike into a parking lot. A great concrete building lurked against the background of redwoods, its surface darkened almost black with the damp. He found a motorcycle space near the edge of the lot and killed the engine. "Looks like a prison block," said Rose, pulling off his helmet.

"It's a dormitory, actually." Randall dismounted and tossed the keys at Rose. "But they built it from a set of prison blueprints. Most of the university was constructed right after the Berkeley free speech movement. Guess the regents decided not to take any chances." They gathered their gear and walked stiffly toward the building, regaining their land legs.

"So who are we meeting here, anyway?" Rose shook out his matted hair. "Either you haven't said or you mentioned it while I was still tripping."

"My elder brother Knox lives here." A heavy door on a piston spring led to an stark entry hall. The only spot of color came from a red number one stenciled onto the whitewashed concrete. Metal stairs wound upward. The wall opposite contained an identical door. Randall mounted the stairs. Rose followed.

The second landing looked exactly the same, except that the institutional number two beside the door had been painted over and replaced. An oriental dragon done in vivid reds and golds curled and contorted into the shape of the number. It seemed alive, mobile, despite a few flaking scales. Someone had ground a cigarette into one of the eyes, leaving it scorched and seamed. The damage only made the reptilian face more menacing. Randall pushed open the heavy door, the dragon dancing in his peripheral vision.

The smell of incense filled the hall beyond. Beethoven's Fifth and Black Dog warred from competing stereos. Most of the doors to the dorm rooms stood propped open. One had been exchanged for a curtain of beads. The door itself lay on the floor at the end of the hall. The curtain parted with a gentle clatter. A woman appeared wrapped in a coarse towel, a rat sitting on her shoulder. She edged past them into another room. Rose peered at the walls, admiring the airbrushed graffiti. "I don't remember jail being at all like this," he ventured.

"Maybe you're still hallucinating." Randall paused before one of the few closed doors. A poster hung from a pair of tacks in the wood, a highly realistic drawing of an eye with just the hint of a death's head in the pupil. Below this a post-it note read: *Grading papers. Kindly fuck off.*

Rose laughed. "I could very well be."

"Listen, Knox can be pretty strange sometimes, and I haven't seen him in quite a while." Randall gestured at the decoration. "Just be ready for anything."

Rose reached around into one of the side pouches of his pack and pulled out a snub-nosed .38 revolver. He spun the cylinder, checking the load, then placed the weapon in some inner pocket of his jacket. Randall watched him incredulously. "Sorry. That's just what I do whenever someone tells me to be ready for anything."

"I meant any sort of strange behavior. I don't honestly expect him to attack us or anything."

"I see." Rose flourished the gun again. "Shall I put this away, then?"

Randall said nothing for a moment. His brows knit. "Keep it." The revolver disappeared inside Rose's jacket. Randall rapped on the door with his good hand. There was no response. They stood there for a few seconds. He knocked again, harder this time. The door opened, fractionally at first, then wide.

"Well, if it isn't the messiah." Knox wore a faded tie-dye shirt and a pair of baggy shorts so gaudy that they had to be swim trunks. "And this must be Judas." He bowed, and swept a hand towards the room. "Please, come in. Make yourselves to home."

Books filled the small, square space. They lined a pair of shelves and the windowsill, spilled across the sheetless bed, and sat in tall stacks on the floor. Several older looking tomes lay open on an ornately carved desk. Crumpled yellow pages littered the floor underneath, gathering in drifts around the clawed feet. Posters and prints covered the walls, overlapping one another. The classic Jim Morrison, shirtless and confused. Pink Floyd's triangular prism. Dali's Hallucinogenic Matador, a cartoon rendering of Jimi Hendrix sipping from a bowl of alien soup, a British subway advertisement for the Kew Gardens, Clockwork Alex, Fritz Lang's *Eve*, *Rocky Horror's* bright red lips, and dominating them all, Klimt's *Salome*, her slender fingers dropping John the Baptist's head into a sack.

"I see things haven't changed much since my last visit," said Randall, "though the books must be different or mildew would have set in by now." He did a sudden double take. "What in God's name have you done to your hair?"

Knox ran his fingers through the centimeter length white stubble, laughing. "First tell me what you did to your hand."

Randall actually blushed. Rose stared in exaggerated amazement. "Well, I was trying to impress some bikers, so I doused it with alcohol and set it on fire."

"Sounds intelligent."

"It seemed like the thing to do at the time." Randall set his pack down on a vacant bit of floor. "Now what about the hair?"

"I shaved it off a little while ago. I'm teaching a small class on nineteenth century American history this semester and there are still of few old photos lurking around. Can't be too careful." Knox gestured at the pile of torn out pages on the floor. "When I have time, I scan through the University's history books. I've almost finished with the ones from the main library. Only a couple more shelves to go."

Rose searched in vain for a place to sit. "How can you have such little respect for those valuable books?" he asked with mock seriousness. "They're public property."

"I'm older than they are." With a broad sweep of his arm, Knox sent half of the books on the bed clattering to the floor. He left them where they fell, tumbled open in a heap of loose binding and musty paper. He gave Rose a little half smile. "And most of them are full of lies, anyway."

"Oh." Rose sat, throwing himself down on the bed. The remaining stacks collapsed into a single pile. "I guess that's all right, then."

Knox hooked a dingy chrome chair out from under the desk and straddled it, arms resting across the back. "Took you long enough to get here, brother dear."

"Unavoidably detained," said Randall. "I took a sort of involuntary nap."

"I understand."

Randall opened his pack and removed a battered envelope. "Does this urgent missive of yours mean that you've finally come around to my way of thinking?" He tossed the letter in his brother's direction. It landed just short of the desk, blending into the pile of crumpled pages.

"Yes and no." Knox looked around the room for a moment, then pulled a metal flask out of the jumble on the floor.

"That's vague yet promising." Randall accepted the flask, took a sip, cringed, then handed it off to Rose. "Would you mind elaborating a little further on that statement?"

"Not at all." Knox leaned back against the desk. "Find some place to sit if you can, this is a bit of a long story." Randall removed the remaining books from the mattress and stacked them on the floor. He sat, looking expectantly at his brother. Knox frowned. "What's the last you heard from Swan?"

The question seemed to take Randall by surprise. He chewed his lip, considering. "A post card a few months ago. From London, I think. Yes, he claimed to be feeding exclusively off whores and tourists, having a wonderful time. Is that right?"

"So far as it goes, yes. Having a permanent address, I heard from him more frequently than you did. He sent me the wildest postcards. I have them here somewhere." Knox turned and began rooting around in the mass of papers on the desk. "There's this one with a woman and a goat. I can't imagine where he found it."

"That's okay," said Randall, "you can show us some other time."

Knox turned slowly back around, hands lingering on the piles of paper.

"Sorry." He stretched an arm out to take the flask. After a couple of hits he capped it and tossed it at Randall, who handed it back to Rose untouched. "As usual, he fell in with street people. Punks. Skinheads. Subway gangs. They'd get wasted and run around the city fucking people up. He always fed alone, of course. But he'd case places with his friends, pick out his next meal. They rolled drunks on the underground for money."

"Sounds like fun." Rose opened the flask and poured the contents down his throat.

Knox talked on as though uninterrupted. "Somewhere along the line he met this girl, a runaway from Dublin. Punk to the bone. Mohawk, genital piercing, the works. It was love at first sight, I suppose. Anyway, they knocked around London together, comparing tattoos and fucking on park benches. Somehow he never consumed her." Knox leaned back, staring up at the ceiling. "That boy is a weird one, all right. Some of the rules just don't seem to apply to him. It might simply be a matter of attitude. Or maybe it's all the drugs he takes."

Rose arched an eyebrow at this, though Randall's expression of gradually thinning patience did not change. Knox seemed to be talking to himself now, paying no attention to either of them. "They developed this little game. They'd dress up in their wildest clothes, leather and spikes and rings hanging from every conceivable portion of their anatomy. If they could, they'd get high, preferably on psychedelics. But when drugs were scarce or they were low on cash they'd settle for getting hammered on Guinness. Once they'd achieved this state of extreme ugliness they'd go to one of the big public attractions and see how obnoxious they could be before security kicked them out. They did all the classic sights. Tower of London. Crown Jewels. Changing of the Guard. Big Ben. Houses of Parliament. And of course they never did anything overtly illegal. Just sneered and talked too loud and breathed in other people's faces. I got postcard after postcard from these places describing just what level of crudity it had taken to get thrown out." He laughed suddenly. "They picked flowers out of the Queen's Garden in Regent's Park. Both had enormous bouquets by the time the custodians caught up with them."

"I trust," said Randall quietly, "that this is all leading somewhere." Rose winced, and knocked back the last hit from the flask.

Knox glanced up at them, looking more surprised than annoyed. "Well you see, one day the postcards just stopped coming. I got one or two a week for nearly half a year. But all of the sudden… nothing."

Randall hunched forward, closer to his brother. "So you figure they finally stepped over the line, got themselves arrested?"

"That's what I assumed at first, yes."

"What changed your mind?"

The question hung in the air, unanswered. "Is there anything left in that flask?" Rose shook his head. "Pity." Knox stood up, slid open a poster covered closet door and began poking around inside. "I think I've got another one in here somewhere." He emerged with a dusty bottle of Wild Turkey. "This should do." He took a drink, hesitated for a moment, then sat back down in his chrome chair. Randall thought he looked a little lost with his bright clothes and his short hair. He wondered, not for the first time, just how old Knox really was.

"Nearly a month after the last postcard, a U.P.S. van drove up in front of the dorm. They brought me a large wooden crate, postage paid. There were tags all over it, but I couldn't tell who it was from. I had to borrow a tire iron from one of the kids in the hall to pry it open." He took another slug of bourbon. "It was Swan."

"What, uh…" Randall had to clear his throat to speak. "What condition was he in?"

"In the sleep," said Knox. Randall relaxed visibly. "But badly damaged. The inside of the crate had been lined with plastic garbage bags. He was covered with dried blood. I couldn't tell who it was at first. And the smell…" Knox trailed off, took another drink. Rose squirmed in his seat but did not ask for the bottle. "He must have escaped from whoever attacked him. Stayed awake long enough to ship himself to me. Or maybe had the girl do it. I don't know."

"You suspect Lisel." It was not a question.

"Or some other elder nasty."

Randall shook his head. "You know the rules. Families don't fuck with other families. There are few enough of us as it is."

"It could have been the brotherhood."

"Not very likely. When's the last time you heard of them attacking another immortal? Decades ago. They were catching too much flack from everybody else. It had to be her."

Knox sat forward, eyes bright. One hand went involuntarily to his scalp, caressing the dead white stubble. "You should have seen him, Randall. It was far worse than anything she ever did to you." He looked at the bourbon, then set it on the floor.

"That would have to be pretty severe," Randall said dubiously.

"There were pieces of him missing." For a while, the two brothers sat looking at each other. Rose surreptitiously took the bottle and drank.

"You have him hidden somewhere, I assume," Randall said eventually.

"Yes, he's safe. She knows where I am, so he's not in Santa Cruz."

"Not going to be more specific than that?"

"I think it's better if only I know. I put him somewhere pretty inaccessible. You know, just in case."

"Yeah." Randall stood and walked through the maze of books to the window. Outside the mist swirled and eddied about the enormous tree trunks that filled the entire view. "How much longer, do you figure?"

"A couple more months at least. Why?"

Randall turned his back to the window, facing Knox. "When he wakes, if he tell us it was her, will you join me?"

Knox put his head in his hands. "I don't know."

"And why the fuck not?" Randall roared. "Got something better to do, have you?" He aimed a swift kick at the nearest stack of books. Pages burst and flew, scattering about the room. "What's so God damn important? Your glorious past?" He stood over Knox now, glowering down at him. His voice dripped with contempt. "Or were you thinking of running for President again?"

"Okay," said Knox, sounding old and tired. "If Swan joins you, I'll join you. Is that enough?" Randall said nothing, just paced slowly back to the window.

After a long silence, Rose curled up on the mattress and went to sleep. When he awoke it was dark once more. The two brothers sat on the floor, the bottle of bourbon between them, discussing the siege of Vera Cruz.

❧

Trees surrounded them. The thick redwood trunks climbed straight into the sky, so dense they seemed to merge with one another at some undefined distance, becoming one solid arch of brown and gently waving green supported by uncounted columns. The damp remains of fallen leaves squelched underfoot. Moss the color of worn felt dusted the high roots protruding from the soil. Clusters of tiny mushrooms grew in the sheltered spots between gnarled arms. The ever-present mist hung in the warm air, swirling languidly between the damp earth and the dome of far off treetops. Randall inhaled deeply. The aroma of live wood and fertile ground mingled with the bite of the mist, teasing at his memory. It smells like November, he concluded, though he knew it to be spring.

They walked without destination, letting the lay of the land lead them on. Rose was unusually silent, looking down at his boots. Randall did not intrude upon his thoughts, or even wonder what they might be. The greatness of the trees, their ancient bulk all about him made him feel concrete and alive. He turned his left hand before his face. Tender layers of pink skin and a pair of partially regrown nails were all that remained of the previous damage. The arm looked as if it had suffered only a mild scald. Randall moved his fingers, articulating each joint separately then flexing them together. The mere physical fact of his hand amazed him. He stared at it in fascination, opening and closing his fist, and nearly walked into a tree.

The magnitude of the thing awed him. A one lane tunnel could have been drilled through it without seriously threatening its stability. Every inch of circumference signified years, possibly even decades of life. Randall laughed quietly to himself. And I thought I was old, his mind whispered. These bastards are the real survivors. He sprinted forward to catch up with Rose, who walked on obliviously. "So," Randall inquired cheerfully, "what do you think?"

"I think," said Rose, "that maple sugar candy ought to be sold year round, and not just during Christmas time." He favored Randall with a lesser version of his insane grin, a hopeful understudy.

"No. I meant what do you think of all this?" Randall swept his hands through the air, turning full circle in his enthusiasm.

"Oh." Rose seemed disappointed. He shrugged carelessly. "Beats rush hour traffic, I suppose."

Randall stopped, and leaned back against a rust-red trunk, hands behind his back. "Do you mean to say that all this doesn't do something to you?" He took a huge breath, exhaling loudly.

Rose did likewise, then sneezed so violently that he staggered backward. "Well, I suppose it does something to me at that," he said, wiping his nose.

"That's not what I meant, either."

"You keep saying that." Rose resumed his random amble. "Why don't you try saying exactly what it is you do mean?"

"Sure thing." Randall followed, keeping a pace or two behind his friend. "I want Knox's help when we square off with Lisel. But he wants to wait and see what Swan-that's the youngest of us-has to say about whoever attacked him."

"I understood that."

"Good. Then you also understand that Swan is in the sleep somewhere, so we can't talk to him for another couple of months."

"Yes, I understand that, too." Rose turned, walking backwards to look at Randall. "I can even guess where this is going."

"Can you now?"

"Certainly." Now his full fledged grin took the stage, transforming his eyes into bottomless pools of mania. "You want to know whether or not I can stand to cool my heels in this hippie haven until baby brother wakes up, yes?"

"That's basically the essence of it." Randall regarded his friend suspiciously. "So how about it? Do you think you can lay low here for a while without going completely berserk?"

Rose's smile collapsed. "I suppose so." He looked around sullenly at the giant trees. "I mean, it can't all be like this, can it?" He turned, skipping lightly down a gentle slope.

"Actually," said Randall, "if what I understand from Knox is true, this place has quite a night life. It's a college town, after all."

Rose snorted. "And what would Knox know about night life? He looks as if he hasn't set foot out of that room for thirty years, except to teach classes and find books to tear up. Did you see what he was wearing? The man could be a poster child for the sixties." He scratched distractedly at his beard. "And to hear you two talk, he used to be a soldier. Incredible."

Randall walked close beside Rose, hands in the pockets of his long brown coat. "Knox was a hard man once. As callous a bastard as you'd ever care to meet. I've seen him order whole platoons to charge cannons when all they had were swords. He shot one of his junior officers through the head once. Some sort of conspirator. No court martial. No firing squad. No last request. He just ordered the man into his tent and blew his brains out. The poor fuck hadn't even finished saluting."

They came to the foot of a long wooden stair leading up the lip of the small valley they were exploring. The clap of their boot heels sounded unnaturally loud and clumsy in the misty silence. Gradually, they worked their way out of the trees and up into bright sunlight. "The Civil War did something to him. I'm not sure if it was anything particular he saw, or just the awesome futility of the whole enterprise. Killing each other. Burning our own land. Before then it had been Mexico, Spain, French Canada, Mother England. But that war… It was like asking a man to amputate his own leg. Anyway, he never fought again. I doubt he even owns a weapon anymore."

The rise terminated in a long deck running the length of the ridge. From the other side, stairs descended into a complex of wooden walks and bridges which linked several small buildings. Tiny streams of weed-choked water wove in and around the sunken supports. Rose hunched forward against the weathered railing, watching people come and go. "They look fairly civilized, Doctor Livingston. Shall we attempt to make contact?"

Randall rested against the rail, looking at his friend earnestly. "I'd like to maintain a low profile while we're here, if you don't mind. Go ahead and entertain yourself, just try and stay out of jail. No hold-ups. No bar fights. No kidnapping the coeds. The more we blend in, the better I'll feel."

Rose said nothing to this, just continued to watch the people below. A young woman in shorts and a halter top emerged from one of the buildings. His eyes followed her across a series of bridges and into another structure at the far end of canyon. He sighed quietly. "What was that you said when you got pissed at Knox?" he inquired. "Did he really run for President once?"

Randall slapped his good hand on the wooden rail. "What do they teach you people in school these days?"

"Just droll dialog and the proper use of firearms. Why? Am I missing something?"

"You certainly are." Randall chuckled. "Knox not only ran for President once, he was the President."

chapter four

"Draw, you lily-livered varmint!"

Rose pulled the revolver from the clunky plastic holster at his side and fired off all six rounds. The cowboy on the projection screen before him collapsed in a heap of cheap costuming and ketchup wounds. "You got me," he breathed, taking a terribly long time to keel over completely.

"No shit."

The screen blanked out, then panned across the facade of a frontier saloon. The batwing doors sprung open, disgorging a Hollywood bandito with a horrendously over-waxed mustache. He held a serving girl before him as a human shield. Her painted eyes pleaded for aid. "You could help me out a little," Rose muttered. "Knee him in the nuts or something." He pulled the six shooter and fired, eager to avoid the bandito's campy dialog. The man dropped away from the girl, shouting random words in Spanish, then mercifully expired.

The woman rushed forward, or rather the camera zoomed in toward her face. "Oh, thank you!" she gushed. "How can I ever repay you, kind sir?" She colored, then looked saucily out from under her false lashes. "I'm just ever so grateful. Come on up and see me some time."

Rose grimaced. "For that I should ventilate you too, you brazen hussy." Big red letters obliterated the smiling face: Game Over. Rose undid the plastic gun belt. "Waste of a perfectly good quarter."

The two brothers wandered over from the air hockey tables. "Whipped your ass again, just like last time." Knox punched Randall playfully in the shoulder.

"The hell you did." Randall folded his arms across his chest, radiating mock belligerence. "I slaughtered you the last time we played. Today you got lucky, that's all."

"Get real. Our last game couldn't have been more than... what... twelve years ago? My memory isn't that bad. You'll just have to face facts, I am the king of ghetto hockey."

"King? And here I thought you were such a fan of democracy."

"Hey guys," Rose interrupted, "let's blow this pop stand. I'm in the mood for some real action."

"Fine with me," said Knox. "I can only take so much of this place at one time." They strolled toward the exit, passing row upon row of videogames. A cluster of teenage boys watched one of their number maneuver a red convertible through a crowded freeway, slamming at the gear shift and stomping the accelerator. An even younger group fought street thugs with joystick-controlled karate. Further on, an attractive woman in an evening dress and pearls blissfully machine-gunned incoming paratroopers while her tuxedoed escort looked on in admiration.

To either side of the main doors, giant glass cylinders bubbled with blue tinted water. Mannequins in old style diving suits stood guard over twin treasure chests, their lusterless eyes staring out the tiny windows of bulbous brass air helmets. "Just what in tarnation are these for?" Rose inquired, stopping to gawk for a moment.

"I've absolutely no idea," Knox replied. "They've been here as long as I can remember. Those diving suits actually functioned at one time, though why anybody thought the mannequins needed fresh oxygen is beyond me." He put his face up to the glass, examining the faded collection of costume jewelry strewn about the tank's floor. "This place is called Neptune's something or other, though it's been ages since the sign burned out."

They pushed through the big glass doors and out onto the boardwalk. All the major varieties of college students strode up and down the concrete shore, from ragged punks with spiked-studded jackets and nose rings to stodgy maidens on an outing from the all girls dormitory. A tight knot of fraternity boys, an endangered species in Santa Cruz, talked loudly amongst themselves. The three men slipped easily into the flow of bodies, heading in the general direction of the carnival rides.

At the far end of the boardwalk, a mildly impressive wooden roller coaster imposed its latticed geometry upon a sky kept bright by an array of mercury vapor lamps. Enthusiastic screams carried across the intervening space. Slightly closer, an over-built Ferris wheel turned sedately in the air. The three passed by a battered merry-go-round. Rose followed the progress of a scuffed looking unicorn until it disappeared from view. "Hey, wait a minute–didn't they film part of a Dirty Harry movie here?"

"Sure did," said Knox. "Some mass murderer or other fell out of the coaster way over yonder and landed on the merry-go-round over here. Pretty good trick if you ask me." He watched the painted horses accelerate, humming along to the organ music. "They filmed a vampire movie here as well. One of the opening scenes, as I remember."

"Which one was it?" Rose peered intently at the whirling steeds.

"It was fairly recent." Knox spread his hands. "The name escapes me, I'm afraid."

"Hold on," said Randall. "You mean that piece of shit with Donald Sutherland's kid and those God-awful Coreys? I hated that film."

"That's the one." Knox nodded his agreement. "I thought it was okay, you know, for a movie."

"I still don't know what film you're talking about," said Rose. He continued on down the boardwalk. "I obviously need to get out more often."

"Maybe if you spent less time in jail..."

"Ha, ha. It is to laugh. You are just such the comedian, Randall."

"Do my ears deceive me, or do I detect just a hint of sarcasm?"

"A drop, perhaps." They passed by a tattoo stand. A muscular man in old fatigues slumped in the chair as though dead while the artist raked a multi-needle fan across his upper arm, coloring in a parrot. Only a twitching knot at his jaw betrayed that he felt anything at all. Another chorus of delighted screams wafted over from the roller coaster. "I'm tired of this teeny-bopper bullshit," Rose complained. "Let's go somewhere totally else."

"Cool by me," said Randall. He looked furtively around at the crowd. "I'm not too keen on being out in the open like this."

Rose heaved a sigh that became a raspberry. "Like anybody's given us a second glance all evening. Really, Randall-you're straying dangerously close to the realm of paranoia."

"Come off it. You're just peeved because that sassy coed left you flat."

"Like that's my fault. Your brother the recluse doesn't even have a telephone."

"He doesn't believe in them. Besides, the number she gave you started with five-five-five."

"It's not that I don't believe in telephones," Knox broke in. "I do not deny the existence of the phone as such. That would be irrational. I just don't like the damn things. Oh, never mind." He jumped ahead of them, into an alley of rip-off game booths and freak show tents. The smooth, insistent patter of a dozen different hucksters assaulted their ears. Hungry eyes followed them, dragging at their attention, while unconnected voices rolled on forever. They ran the gauntlet successfully and exited the boardwalk through a revolving door of horizontal bars.

Once they hit the street, Knox slowed to walk even with his companions. "So what's it to be, then? Drink and debauchery? Live sex shows?"

"Nah." Rose waved a dismissive hand. "We did all that yesterday."

"I know this great little Chinese restaurant, if you're in the mood." Randall covered a laugh. He had never see his brother behave like this before. Rose seemed to bring out the tour guide in him. "Or the Saturn's probably still open. They make a mean cappuccino." Randall lost control and giggled audibly, but the other two did not seem to hear.

"I'm not hungry, exactly." Rose draped an arm casually over Knox's shoulders. "Think of something more adventurous."

"We could go hear some jazz. Or a thrash band, if that's more your scene." He looked down at his flimsy t-shirt as if just noticing it for the first time. "Though, come to think of it, I'm not dressed properly for a mosh pit."

"They'd cut you to ribbons, no question." Rose halted suddenly, dragging Knox to a stop with him. Randall sidestepped them both nimbly. "I've got it!" Rose declared, smacking his forehead with his free hand. "Let's go hot tubbing!"

Knox ducked neatly out from under Rose's arm, his friendly expression darkening toward anger. "What do you think?" he asked Randall. "Should we castrate him and kill him, or just castrate him?"

Randall appeared to consider this. "Either one," he said finally. "But let's wait a while, get him when he isn't expecting it."

"Oh, I agree." They shook hands formally.

"Uh, it was just a joke guys." Rose swallowed nervously, running a hand through his mop of hair.

"Sure, sure," said Randall, starting off down the sidewalk. "Come along,

Renfield." They walked aimlessly for a while, passing nightclubs, head shops, and used records stores.

"Hey, I know where we can go." Knox looked around, then turned a corner. "You guys'll love this place. It's kind of a ways. We should probably take the bus." They walked a couple more blocks, stopping before one of the shabby wooden shacks.

Rose found the schedule, half buried under a crust of bar coupons and concert advertisements. He squinted at it in the dim light of a nearby street lamp. "Should be here any minute now," he announced. As if on cue, a bus rounded the corner, grinding to a halt just far enough up the street to envelope them in exhaust fumes. "Ah," said Rose, fanning futilely at the air, "I do so love public transportation."

The doors squeaked open and they clambered in. Knox flashed some sort of campus I.D. and the driver waved him through. Randall counted out coins and fed them to the sorting machine.

Rose padded at his various pockets. "I don't suppose you can change a five? No? How about barter?" He displayed half a pack of cigarettes. Randall slapped a jumble of change into his hand. "Thank you, my savior." The driver closed the door and started off while Rose sifted through the coins. As they lurched into traffic, the interior lights went out. "Air raid!" Rose yelled, grabbing onto the nearest pole for support, spilling money everywhere. Growling in disgust, he stooped down to the floor and groped for the scattered coins. Cursing under his breath, he dumped the whole handful into the sorting machine and staggered blindly toward the rear of the bus. "I'd like everyone here to know that I think this fuel economizing shit has gone too far."

"Sit down, you idiot," Randall called from somewhere.

"Insult me again so I can find you."

"Oh, like we want you next to us." Rose flopped into a seat at random. As they passed a street lamp, he made out Knox and Randall just across the aisle. "So where is this hell carriage taking us?"

Knox said nothing for a moment. "You'll just have to wait and see." Mischief danced in his eyes. Rose groaned.

"It's not a gothic club, is it?" Randall asked suspiciously. "Cause if it is, I'm going to leap out the window right now. The last thing I want to do is hang out with a bunch of pasty humans on speed listening to the latest Nine Inch Nails single."

"Oh, it's even better than that."

Randall leaned over towards Rose. "I don't think I like the sound of this. Not one little bit."

"Forgive me for the hot tub crack and we'll tag team him."

"Deal." The bus ground to a halt. The pneumatic door hissed open and the lights flashed on. A collective grunt of blinded betrayal echoed around the bus. Someone in hard heels stamped up the steps as the passengers rubbed at their eyes. The door closed, and darkness fell once more. "This is obviously some new development in urban warfare," said Rose. "Chinese bus torture. Think I read about it in *USA Today*."

"We're almost there," Knox assured him.

"Joy." Passing cars sent rays of light searching through the windows. Rose caught glimpses of faded ads and route maps in the brief spears of illumination. He glanced down at his seat, surprised to find that it was a deep red instead of gray or black. After several minutes in traffic, the bus finally stopped. Rose closed his eyes this time, blinking rapidly when the lights popped on.

"This is us." Knox stood, ushering the other two forward. They filed reluctantly out onto the pavement.

"I'm warning you, brother dear," Randall began, "if this is some stupid…" He stopped, staring at the neon sign above the building before them. Sharp red letters stood out against the black facade: Vampyre Café. "You can't be serious."

"Come on," said Knox, pulling open the door. "You'll love it."

The interior seemed designed to confuse. Murals covering the side walls depicted Mediterranean arches of worn stone with darkened streets beyond, giving the room a false airiness. The tiled floor imitated cobblestone, though the pattern of artificial rocks repeated itself visibly. The low ceiling had been painted to resemble a cloth canopy. Fire sprinklers pierced the illusion at regular intervals. Small tables with checkered cloths sat scattered about in no particular order. A counter with accompanying stools facing a narrow window onto the kitchen ran along the back wall. Posters, photos, and press cuttings covered this wall, all to do with vampires. Randall examined the images of every pop culture demon from Lugosi to Lestat. He shook his head. They all looked so artificial, so on stage.

So did the patrons. There were a few classic vampires, cape draped, decked out in widow's peak and white face. Most of them sat alone, taking the occasional sip of tea and giving one another ominous looks.

The rest of the crowd had opted for the modern variation. Black trench coats and bolo ties. Or leather jackets, punk hair cuts, and a sprinkling of face powder. A quartet of women wearing dark evening gowns and gigantic costume jewels clustered around a table by the wall.

"Unbelievable," Randall murmured.

The three sat down at a vacant table. Rose put his boots up on the pristine tablecloth, leaning back in his chair. He looked all around slowly, then blew a whistle at his shaggy bangs. "You come here often, do you, Knox?"

"Only when I need a laugh."

"These people are disgusting," Randall said, quite loud in the relative silence of the room.

Knox sunk gradually down in his seat until he had achieved a comfortable slump. "I was thinking you might want to recruit them. They seem awfully keen on the lifestyle."

Randall snorted, practically spitting on the table in indignation. "Look at them. What they want is death. They're not living now, so why give them more life?" He dismissed them all with a slashing sweep of his arm. "This whole place is one massively idiotic skullfuck."

A waitress stepped briskly up to the table. The cheerful animation of her young face seemed an almost deliberate contrast to the vacant expressions of the customers. She wore the uniform of waitresses everywhere: a neat pink skirt and blouse, pleats ironed; comfortable shoes; and hair in a bob. An embroidered doily pinned to her pert bosom declared her to be Nicole. She looked scrubbed and alert and entirely too vivacious. "Good God," whispered Rose, "it's the competent American waitress from hell."

She drew a pen from her apron pocket and held it poised above her order pad. "And what can I get you gentleman?" she asked.

"How about a menu?" Rose returned.

"We don't have one." She smiled demurely. "You'll just have to wing it, I'm afraid."

Rose swung his feet back to the floor and took a better look at her. His maniac smile pulled at the corners of his mouth. "And here I thought I had you." He scratched at his beard, considering. "No menu. Well, in that case, I'd like a B.L.T., a basket of fries, a slice of apple pie a la mode, and a Coke, no ice." He watched while she scribbled furiously at her pad.

"Pepsi okay?"

"Perfect."

Knox leaned toward Randall. "I though he said he wasn't hungry."

"He isn't."

"And what would you like, sir?" Once again, her pad stood at the ready.

Knox beamed up at her. "Oh, just coffee, please."

She didn't even bother to write it down. "And you?"

"The same." Her sprightly voice and efficient movements had begun to grate on Randall's nerves. He gave her a grim look, then forced his face to relax after catching a glimpse of the other patrons. Maybe it's her, he thought.

"And would you like anything with that? Cream? Sugar?"

"Black is fine," Knox replied. Randall said nothing while he contemplated his negative reaction to her vitality. He looked up at her once more, this time feeling the red lust prickle at him.

"Sir? Would you like anything special in your coffee?"

He smiled. "Bleed in it."

She bustled off toward the kitchen.

The front door swung open and a couple walked in. The other regulars acknowledged them with silent nods. The man seemed to be an extreme example of the type. His unevenly cut black hair stood away from his head in unwashed tufts, though his pale face was smooth and clean. A shapeless black duster hung down to his knees, partially concealing dark jeans and a slashed up Cure t-shirt. His Doc Martens squeaked with every step across the linoleum cobblestones.

Randall dismissed him from notice almost immediately, focusing instead on the woman. She was short-noticeably so-and Asian, though he could not place the country from her features. Glossy black hair hung straight down her neck, blending into the bulky jacket slung over her shoulders. Bright eyes and a sharp nose gave her an air of alert observation, though she walked casually enough beside her companion. Randall recalled a statue he had once seen of Kali, the Hindu mother of creation and destruction. The face was much the same. He had the disconcerting notion that if the woman dropped her jacket, she would reveal a dozen delicate white arms, each hand clutching a knife or a lotus blossom.

As soon as he was seated the man adopted a pose of melancholy contemplation, chin in hand, staring off into space. For her part, the Kali woman looked her companion over with naked calculation. After a moment or two, she tired of him and shifted round in her seat to examine the crowd. Her gaze lit on Randall eventually, and he returned her stare with casual intensity. She looked away first, though not quickly.

The frightfully cheerful waitress returned, bearing drinks. She set them down in the correct places and paced briskly away. Randall's coffee had a distinctly reddish tinge. He considered it for a moment, puzzled and more than a little disconcerted. Finally, he ventured a sip. Grenadine. It ruined the taste completely, but he decided to feel relieved.

"I think she likes me," Rose declared. He took a gigantic swig of his Pepsi.

"Who?" asked Randall. "Miss Teen U.S.A.? I didn't think you went in for the wholesome type."

"You of all people should be aware of the joys of corrupting the innocent." Rose looked critically at his drink. "I wonder if they give free refills?"

Knox had been examining the couple ever since they entered with a covertness Randall found somewhat ridiculous. Now he dragged his chair a little closer towards their table and tapped the young man on the shoulder. He turned his head to look with affected disinterest, saying nothing. "Excuse me," Knox began, "but I was just wondering why you were staring off into nothing like that." Knox gave him the knowing look he usually reserved for his students. "Tripping on something good, are we? Get a hold of a potent blotter?"

The pale young man shook his head. "I am contemplating the misery of my fate," he explained in a voice that implied it should have been obvious. Kali's attention snapped back to the conversation. She sat upright in her chair, the big jacket concealing her body like a cape, her vividly anxious face focused entirely on the two men.

Knox did not seem to notice the additional scrutiny. He was far too interested in the callow youth. "What fate would that be, precisely?" His voice showed only genuine curiosity, though Randall could see condescension in the set of his shoulders, the tilt of his neck.

"I have become a creature of darkness," the young man confided in a stage whisper. His whole face seemed to sag. Kali's eyes glittered.

"Ah, I see." Knox turned back to his own table as if this answer had satisfied him completely. Hunching down close to Rose, he pointed a covert finger. "This guy over here, he says he's become a creature of darkness. Isn't that fabulous?"

Rose had finished his soda and was twirling the glass lightly between his hands. "That's rather vague, isn't it?" He raised the glass up over one eye and peered through the bottom. "You didn't delve any further?" Before Knox could answer, Rose had dragged his own chair over to the other table and accosted the man himself. "Sorry to bother you," he said. "My friend tells me you're a creature of darkness. Now, I'm very curious. What type of creature would that be? I mean, specifically?" His eyebrows launched themselves up his forehead, emphasizing the question.

The man turned even more slowly than before, veritably limp with sorrow. Kali's features seemed to sharpen. The man opened his mouth, saying nothing, then closed it again. He leaned toward Rose, collapsing forward without his own volition. "I am the wampire," he breathed.

Rose nodded tersely, then scooted his chair back to his place, legs scraping loudly on the tile. "Randall," he said, barely holding in his mirth, "this boy says he is the wampire."

Randall made a show of looking him over. "He is the wampire?"

"I am the walrus."

"Coo coo caju."

"Come again?" said Knox confusedly.

"Pop culture reference." Randall looked curiously at his brother. "What was the last band you really liked?"

"John Philip Sousa." Knox pounded his fist on the table decisively. The flatware jumped. "Though, come to think of it, he didn't really have just one band, did he?"

"The prosecution rests."

The sprightly waitress returned with Rose's meal, dessert included, and fresh drinks for everyone. Rose neglected to make a pass at her, jilting her temporarily in favor of his french fries. She stopped at the couple's table and poured two coffees. Randall looked around, but she seemed to be the only waitress in the place. He wondered if she did the cooking as well. She disappeared into the kitchen, the swinging door rustling the posters and papers on the wall.

Randall examined his second cup of coffee. More grenadine. He wondered if she was toying with him, or if it was some sort of house special. Well, he thought, at least there's no cherry. Taking up his original mug, he saluted the couple at their table. "Here's rest for the weary," he exclaimed, "and peace for the damned." He tossed down the bittersweet liquid. The aftertaste was actually quite pleasant, like the lingering flavor of a child's cough drop. He considered the next cup.

The pale young man's drooping eyes lifted from the floor. He wrestled himself around completely, then staggered into a standing position. "You!" It was less of yell than a wail. What little conversation there had been died. All the faces in the room swiveled towards him. Kali stared as though she meant to burn holes in his back.

"You dare to mock my affliction?" He looked around at the crowd, meeting with nods and harsh smiles. They were with him, all right. Death to the interlopers. "Our affliction," he amended. He pulled at one of the holes in his shirt, revealing flesh as pale as paper. "We are the undead," he continued raggedly. "Do you know what a terrible curse this is?" The regulars had begun to mutter among themselves. Rose's hand crept into the interior of his leather jacket while Knox looked about in bemused surprise. The youth lurched forward. "Our eyes have seen civilizations come and go like... like..." He trailed off for want of a decent metaphor.

This can't be happening, thought Randall. A mob of costumed punks led by a drugged-out zombie wannabe are going to jump us. This is just too stupid to be real. But as he looked around the room, he saw quite clearly that it was indeed happening. No question. All over the café, chairs scooted away from tables and hands went into pockets, purses. Faces and bodies tensed. Eyes stabbed at him from all directions. They could snap in a second, would snap soon enough even if he did nothing.

Randall wanted to laugh. They were so pitiful, clinging to the trappings of death, worshipping it as though it were something ultimately sensual. I've been there, he thought. I've been there and it's nothing. Literally nothing. Total absence, without even a tinge of mystery. But here they were, oblivion's tramps, ready to tear him to pieces in defense of Death's glamour. To hell with them, he thought. If they want a fight they've got one. He looked at the pallid youth standing before him in his ragged black clothes, listing on his squeaky boots as though punch-drunk already.

Even before the back of his chair hit the floor, Randall stood within inches of his adversary, the tip of his hunting knife resting just below the shaven chin. Rose's gun was out, for the moment pointed towards the ceiling. Several people in the crowd who had started to stand now thought better of it. Knox continued to look around in perplexity, as though he'd walked in on the middle of a movie.

"So you've seen civilizations come and go, have you?" Randall stared into his accuser's eyes, but his voice carried to the entire crowd. "You're ancient. Damned. Oh so weary of this vale of tears." He stood back a little to look at the rest of his audience, though the knife remained rooted in place. "Do I have the general idea?" No one answered. "You're looking for death but you just can seem to find it. Never returns your phone calls. Always out of the office when you drop by." He returned his attention to the youth. "I sympathize. I'm here to help." He jabbed the knife upward minutely. The youth flinched. Blood beaded on the blade. "Here it is, my handsome friend. The underworld on a plate. All you have to do is say the word." Randall's smile twisted into a wicked grimace. "So how about it, boy?"

He stared intently into the youth's eyes until they seemed to recede in fear. Behind him, Kali looked as if she were about to burst into flame from inner tension, her face flushed red, jaw clenched and quivering. Randall waited a long moment while his adversary said nothing. He scanned the crowd. Most of them looked away.

When it had become painfully clear that the youth was not going to risk saying anything, Randall withdrew the knife. The pale young man fell back into his seat, shivering uncontrollably. Kali deflated visibly, her sharp features conveying a vast disappointment. "I thought not," said Randall quietly. Part of his mind urged him to stop here, to depart while the stunned silence lasted, never to return. But the rage he felt towards these people would not allow that. He had stepped on stage with them, and he now would stay. "In that case," he said more brightly, "I have another offer." Placing the knife between his teeth, he rolled up one sleeve of his brown trench coat, revealing the pink hairless flesh of his newly healed left arm.

Knox blanched, then leaned in close to Rose. "He's not going to set himself on fire again, is he?"

"Don't know. I missed it the first time." Rose glanced over the crowd. All eyes were on Randall, so he slipped his pistol back into his jacket.

Randall took the knife in his right hand. He brandished it above his head so that everyone could see, then brought the blade down to rest lightly on his left wrist. With a patient movement, he drew the gleaming edge across his flesh. Blood welled from the wound, falling to the floor in audible pats. He held the hand up and blood flowed down his arm, dripping from the elbow. "Who wants to live forever?" Nobody spoke. The entire crowd stared at him as though flash frozen.

"Come on!" he yelled. Placing one boot on a vacant chair, he vaulted onto the couple's table, scattering crockery. His blood spattered the checkered tablecloth. "I'm offering eternal life here! Watch your friends age and die, see cities grow and wither. Yours for no money down." He shifted his stance; the table sagged. Kali stared up at him from the confines of her enormous jacket. For a moment he could not read her expression. It was not fear, not awe. Nothing he might have expected. If anything, she looked fierce, prideful, triumphant. Randall flicked his hand at her, spotting her with blood. She didn't even flinch. Feeling strangely appalled, Randall leapt down from the table, sending it crashing to the floor.

"Isn't anybody interested?" He paced slowly from table to table, wounded arm extended, bleeding into cups and plates of food. "Nobody at all?" He sighed in disappointment, then whipped his arm around. A crimson stripe slashed across the cluster of women in evening gowns, trailing off onto the wall behind. They stared at him in mute horror. One woman put her hand to her face, pulling away sticky red fingers. Randall thought she might vomit. "How vastly tragic," he declaimed. "And here I thought I was running with the wolves." The flow from his slashed wrist began to slow, the blood on his forearm drying to a brown crust. With all the contempt he could muster, Randall spat upon the cobblestone floor. "Fuck the lot of you," he declared. Without a glance at his comrades, he walked out the door and into the night.

After an interval of silence, Kali shot up from her seat and bolted out of the café, jacket flapping from her shoulders. Her pale escort watched her go but did not follow. The crowd began to mutter loudly to itself. The blood-stained women moved as one towards the ladies' room.

"You know," Rose said thoughtfully, "I don't think Randall likes this place."

Knox favored him with a black look. "What do you think? Should we go after him?"

"To hell with that. I haven't finished eating." Rose drained his second Pepsi, then looked around for the waitress.

chapter **five**

Randall walked without purpose, his slit wrist jammed into the pocket of his long brown coat. He moved straight away from the café until the whim of the traffic lights prevented further progress in that direction. Without thinking, he turned the corner and walked on. He needed motion, not destination. Motion dulled the anger, kept his mind from returning to the scene he had just left. The scene he had created.

Why did I do it? He asked this several times each minute. Why did I do it? I wanted secrecy, anonymity. I wanted to blend into the city and fade from the notice of the night. So, why? Why? He scourged himself with the question. What was the point? Do I need to feel superior so badly that I parade myself before a restaurant full of listless freaks? Where's my restraint? He growled in self-loathing. Though the bleeding had stopped, his wrist throbbed in time with his beating heart. Pain is a primitive form of guilt, he decided. The body telling you that you've just done something stupid.

He came to another corner, more traffic. Not wishing to double back, he forced himself to stop and wait. Reality hammered at his mind, forcing him to take notice. The world had a brazen solidity that offended his soul. The cars shoot by in the half dark, white headlights blurring as they passed, transformed into fleeing red. The pale street lamp arched above him, shaped like something out of *The War of the Worlds*. The people walked by, oblivious, their lively faces scraping at the raw edges of his lust. The blood loss did not help at all. Salt in an open wound.

Too much, he thought, and closed his eyes. The absence of sight brought some relief, though the rumble of the traffic intensified. Wind from passing cars whipped his coat, tugged at his hair. He groped for the lamppost, felt his fingers brush the cold metal. Gratefully he slumped against it, gave it his weight. Traffic roared past.

How, he thought, am I supposed to react when you usher me into a room filled with shadows? Did Knox think I would find them entertaining? Enough of our own people get like that eventually. This is exactly what I'm fighting. Can't he see that? Or maybe I have a death wish after all. If we screw this up, we die. If we win, I die. Either way, I'm gone. But what's the use of just existing? Oh, fuck it. Never mind me. Just skip me for a second. When you get right down to it, nothing makes any sense. This whole planet is a practical joke. In a cosmic blink, the lot of us will be so much free hydrogen blowing through space, no matter how many pretty symphonies we've written. Now or later, what's the difference? It's all a matter of style. So on with the God damn show.

Randall opened his eyes. The oncoming light glowed green, so he started across the street. His wrist ached just enough so that he could not ignore it. The skin around the wound itched. He repressed the urge to scratch at the newly formed scab. Both hands clenched and unclenched in their separate pockets. A woman in a floral print jumper and sandals came toward him going the opposite direction. He found himself watching her as she passed, eyes lingering on her freckled shoulders.

It's too late, the red lust whispered. Do you honestly think your flagrant performance of this evening will go unnoticed? Rumor has swift wings, and word has already begun to go round. So why not go for broke? You may as well. Nothing more or less will come of it. Besides, the lust continued languidly, it's been so very long. Months, is it? Or perhaps more like years? A trickle here, a dribble there. Coyotes and house cats. How can you stomach that? A person dies for every beat of your heart, so why not one for you? They won't be any more dead, after all. Or any less.

Randall had learned long ago to deafen himself to the blood lust. It was, in many ways, the most inconvenient condition of his long existence. This urge, this ritual need. But he had caged it and starved it and fed it scraps to keep himself alive. The lust was the prisoner of his will, and not the reverse. But tonight-after his sourceless rage, his self mutilation, after the iron reality of the street and the people-he found himself listening to the voiceless whisper.

He toyed with the idea as a collector toys with a loaded gun, aware of the danger but unable to resist handling it. And why not? he thought. This fine city has some of the highest murder statistics in the world. Half the population are psychopaths of some kind. What's one more body in an alley dumpster? Nothing. A cough during an earthquake. I've become paranoid, renounced my heritage. I need this. Someone dies tonight. He savored the idea for a long moment. Then, having tasted its power, he locked the thought away.

Hoping to find some street animal to satisfy his hunger, he ducked into an alley. Rats skittered into piles of rubbish. Too small. He examined battered trashcans and crumbling cardboard boxes. Nothing suitable presented itself. More annoyed than disappointed, he exited the alley. Traffic was light, so he crossed the street from the middle, edging between parked cars. It was then that he spotted Kali, trailing him. The oversized jacket concealed her arms and torso like a shroud.

Just what I need, he thought. A groupie. Or maybe she just wants to beat the shit out of me for insulting her boyfriend. He considered ditching her, leaping into a side street and climbing the first fire escape he came to. But something held him back, a desire to tack a better ending onto the foolish scene he had just played, a need for resolution. So he walked at a normal pace, ignoring her presence behind him. A pool hall occupied the next corner. On impulse he stepped inside.

Stale smoke and the clatter of billiard balls blended with the restless patter of the players. Randall looked casually around. No women. And all of the men looked sharp and starved and a thousand years old, hustlers taking a break from the college tables, sharking one another for the price of a pitcher of draft. Randall sat at the counter and ordered a beer. Okay, he thought, let's see how badly she wants to talk.

He kept an eye on the door. Soon he saw her stroll past the grimy window. Their eyes met. She moved on. Randall laughed silently to himself and took a sip of beer. Then she was back, coming from the opposite direction, pushing boldly through the door. None of the players gave her a second glance. They had sacrificed the sex urge to the god of the game long ago. She sat down on the stool next to his.

Again Randall had the unsettling impression of some supernatural physical feature concealed by her jacket. He pictured a dozen milk white hands passing trinkets back and forth in the humid darkness. Hat pins. Snuff boxes. Voodoo dolls. Or perhaps the bulky garment hid a thousand eyes, moist and blinking, looking out of a thousand puckered scars. Just as this image passed through his mind, she shrugged the jacket off her shoulders. It was all he could do not to laugh aloud. A loose cotton shirt revealed her lack of a brassiere, and a small brown mole near the base of her throat. There was nothing else unusual about her. She turned towards him, unleashing a beautiful white-toothed smile. "Buy a lady a drink?" she asked.

Randall felt determined not to let her off so easy. "Introduce me to her, and I'll think about it," he replied.

She chose to misinterpret in his favor. "Lisa Robinson." She extended a slender hand.

This time he decided to play along. "Randall Springfield." She possessed a firm, warm grip that somehow matched her smile. He signaled the bartender and bought her a beer without asking what she wanted. She did not object, just thanked him politely.

Lisa took a healthy gulp from her glass. "So," she began conversationally, "how did you do that trick at the café?"

"Which trick was that?" Randall smirked at her over his drink.

"You know." She held up her left hand and made vague slicing motions over it with her right. "That trick with your wrist."

"Oh," said Randall, feigning surprise. "That wasn't a trick." He pulled his hand from its hiding place in his coat pocket, laying it palm upright on the bar. "See?" A rusty clump of dried blood sealed the deep cut along his wrist. The surrounding tissue had turned red and puffy. Randall prodded the wound with his right index finger. Clear liquid ran from a crack in the scab while the swelling lessened noticeably.

"Jesus," Lisa hissed, and held out a trembling hand to touch the injury. The brush of her small fingers made Randall's wrist tingle in a way that felt both pleasant and repulsive. Her light touch crossed from one end of the cut to the other, then back again. He wanted to tell her to stop but could not, as though he were unconsciously exploring the wound himself. After a final excruciating pass, she took her hand away.

"So," she started, and her voice broke. She coughed furiously, waving embarrassed excuses with one hand. Another hit from her beer restored her. "So," she began again, blushing. "You're one of... You're... Oh, God." She put her head in her hands, flushing crimson now. "I can't say it. I don't even know what to say." She shook her head ruefully.

Randall stalled by taking a drink. He found it hard to reconcile this sudden display of nerves with the blazing look of victory she had given him in the café, her persistence in following him here. She must be acting now, playing a role. But why? To what end? Did she seriously intend to charm him? The notion amused him, and he decided to humor rather than confront her. "Put simply," he said, "I don't die." He gave a self-deprecating laugh. "Well, not easily at any rate. Suicide is pretty much out of the question." He flourished his slashed wrist in her direction before returning it to his coat pocket. "You believe me?"

"Yes," she answered without hesitation. "But then, I've believed others before you." She shrugged as if to say that was all behind her now. "So far you've presented the most compelling evidence." She looked him in the eye, and something of her previous intensity returned. "There's nothing I want more, you know. My life, my consciousness. I enjoy myself always, have one hell of a good time. I want it to last, forever if possible." The fire dimmed, and she returned to her drink.

"So what do we do about it?"

"Anything," she replied casually. "Whatever it takes to make me like you. I don't care what it involves."

Randall winced inwardly at this. He'd heard it before, many times. Whatever it takes, master. I'll kiss toads, drink blood, wash your dirty socks. Just give me the red flower. Instead, he gave her the same lecture he had once given Rose. "This isn't like buying a new car, you know. It isn't something I can just do. If you decide to join me, you'll be entering into a rather complicated situation. And a dangerous one. There'll be a certain risk before your reward. There's even a chance that you'll die, and by that I mean permanent oblivion." He took a long drink of beer. "Still interested, Lisa Robinson?"

She stared soberly down at her drink. "A certain risk of death, you say?" An intense frown creased her face. She said nothing further, seemingly bent on examining her half-empty glass.

Randall finished his beer while she contemplated. The bustle and clatter of the pool tables droned on in the background. White noise. He wondered briefly what Knox and Rose were up to. Probably getting hammered on whiskey and plotting a panty raid on the all girls college. Recently those two behaved like they were living a teenage Friday night for their entire lives. In less than a week they had become comrades in arms. If nothing else, it was another hook into Knox. Another reason for him to join the crusade. Randall pictured them walking shoulder to shoulder along the boardwalk. Let them play, he thought. That's their end of the bargain.

When Lisa spoke it was to pose a question. "So what do you do with it, Randall Springfield?" She turned towards him, pensive. "Do you collect stamps? Read whole libraries? Screw lots of women?" She leaned closer. "What's your purpose, if you've got one?"

Reading my mind? Randall wondered. How much do I tell you? How much would you believe? Mother. The bikers. My plans for the colony. How much do I need to give to hook you? Or are you hooked already? "Let's just say that my purpose and your desire happily coincide."

She hoisted her glass, clearly unsatisfied, but unwilling to push the issue. "Show me where you live."

"It's not much," Randall asserted. "I haven't been there long."

"Show me anyway."

Her smile made him wary. She was acting again, taking the long way around towards something. It doesn't matter, he assured himself. Our goal is ultimately the same. I've kept things from her. So what if she doesn't give up her soul on a plate? She wouldn't betray me. She can't betray me and still get what she wants. "I could introduce you to the others, I suppose."

"Sure." She hopped down from the bar stool, loose breasts yawing to one side. "Anything you like." She wadded up her jacket and stuck it under one arm.

He followed her to the door, then held it open while she stepped through, her kilowatt smile cranking up a notch at his chivalry. Randall shook his head, perplexed. For a fleeting second, as they walked out into the night he felt... normal. Just a man walking with a woman, vaguely hopeful, vaguely happy. No weight of unnatural age, no awareness of difference. Just a simple human being once more. As they sauntered down the street, she took his hand in hers.

Suspicion flowed into him. The warmth of her skin, the lazy grace of her walk beside him, these were weapons to fear.

Randall led her inland, away from the boardwalk and the adjacent nightspots, towards the city center. "So where are you from, Lisa Robinson?" he asked to get her talking. Her silence had an unpleasant air of calculation.

She squinted in a way that emphasized the almond slant of her eyes, batting her lashes mysteriously. "Sacramento," she replied, then giggled.

He laughed, a little woodenly, far too aware of her small hand clasped to his. "I meant originally."

"Cambodia." Her smile flickered and went out. "I don't really remember it. Mother brought us here when I was very young." But he could see by the grim set of her face that she was remembering something quite vividly indeed. The muscles of her jaw bunched into tight knots that unraveled gradually into an expression of pleasant enjoyment. After a moment or two it looked almost natural. He led her on through the musty cones of light thrown down by decrepit street lamps.

A city bus pulled up to the curb just ahead of them, grinding to a reluctant halt and disgorging a group of chatty women, either higher class whores or lower class secretaries. The bright skirts and tight little blouses were the same. "Shall we?" Randall gestured at the bus with his wounded hand.

She ran ahead of him and scampered aboard, blinding the driver with a grin while she fished in the pockets of her jacket for her student ID. When Randall had paid, she took him by the hand once more, dragged him toward the back. She chose the seat over the rear wheel, squeezing in by the window. The hump of the wheel housing forced her legs against his. She pursed her lips flirtatiously, eyeing him with ludicrously overdone lust.

The doors hissed closed and the lights went out. Oops, thought Randall, I'd forgotten about that. The bus launched itself into the street. Almost immediately he felt her hand pull away from his. He winced, positive it would pounce again soon. But when it came, the touch on his chest was light, tender. For a while her fingers played softly up and down his abdomen, seemingly content with this limited domain. Her legs pressed against his. Her head rested on his shoulder. The clean scent of her hair filled his mind.

So gradually that he could not object, her hand ranged farther and farther down. The fingers caressed his stomach, traced the puckered scar of his first birth, the only one that never faded. The descending hand reached his jeans and held still for moment. He thought that she might stop there. Then he thought she might try and reach inside. The image filled him with alarm. Just as he tensed, she ran her hand down the outside of his pants to grip his inner thigh. Her tongue found its way into his ear. He pulled away, facing her in the dark. "Mrs. Robinson," he said seriously, "I think you're trying to seduce me."

She laughed, a completely natural half-snort of surprise no art could stifle. "Nonsense," she returned, "I've been friends with your parents for years." She fell back against the window, still giggling. "Believe it or not," she said when she could speak, "nobody's ever pulled that one on me before."

"You're right," said Randall. "I don't believe you."

Suppressing a residual chuckle, she leaned against him once more, put an arm around his waist. But the tension had gone, and her embrace felt merely friendly. She yawned, and snuggled deeper into his shoulder.

The bus ground to stop. The door opened and the lights flashed on. Once his eyes had adjusted, he looked down and caught her staring at him with such a frank expression of evaluation that he blinked in surprise. The look melted instantly away, replaced by sleepy affection. She nestled happily against him.

It doesn't matter, Randall told himself. The lights went out again.

❧

"Here we are."

"Oh my God. You can't be serious. A fucking mortuary?"

"It wasn't really my idea." Randall had tried to convince Knox to vacate Santa Cruz altogether. Finally, reluctantly, he agreed to leave his dorm room behind in favor of more obscure digs. But that was as far as he would budge. He insisted on continuing with his classes and his public life at the university.

They had lucked into the rooms above the mortuary. The previous occupants had just been arrested for dealing heroin. And in a town like Santa Cruz, there had been no end of applicants for the three separate rooms, one bath. Knox had carried the day with the funeral parlor's owner, a mousy, surprisingly squeamish man. Compared with the demented carnival that had been parading through his doors, the three of them looked downright respectable. And when the fellow heard that Knox was a tenured professor, that clinched it.

Randall liked the place, actually. It was clean, conveniently located, and inhumanly quiet except for the occasional bout of hysterical weeping leaking up through the floor. But that gave it a little character. Randall put an arm around Lisa's slim shoulders, directing her to the side of the serene white building. "It's not what you think. We live in the rooms

72

upstairs. It's not as if we sleep in coffins, or anything morbid like that."
He shuddered. "Frankly, that sort of thing has never appealed to me. I
have this irrational fear of accidental cremation."

"Still, don't you think it's a bit obvious?"

"Not if you think about it." He led her into a back alley and up a rickety
flight of wooden stairs that had been tacked on the building for the
convenience of the tenants.

"Okay," said Lisa, "I'll bite. How is a funeral home not an obvious
place to look for vampires?"

"What would creatures who feed on the living want with a bunch of
dead bodies? Embalmed at that. You ever smelled formaldehyde?" She
nodded, sharp nose wrinkling. "Well, it tastes about a thousand times
worse."

"Yuck! You mean you…" She could not bring herself to finish.

"Only once, by mistake of course." At the top of the stairs he pulled
out a ring of new keys and sifted through them, trying to remember
which one opened the door. "I was very drunk."

"No doubt."

Randall tried a key at random. It would not even go into the lock. He
tried a second, which fit. Opening the door, he ushered her into an
immaculate white hall with hardwood floors. The refurbishing had only
been completed a couple of days earlier, and the air smelled of paint. A
few scuff marks ran from the four interior doors back to the staircase,
results of the police seizure of the old furnishings. But the mousy
mortician and his wife had been at it with varnish, glossing over if not
repairing the damage.

Randall and Knox had taken the rooms to the right, with windows at
the back. Rose got the windowless room adjacent to the bathroom, as he
was the only one who used it much. Randall went over to Knox's door.
A post-it note hung at eye level. *Still grading, so piss off. This means you,
Randall.* Light leaked from under the door, though he heard nothing.

"Doesn't sound like the best time to meet him," said Lisa, reading
over Randall's shoulder.

"No, it doesn't," he agreed mildly. He turned to Rose's room, raised
a fist to knock, then stopped himself. Leaning an ear against the door,
he motioned at Lisa to remain silent. A verse of "She'll Be Coming
Round the Mountain" sounded faintly through the thick wood. Another

voice, female, moaned in harmony. Randall thought he caught a hint of creaking bedsprings, but he probably just imagined them. "Not the best time to meet Rose either, it would seem."

"What a shame," Lisa replied, smiling radiantly. "You can show me your room, at least." She stepped closer, taking hold of his arm. "After all, we have plenty of time. I haven't even gotten to know you yet."

Randall fiddled with his keys, then opened the door to his own room. Lisa preceded him inside, instinctively switching on the light. "As I said, I haven't done much with it so far." White walls, newly painted, nothing on them. Single bed with white sheets, crisp and unslept in. Rickety metal desk under a fire escape window, folded metal chair leaning against it. White dresser, almost empty, no closet. White mini blinds. Wood floor. Tile ceiling. The only color in the room came from a small stack of hardbound books sitting on the desk, on loan from his brother.

A small art print, also a gift from Knox, hung on the back of the door. It portrayed the venomous face of an intensely angry woman, all done in bold strokes of bright color, almost like finger-paint. "Jesus," said Lisa, examining the piece, "how can you sleep with that looking at you?"

"I don't need to sleep." He unfolded the metal chair and sat in the middle of the room, watching her.

She dumped her jacket in a heap beside the door. The painting glared over her shoulder. "Then what's with the bed?" The corners of her mouth twisted knowingly.

"It came with the room."

Lisa smirked at this, as if she had heard it before and had not believed it then either. He watched as she turned a slow circle, getting the ambiance. Her smile shifted up another gear. "I still don't believe you, you know."

"Honestly," said Randall, a bit confused, "it really came with the room." He leaned forward, elbows on his knees. "The owner and his family used to live up here when they were starting out."

"That's not what I meant." Lisa tilted back, leaning against the door. Her dark hair shrouded the malign gaze of the painting. "I meant that I still don't believe you can't make me one of you any time you like."

Great, Randall thought, back to this already. "It doesn't matter whether you believe me or not," he replied somewhat coldly. "There's something I have to do first," he continued, trying to put a friendly face on his denial, "something you can help me with if you like."

She hardly listened. "Can't it wait?" She pouted, biting her lower lip. "What do I have to do to show you how much I need this?"

Ye Gods, thought Randall. She can twist, but good. Best cut this off right now. "Just drop it," he said, letting anger edge into his voice. "I can't do it yet, that's all there is to it."

"Sure," she said, radiating disappointment. "Never mind." She stood silently for a moment, wringing the bottom of her shirt in her small hands. Looking up, she caught his eye. "So, Randall Springfield, would you like to fuck?"

"Listen Lisa," he began, "if you think that by..."

She stepped towards him, invading his space, cutting him off. Her small breasts hung before him at eye level beneath a thin layer of cotton. He saw that her nipples were hard. With effort, he looked up to her face. "I don't think anything," she said, returning his gaze. "I just want." Oh shit, thought Randall. Her smile shifted into overdrive, creating little dimples in her cheeks. She pulled off her shirt, tossing it after her jacket. A dozen small, circular scars dotted her breasts. Cigarette burns.

She sank forward onto him. Her warm flesh pressed against his chest. She planted light kisses on his neck, working her way up to his ear. He resisted the urge to clasp her to himself, but she did not seem to need encouragement. "Listen," he said, as she began to chew on his earlobe, "this is stupid, dangerous." Her tongue was back in action, probing wetly. "If this goes on..." He was having trouble speaking, finding words to say. "If you keep this up, I could... I might..."

"What?" she whispered hoarsely. "Kill me?" She kissed his forehead, his eyes. "I don't think so." She shifted, hitching herself farther up onto him. The folding chair groaned in protest. Pressing her breasts into his face, she clasped his head in both hands, holding him against their soft and yielding warmth. He let out a small groan. "That's the way," she said. Her hands slid down his shoulders to catch his own. With gentle force she placed them on her bare back, leading them in a first caress.

Half against his will, Randall felt his body respond. In truth, he had been celibate for quite some time, ever since making his decision to destroy Lisel. Sex led almost invariably to death, and a human corpse would reveal his location to her like a beacon in the night. So he stayed away. But now, with Lisa straddling him, his body sang like vibrating metal. Not from the red lust, he noted with amazement, not the blood hunger. But animal lust, as old as life. The scent of her hair, the taste of her skin, the pressure of her body on his conspired to inflame his smothered longings. He wanted her. And in one reckless instant he decided to take her.

He hugged her body to him, kissing her breasts fiercely. Sensing victory, Lisa stood, stepping away. Her smile had dimmed a little, but her eyes bored into him with blatant anticipation. One hand lingered, sweeping from his shoulder down his chest to spring lightly from his thigh. Slowly, she undid each button of her patched jeans, then let them drop. No underwear, thought Randall. How nice.

Suddenly he was standing, tearing his clothes off. Or she was, he was not entirely certain. Coat, t-shirt, boots, jeans, and boxers flew in all directions, striking the white walls before falling to the floor. Then he was upon her, pulling her close, his hands grasping her buttocks, her pubic hair tickling his erect penis. In one motion he hoisted her from her feet and dumped her onto the immaculate bed, crashing down on top of her. They kissed greedily for few minutes, hands racing up and down each other's naked bodies, rubbing against one another, establishing a rhythm. When he entered her, it was almost more than he could stand.

She wrapped her legs about him, raked his backside with her sharp fingers, pulling him deeper. Her mouth surrendered his ear and she began a low wail of pleasure, punctuated by grunts and small shrieks of delight whenever he changed his angle of attack. She moved with him, her body rising to meet his. Her hands alternately crushed him to her or slashed across his flesh in involuntary spasms. She sucked at the juncture between his shoulder and neck, returning gradually to his ear. "Take me," she whispered.

Deep within Randall, the blood lust stirred. The sound of her heart kept time with their furious rhythm. He thrust deeper, hugging her body tightly in an effort to drown out the red whisper with the intensity of his pleasure. He felt her blood flowing beneath him. She moaned, loud and long, trailing down into silence. "Take me," she whispered. "Do it, Randall." The red lust coiled, listening. "Take me." And the red lust answered.

Opening his jaw as wide as it could go, Randall bit down full force on the juncture between her head and neck. Lisa screamed. It could have been pleasure or pain. Holding his mouth to the wound, Randall let the hot liquid jet down his throat, searing. Lisa twisted beneath him. Blood sprayed his face and chest, spattering the crisp white sheets. She screamed again, this time in obvious terror. To silence her, he clamped his teeth on her throat, slowly crushing. Blood welled from the new wound, flowing down her neck, staining the pillow crimson. Hungrily, Randall sucked at the steaming liquid as it seeped from the ragged punctures. Wasted blood spread across the bed sheet in a growing pool. She beat against his back with weak fists, gradually ceasing as her heartbeat faded to nothing.

❦

"So what have you got?"

"A pair of threes."

"Ha! I've got jacks. You lose, pretty boy." Nicole raked the pile of loose change over to her side of the bed, then tipped her cigarette ash into the coffee mug that sat between them. "Your deal, ace."

Rose shuffled the cards. "You know, I've never played poker after sex until now." He flicked cards rapidly into two neat piles on the wrinkled sheet.

"We have to do something to unwind." She took a long drag on her cigarette, then dropped the stub into the mug. "And I don't smoke."

Rose grinned. "For some reason I don't buy that. Call it intuition."

She shrugged, unconcerned. "I have to get rid of all my tip change somehow."

"But you're winning," he pointed out.

"Very clever of you to notice." She tapped at her temple with an index finger. "Intuition?"

Someone knocked on the bedroom door. Rose shook his head. "Just ignore it." He took up his cards, examining his hand. Whoever it was knocked again, hard and rapid. "Okay, just a minute." Throwing down his cards, he gave Nicole a wan smile. The knocking continued. "Hold your water a second!" he called. "Just let me hide my hard-on." He pulled on the nearest pair of underwear, hers, while she hid beneath the sheets. Thus minimally covered, Rose opened his door.

Randall stood outside in the hall. Blood smeared his naked body, covering his face, chest, hands, drying in his hair. His eyes looked far away, not entirely lucid. "We have," he said, "a slight problem." Behind them, Nicole shrieked and bolted into the bathroom through the adjoining door.

chapter six

"Jesus, Randall," Rose exclaimed, "you look like you went wild at a barbecue pit." He looked him up and down, surveying the full extent of his blood-stained body. "What did you get this time, a fucking bull moose?"

"Not exactly, no." Randall collapsed against the door frame, his features squeezed into a tight knot. His heartbeat pounded in his temples while his stomach churned. Too much all at once, after so long. He thought he might retch. Even his jaw hurt. The sensation passed, and the sound of his own blood receded. He stood upright, massaging his forehead. "You better just come and see."

Without bothering to put on any more clothes, Rose followed Randall into his room. He froze when he saw Lisa's naked corpse laying on the blood-soaked bed, then gave a low whistle of amazement. "We wondered if she'd caught up with you. Hell of lot of good it did her." Walking gingerly over the to the bed, he examined her more carefully. "So," he asked, his voice strangely flat, "did you tear her throat out before or after you got off?"

"It wasn't like that."

"Oh, really?" Rose rounded on him. "And I suppose some hippy pervert climbed in the window, stripped her and fucked her during the thirty seconds you spent in my room. Guess some necrophiles like fresh ones, eh?" He punched Randall in the chest. "You only killed her. That makes it okay." He hit him again, hard. "You evil shit!"

"Now listen!" Randall grabbed Rose's shoulders, squeezing until his fingers turned white beneath the drying blood. Without letting go, he drove his friend backward against the bed, shoving him down close to the dead girl until his bearded face hovered near the ruin of her neck. Rose strained upward, muscles standing out like cords, just to keep himself above the gaping wound. "This is what we are," Randall hissed. "This is what you are trying to become." He thrust Rose's face closer to the bloody mass. "This is the price, God damn you. This is what we do to survive. Some day you will, too. So save your morality trip or get the fuck out of this right now." He released him so abruptly that Rose over-balanced and fell backward onto the floor. Randall stood over him, face livid with anger.

"Well, if this isn't an incredible tableau." Both men turned their heads to find Knox standing in the doorway, wearing a full-length nightshirt. "It would make a wonderful still life. 'Blood covered man with catamite, female corpse in background.'" He took a step into the room, frowning. "That better not be one of my students."

"No," said Rose, picking himself up off the floor. "It's that girl from the café, the one who followed him out." He looked down at the frilly blue panties stretched to the limit over his crotch. "Did you say catamite?"

Knox ignored him. Striding forward, he grabbed one of Lisa's wrists, looking for a pulse. The dead limb bounced a little when he let it drop. "No use calling an ambulance," he said distractedly. He turned to look at Randall. "What the fuck have you done?"

"I should think that would be pretty obvious." The anger washing through Randall had drained away. Now he felt tired, sore, and rather sick. He sat down heavily in his folding chair, wishing he had kept quiet.

But Knox was not finished. "You're the one who kept going on about security, maintaining a low profile. Hardly a week in this new place you insisted I move to and you consume a girl two dozen people saw chasing you after that scene you pulled." Knox kicked the chair with his bare foot to regain Randall's waning attention. "Good God, what the hell were you thinking?"

"I'm sorry," Randall began. His head hurt, and his vision was painfully sharp. "It wasn't like I set out to do it. She wanted to join us, be like us. I told her I couldn't do it yet, but she just didn't believe me."

"Wait a minute," Knox interrupted. "Are you trying to tell me that she seduced you?" Randall nodded. "Bullshit!" Knox kicked Randall in the chest, spilling him to the floor. The folding chair collapsed with a clatter. "Bullshit!" He kicked him in the side, receiving only muffled grunt in response. "That's the biggest lie I ever heard!" He kicked furiously, bare feet lashing out from under the hem of his nightshirt, impacting against Randall's unresisting body.

Rose grabbed him by the arms, pulling him away. "Come on man, cool it." He tightened his grip as Knox launched another series of kicks. "I started to get pissed, and you saw what he did to me."

"I ought to rip your fucking head off!" Knox wrenched himself away from Rose, but did not approach Randall. "You wanted to find Lisel? Well, little brother, this should bring her right to our God damn doorstep!" He vented a last kick at the wounded folding chair. "You idiot." Shaking his head in disgust, he sat down on the floor, knees splayed out beneath the fabric of his nightshirt.

For a while no one said a thing. The thin moan of wind through the back alley blended with the brothers' ragged breathing. Knox sat on the floor as though stunned. Rose stood behind him, eyes closed wearily. Sprawling where he fell, Randall whipped himself mentally. Why? Why the scene? Why the girl? Why had he let her go so far? Why had he taken her? Because it felt good. No, better than that. She had been fantastic, the sky breaking open after a long drought. But that was less than an excuse. Even without his purpose and his plan it was still foolish, stupid in the extreme. He should never have brought her here. After all, he thought, I'm not living for just myself anymore. My life is for Rose, and Knox, and Swan if he decides to play along. But it's too late to undo it now.

Randall cleared his throat and pulled himself into a sitting position. "If I may raise a practical question at this point, how do you think we should dispose of her?" He stared fixedly at the ragged tears in Lisa's neck.

"Well," said Rose, almost brightly, "we are conveniently located above a funeral home."

"Too obvious," Knox broke in. "If our landlord should happen to notice an extra corpse-mutilated, at that-laying about his place of business, who's he going to think of first, eh?" He shook his head.

"I didn't mean to just ditch her there and wander back upstairs." Rose rolled his eyes comically. "I was thinking they might have a crematory or something."

"I neglected to ask when we signed the lease. My apologies." Knox ran one hand unconsciously through the white stubble of his hair. "Still, I don't think we should risk it. I noticed plenty of security cameras down there. This town is full to the brim with deviants."

"No bullshit," said Randall.

Knox gave him a harsh look. "I don't think we should risk doing anything with the body this close to home. We could drive her out to Rio Del Mar and dump her in the river. This is homicide city, after all. Even if she's found, one more body in this place isn't going to start a manhunt."

Rose blew an explosive breath in the general direction of his bangs. "And how are we supposed to get her out there? Drag her on the bus? 'Never mind our friend. She's had a little bit too much is all. The blood? A nose bleed, sir. She's a hemophiliac, banged her head on the bar. Terrible, isn't it?' Yes, I think they'd buy it." He leaned back against one of the bare walls, shaking a little. Randall could not tell if it was laughter or shock setting in.

"We'll just have to get my car," Knox returned calmly.

"You have a car?"

"Sure, Randall. The same one I had when I first settled here. You remember it."

"That antique still runs?"

"I presume so." Knox pulled his flannel-swathed knees up closer to his chest. "It's been in storage for about a decade, give or take."

"Wonderful." Randall levered himself gradually up onto his feet. He swayed slightly, legs akimbo, then found his balance. "Do you even remember what garage you put it in, give or take?"

"Of course I do." Knox stood as well. The three men looked at each other awkwardly, shadowed by their previous hostility.

"Well, good." Randall looked himself over. "I guess this means another shower." He grimaced. "Why don't you change and dig out your keys while I clean up."

"Uh, you might want to skip it," said Rose, suddenly even more reluctant to meet Randall's eyes.

"Why?"

"You remember the girl in my room? The waitress, Nicole? She's locked herself in the john."

⚕

Randall scratched at his chin as he and Knox descended the wooden stairs at the side of the mortuary. He had scrubbed his face and hands with a dry nail brush until they looked acceptable. The black t-shirt and jeans covered the majority of the stain. Far from feeling clean, his abraded skin felt raw and wounded, certain to attract attention. Inside his clothes, dried blood flaked and fell with his every motion, teasing at his nerves. It was, he thought, no less than he deserved.

They had left Rose in his room, still talking to Nicole through the adjoining door. It had taken him a quarter of an hour to get her to respond at all. Her first words had been a volley of obscenities so vile that even Rose's ears had gone a little red. When the brothers finally left she had still been cursing, albeit more quietly. They had taken this as a positive sign. Carefully closing and locking Randall's room, they went to retrieve the car.

During the bus ride out to the city center Knox said practically nothing. Randall chose not to break the silence, partly for fear of what the others on the crowded bus might hear and partly to avoid reviving his brother's antagonism. Knox was still mad. Seething, probably. The tense set of his shoulders, the blankness of his expression, these signs did not bode well. So Randall simply sat and thought, running the disposal of Lisa's body through his mind.

Rio Del Mar lay considerably south of town. He vaguely recalled passing signs for it on the way up. If memory of previous visits served, the river was small and sluggish, and joined the sea right in the middle of a public beach. But further inland it ran through some decently thick forest and became almost marsh-like at several points. That would be ideal. Still, if the body should float along far enough and somehow run aground at the beach, that could definitely be trouble. Some further mutilation might prove necessary. Or maybe weights.

"You know," Knox said eventually, "I've never asked you why you've taken it upon yourself to do this."

"No," Randall replied, "you haven't." He did not want to provoke a scene, but his brother had touched a nerve. There was no way he would let him back out, not until they had spoken to Swan.

Knox did not rise to the bait. If anything, he looked less tense than before. "Swan and I are content as we are," he said.

"Maybe." Outside the darkened bus, night traffic slipped by like stock footage on a theater screen.

The garage turned out to be a place that specialized in long-term storage and maintenance. With the school providing free public transit, large numbers of students simply parked their cars for the duration of their academic careers. Randall's mood brightened somewhat. He had not really expected Knox's car to be accessible, let alone drivable, and the prospect of renting one at this late hour did not please him in the least.

They wandered through the ground level past rows of battered sub-compacts and love buses. A pristine white Lotus sat astride two spaces; apparently the owner had splurged. In the center of the garage a small glass-walled office stood guard over the automobiles. A slight elevation made it ideal for watching the lot, though a hoard of screaming urban lunatics could have run off with every hubcap in the place for all the attention of the teenage attendant. He sat with his feet up on a small desk, headphones covering his ears, reading a comic book.

Knox rapped on the glass, to no effect. He knocked harder, shaking the entire structure. The attendant dropped his comic book and came to the window. He pulled his headphones down around his neck. Jane's Addiction blared from the tiny speakers. "Can I help you?" he asked loudly, as though to someone deaf.

"I'd like to pick up my car," Knox hollered back. He handed over the yellowed claim ticket.

The attendant studied it for a minute, then turned off his music. "You're kidding, right?" He waved the paper under Knox's nose. "This ticket's sixteen years old."

"I'm perfectly serious," Knox replied. "I want my car." He put one hand to his chest to reinforce the statement.

"If you say so, man." The attendant searched briefly through a file cabinet, removing a manila folder. He came out of his booth, locking the glass door behind him. "It's down a couple levels." He led them towards a stairwell. "With long term storage we try and start the car once a week, and we charge the battery every couple months." He flipped through some of the papers. "If it doesn't turn over, we'll help you jump it, no extra cost."

They descended two flights of metal stairs and came out into a dimly lit sub-level packed with cars. A neatly disassembled Fiat sat on blocks near the entrance. Labeled gears sat below it on a tarp. Mercury vapor lamps hung from the low ceiling on short chains. They had to dodge them as they searched the rows of close-parked automobiles. "There it is," said the attendant, pointing ahead. "Nineteen sixty-seven Plymouth Barracuda, California license YHS 813." He scrutinized the dusty blue plate. "Your registration expired." He squinted. "In seventy-eight."

Knox said nothing in reply. He stared at the car, which looked like someone at Chevrolet had decapitated a Plymouth Fury then stretched it in a taffy puller. A smile gradually formed on his face. Grime coated the sharklike chassis. Randall could not even tell what color the paint was, and did not remember. The upholstery had fared better. Beneath a wooly accumulation of dust, the interior was obviously white. They had stored it with the top rolled back. But the tires looked firm and the taillights clean.

The attendant opened a long envelope and shook out a pair of keys. "Is it okay if I just hop over the trunk?" he asked. Knox nodded. Neither of the two large doors could have been opened more than an inch without denting the cars on either side. The teenager clambered into the driver's seat, leaving long smears in the dirt and dust. He turned the key in the ignition. After a few seconds of ominous grinding the engine caught. He fed it some gas and the car responded with a fierce, healthy growl. "Hot damn!" he shouted, smacking the steering wheel and setting off the horn. With great caution, he backed the car out into the aisle.

Knox grinned widely now, the same kid-in-a-candy-store look that sight-seeing with Rose had given him. Randall began to smile himself, then remembered the reason for their errand. His spirit sank. He only hoped Knox remained in a good mood.

"All yours," said the attendant, holding open the driver's side door. Knox settled into the seat. Randall walked around and hoisted himself into the passenger side.

"How much do I owe you?" Knox asked.

"Nothing," said the attendant. "In fact, we owe you." He pulled another envelope out of his file, handing it over to Knox. "You left us enough for two decades. That's what you haven't used yet."

Knox leafed through the bills, counting. "Honest kid," he said to himself. He removed a twenty and stuffed it into the attendant's shirt pocket. "Go buy yourself a hearing aid." The boy had just begun stammering his thanks when Knox stomped the gas pedal to the floor, pushing Randall back into the padded bench seat. The car spiraled up and out of the parking garage, hitting the street at near freeway speed.

Knox squinted down at the dash while darkened buildings swung by overhead. He tapped at the gas gauge, whipping the car around a corner one handed, not even looking at the traffic. Randall searched the crack between cushions for his seat belt. He had forgotten his brother's driving. "The tank's almost empty," Knox complained disbelievingly. "What did they do, drive up to San Luis and back every Friday? I swear I left this thing at least three quarters full." They careened into an intersection. Knox changed lanes without bothering to check behind him, nearly chopping into a Toyota flatbed. Horns sounded. "Stupid asshole," he muttered, adjusting the rear view mirror.

"You left it sitting for a decade and a half," Randall reminded him. "Maybe it went flat." He clicked the belt in place across his lap, wishing vainly for a shoulder strap.

Knox snorted. "Gas doesn't go flat," he declared. "Does it?" Randall shrugged. Glancing up, Knox noticed a filling station on the opposite side of the road. He slammed on the breaks and turned, leaving the long car straddling the painted divider. Almost immediately he stomped on the accelerator, sending them lurching through a break in oncoming traffic. He pulled up to the nearest pump.

"You'll have to move to the next island," said Randall. "This whale won't burn unleaded."

Knox stared at him in confusion for a moment. "Oh, yes," he said finally. "I'd forgotten about all that." He swung the car around to the proper set of pumps, then jumped out with the engine running.

"I'll go pay," said Randall, hoisting himself over the passenger door while Knox fiddled with the gas cap. He padded the pockets of his coat, hoping he had remembered to bring money.

"Don't be stupid," exclaimed Knox, nozzle in hand. "You've no idea how much it is yet." Randall just shook his head and went into the store. Knox had not adjusted to the change from horses very well. He drove like he expected the car to keep itself out of trouble. Miraculously, he never hit anything large or living. He just came way too close, way too often.

"Twenty on number three." Randall handed the cashier a bill. The man pressed a button on the grimy console behind him. Through the window, they watched Knox's astonishment as the seemingly defective pump spurted gas onto his shoes. With any luck, he might set himself on fire. Randall remembered Lisa's body, the soft black hair soaked in blood.

Nodding to the attendant, he left the store and paced back to the car. Driving had blown some of the dust off, and he could now see the bright red paint underneath. Of course. How could he have forgotten? Candy-apple. How very Knox. He dipped the complimentary squeegee in a bucket of water and began to clean the windshield. "Do you have a gas can in this thing somewhere?" he asked.

"I think so." Knox held the nozzle suspiciously as gas gurgled into the gigantic tank. The numbers on the pump ticked by. Twenty was not going to fill it. "It must be in the trunk."

Randall finished with the window and replace the squeegee. Coming round to the trunk, he held out his hand for the key. "The lock's busted." Knox never took his eyes off the nozzle. "Just give it good kick."

Obediently, Randall slammed the heel of his boot into the lock. The trunk popped open and he retrieved the ancient, cylindrical gas can. Mutilation, he thought.

�

They returned to find Rose alone and fully clothed, pacing the hall outside Randall's locked door. "It's cool," he informed them. "I convinced Nicole that you're some sort of screwball special effects artist who enjoys freaking people out. But she says if you ever set foot one in the café again, she'll brain you with a fresh pot of coffee."

"I wasn't planning a return engagement." Randall unlocked his door and thrust it open. The smell of spilled blood washed over them, half mildew, half meat. Rose gagged. Randall walked across the room and, leaning over the body, flung open the window. "The car's in the alley. Should we take her down the stairs or the fire escape?"

Knox stepped into the room. "We can't use the fire escape unless you plan to drop her the last fifteen feet. Those steps end in a ladder." He turned to Rose, who still hovered in the doorway. "Go find some garbage bags, or a tarp or something." Rose nodded, then vanished.

"And some weights!" Randall called after him. He stood for a moment, staring at the terrible wounds he had made in Lisa's neck. Her blood filled him still, making him feel alternately sick and strong. The strange vitality in his limbs, the sudden sharpness of his vision, they were hardly familiar anymore. It had indeed been a long time. But the sight of Lisa's pale face, blue lips, and torn throat filled him with remorse. "Well," he began awkwardly, "I suppose we should strip the bed or something." He moved to the foot and began pulling the fitted sheets from the corners.

Knox freed the sheets from the head of the bed, and together they folded them over the body. Rose returned shouldering a cardboard box. "Heavy duty trash bags." He tossed them to the floor. "Twine." A brown, fraying ball followed. "Duct tape." He let the box drop. "No weights."

Randall stared at him incredulously. "Where did you find all that so quickly?"

"The bathroom closet." Rose smiled wickedly. "Maybe the previous occupants did this kind of thing a lot." He kicked the box, spilling rolls of duct tape. "Or maybe that mortician and his wife are secret cult weirdoes. It's a good thing we decided not to venture downstairs. Who knows what we might have found?" His eyebrows fluttered dramatically.

"Cut the crap and hand me a trash bag." Randall lifted the head end of the shrouded corpse off the mattress while Knox pulled one of the plastic sacks down to about waist level. They repeated the operation with the leg end of the body, the bags just overlapping. Randall sealed the juncture with duct tape, ponderously turning the limp weight over. He motioned to Rose. "You direct, we'll carry." He grasped unseen shoulders. "Ready?" Knox took hold of the feet. "One, two, three." The corpse sagged between them like a swayback horse, nearly brushing the floor. Dark blood stained the top half of the mattress.

"Stay put," said Knox. He took a couple stiff steps backward, stretching the body out almost straight. "Rose, check the hall."

"All clear." They hobbled out of the bedroom. Rose poked his head out the front door, then gave them the thumbs up. Knox walking backward, they descended the wooden stairs at the side of the building. Everything went fine until they came to the hairpin turn, the path of the stairs folding back upon itself through a series of triangular steps. "Just take it slow," said Rose, "I'm right behind you if you slip."

Knox put a foot back, missed the step completely and tumbled backwards into Rose. Randall felt the slick plastic wrenched from his grasp. Lisa's head hit the boards with an audible crack. The body clattered down the stairs, smacking feet-first into Knox and Rose, who had yet to regain their balance. The three of them rolled and thumped down the last flight, landing in a tangled heap on the pavement. "You know," Rose moaned from the pile, "maybe we should have dropped her out the window after all."

Randall hurried down the stairs and helped them up. He hoisted his end of the body. Knox dusted himself off, then lifted the feet. Quickly, they hustled their burden into the alley. As they rounded the corner, Rose doubled over with laughter. "That's your car?" he giggled. "It looks like something Billy Joel would drive."

"Kick the lock on the trunk, you degenerate," Knox ordered. "It's the only way to get it open." Rose gave it a solid boot and the lid sprung up. The brothers dumped the body in over a litter of tools and snow chains. Knox slammed the lid back down. "Let's get the fuck out of here and get this over with." They piled into the car, Rose draping himself over the back seat. The Barracuda screeched out of the alley and hurtled into the night.

"Watch your driving," said Randall. "We don't want to get pulled over."

"You got that right," called Rose, who had begun his own search for a seat belt. "This flying slab of yours is about as inconspicuous as a bomb going off."

"What's wrong with my driving?" The light at the intersection ahead of them turned yellow. Knox accelerated, cutting off an El Camino that had been trying to turn left. "I even had a license once."

"Christ," muttered Randall, and closed his eyes. For a while he listened to the howl of the air sweeping over the windshield. He felt the car lurch this way and that, accelerate. Tires squealed and he was thrown forward. The car turned and he slid into the door. He leaned back against the seat again, trying to relax. He felt so alive it was painful, strong enough to smash steel but on-edge and sour-stomached, as though he had overdosed on speed.

Soon they were on the Coast Highway, barreling south at top velocity. The headlights bored twin holes into the darkness ahead, illuminating the gray tarmac. They were alone on the road. The wind ripped furiously at Randall's hair. He felt certain that if something stationary burst out of the darkness ahead they would have no time to avoid it. He looked at the speedometer; the needle was buried at one hundred. He looked at Knox; his brother was smiling.

The car flew smooth and comfortable, only the wind and the whirling scenery giving evidence of their speed. They came to a jump in the pavement leveled into a short rise with gravel and tar, a reminder of the most recent quake. The front end rose into the air then dipped back down with a crunch, the bumper scraping sparks off of the road. "This thing drives like a missile," Rose hollered from the back seat.

They passed the sign for Las Gatas, then the first sign for Rio Del Mar. Knox slowed reluctantly, not so much braking as taking his foot off the accelerator. They flashed by the exit still doing eighty. Knox stomped on the breaks, sending the car into a long skid. The tires howled and the Barracuda fishtailed, veering into the next lane. When they had jerked to a stop, he put the car in reverse. Glancing over his shoulder, Knox brought them speeding back along the path of the skid, black lines appearing before them as if the tires had been dipped in ink. When they had passed the exit again he stopped, throwing them all against their seats. Putting the car in drive, he idled down the ramp.

The road forked at the bottom. In one direction, two paved lanes led towards the coast and the public beach. In the other, a dirt track ran off into the brush. Knox eased the Barracuda off the tarmac, the low-slung automobile bouncing on its aged shocks. He drove as fast as the terrain would allow. The car shook and shuddered its way up the road leaving a rising cloud of dust behind.

They drove in this way for nearly a half an hour, rattling along, tires spitting rocks into the brush. The trees got thicker, taller. The road became narrower still, until they could not have passed oncoming traffic had there been any. Trunks leaned overhead and roots jutted out into the road. They drove over the intruding limbs with bumps that cracked their teeth together. Knox seemed determined to maintain his speed, no matter what obstacles presented themselves. Rose leaned over the front seat. "Is it much farther?" he asked. "I think I'm getting sea sick."

Knox peered into the patch of light ahead. The misty gloom looked the same as it had since they left the highway. "I guess this is far enough." He took his foot off the gas and the car bounced slowly to a halt. The sound of gently running water played over the dull hum of the engine, coming from somewhere in the forest to their left.

"Leave the lights on a minute," Randall said, stepping stiffly out of the car, "there's something I have to do." Rose eased himself over the door and gave the trunk a swift kick. The lid remained in place. He kicked it again, but the lid stayed down. "Let me try." Randall stood close to the car and brought his boot heel down on the lock. Nothing happened. "Crap."

"You just have to have the right touch," said Knox, joining them. He contemplated the lock for a moment, then gave it a well-placed kick with one deck shoe. The trunk stayed closed. Knox laughed. "It's just sensitive, is all." He kicked it again, to no effect. And again. He stood back, glaring at the trunk in frustration. "I'll be damned if I'm going to leave a dead body in my car." He gave the lock a truly savage kick, then sprung back. "Shit!" He sat down heavily in dirt, clutching his foot. "Son of a bitch." The trunk was still closed.

"Stand back," said Rose. He pulled the revolver from inside his jacket. Gripping it with both hands, he took aim and fired. The bang echoed off of the surrounding trees. The lock exploded in a small burst of shrapnel and the lid lifted slowly into the air.

"Nice work, Doc Holiday." Randall gestured at the splintered metal. "How the fuck are we going close it again?"

Rose blew at the cordite smoke seeping from the muzzle of his pistol. "I figured we'd burn that bridge when we got to it." He fingered the short bore to see if it had cooled, then tucked the weapon away.

Randall manhandled Lisa's body out of the trunk. Knox had removed his shoe and was examining his foot in the red glow of the taillights. Ignoring him, Randall hauled the body, leg end dragging, into the pool of illumination before the Barracuda. He let her drop, then sat down next to the shrouded form. Wearily, he began to tear away the duct tape holding the two trash bags together. He pulled the top bag off, then unwound the bloody sheets. Beneath the rusty stains, her naked skin was blue and cold. The cigarette burns stared back at him, white and blank. Rose came up behind him. "What are you doing?"

Randall pulled her arms free of the tangled sheets. "Go back to the trunk," he said without looking up, "and bring me that gas can." Rose stood behind him for a long moment, then walked back to the rear of the car.

Randall splayed Lisa's hands out at her sides, palms up. "Here," said Rose, and set the gas can down beside her. Randall stood and removed the cap from the spout. Tipping the can, he poured some gasoline over each exposed hand, soaking the sheets beneath. The fumes stung his eyes. Quickly, he dumped the rest of can's contents onto her face and neck.

"Got a match?" he asked, still gazing down at the pale body. She seemed smaller than he remembered, somehow more frail. Rose pressed a matchbook into his hand.

Randall tore out a match and struck it, holding it until it almost burned his fingers. He let it fall onto the body. The gasoline lit all at once. Her dark hair blazed, then withered. The bloodstains boiled. Her pale flesh began to blacken and smoke. Rose coughed and turned away, but Randall continued to stare down at her burning face. "Jesus Christ," said Knox, stepping up beside him, "you could have at least closed her eyes."

"Too late for that," he replied.

chapter **seven**

The pool hall had no real name, so far as Randall knew. The Chinese barman, apparently the owner, spoke English so broken it should have been put in traction, though he claimed to have lived in California all his life. He crouched behind the formica counter seven nights a week, slinging dollar shots of saké and toying with the ends of his vestigial moustache. When asked, he had informed Randall, "I born Malibu, Yankee citizen."

Four coin-operated pool tables huddled close together in the tiny space, making shooting cramped and difficult when the place was full. Randall chalked up a warped house cue and sighted down the table. He pulled his stick back, then gave the cue ball a sharp tap. Too hard, he could tell instantly. The ball rebounded from the far end of the table and rolled to a stop just touching the velvet rail near his hand.

"That really lagged," said Rose from his perch on a bar stool. Knox snorted and hastily set down his beer.

"Cute." Randall thrust the cue stick at Rose. "Your break, wise ass."

Randall had confined himself to his room for over two weeks, partly to wait out any heat caused by Lisa's disappearance, and partly as a kind of penance. He sat at his metal desk by day, reading history books borrowed from his brother. Many of them amused him greatly, particularly those dealing with the conquest of Mexico. By night he roamed the university's wooded hills, feeding on insignificant creatures. Knox continued to teach his classes and advise his students, ignoring Randall thoroughly.

The red Barracuda stayed parked in the back alley, seemingly forgotten. Rose kept indoors for a few days, agitated and withdrawn. Finally he stomped out the door and down the stairs late one night, returning with female companionship just before dawn.

Gradually, Knox and Rose renewed their tour of the city. At first they ventured out only to buy food for Rose. From restaurants they progressed to nightclubs and bars. When Fire House played at the Catalyst, Rose insisted on dragging Knox to the concert, properly booted and spiked for the slam pit. They had returned-bruised, bleeding, thoroughly drunk-staggering against each other and laughing like idiots. After that it had been an endless succession of pool halls and poetry readings, symphonies and strip joints. Rose even began sitting in on Knox's lectures. Randall stayed in his room, reading history. A week into his confinement a sheet of paper slid under the door. The flyer described Lisa Robinson as missing and gave her particulars. Randall did not know whether or not to feel relieved. The paper made no mention of him, saying only that she had last been seen at the Vampyre Café. In any case, Randall remained cloistered in his room.

Shortly thereafter, Knox and Rose had drawn him out. Hopping into the Barracuda, they spied him reading on the fire escape. "Ahoy there!" Knox shouted. Randall politely set down his book. "We're going over to Cheap Saké Billiards. Want to came along?" Rose motioned for him to leap down into the car. Why not? thought Randall. It's probably safe by now. And I'll behave myself this time, I promise. He tossed his book through the window and clambered down the iron ladder.

They parked in a municipal lot and walked from there. The narrow building sat squeezed between a laundry and an adult bookstore. Stolen movie marquee letters of various sizes taped to the plastic window spelled out *Cheap Saké*, and further down, *Billiards*. They stayed until closing, shooting game after game on the quarter-a-play tables. Now they were practically regulars.

Rose placed the cue ball on the green then sighted down the stick, his face pinched into a tight squint as though he were examining a jewel. He drew the stick way back, then rammed it forward. Balls rattled and crashed up and down the table, some of them becoming airborne. The eight ball spun lazily towards the left corner pocket. Knox leapt at it, but failed to catch it before it sank. "Game, set, and match!" cried Rose. He thumped the butt of the cue against the floor. "Am I hot, or am I hot?"

"Table scratch," said Knox, picking the cue ball up off the floor. "Randall wins."

"Unfair! Unfair!" Rose stomped up to Randall, chest puffed out and cue held at the ready. "The best shot of my life and you mean to deprive me of the game through some technicality?" He brandished the cue warningly. "You unprincipled cad!"

"Rules is rules," Randall replied, taking the cue. "Now be a good lad and feed the beast another quarter so we can play a real game."

"Surely we can play without the eight ball," Rose objected, giving Knox a pointed look. "Unlike some people, I do not operate on anything like a fixed income."

"So what do you suggest we do to end the game, then?" Randall asked.

Rose shrugged. "Wrestle?"

"Cool by me. I outweigh you."

Rose switched on his maniac grin. "Ah, true. But you have failed to take into consideration the debilitating effects of my withering halitosis." He exhaled loudly in Randall's direction.

Knox chuckled. "My money's still on you, brother."

Rose smiled sweetly at him through his beard. "Since you have cash to spend, why don't you spot us a quarter for this game?" He looked around the bar. "I don't think there's enough room in here to wrestle, anyway." Indeed, the place had been filling up. A grungy looking group of students had taken the table behind theirs. One of them had his own cue, which the others borrowed. A fair crowd had accumulated at the bar, hounding the Chinaman for shots of saké.

Knox fished a quarter from the pocket of the jeans he had taken to wearing since the Fire House concert. With the deck shoes and grey sweatshirt, he looked almost normal. Only his dead white hair stood out. "Alright," he said, "but if you lose this time you owe me a drink."

"Well, there's no chance I'll ever have to pay that off. I'm invincible." Rose chalked up while Knox fed in his quarter.

The table released the captive eight ball. Knox re-racked, spotting carefully. "Your break, Randall." He lifted the triangle away. "Murder him for me."

"Promise." Randall sighted and shot. The rack broke cleanly, balls scattering throughout the green. The thirteen rolled with teasing slowness toward the right corner, then sank. "Ten, side." Randall tapped the cue ball lightly, giving it just enough force to nudge the blue stripe into the pocket. "Eleven, corner." He sank that too, but left the cue ball between a group of solids and the rail. "Crap." Without bothering to call anything, he sent the white ball down the rail into a cluster of stripes at the opposite end of the table. Nothing sank. "All yours, Mr. Hot."

Rose hefted his cue stick and paced slowly around the table, examining possible shots. "Hey there," called a voice from the bar, "how about letting somebody else play?" A tall man lurched away from the counter, highball glass in hand. His dark hair hung loose and tangled to his shoulders. He wore new designer jeans and a gaudy pair of red and green snakeskin boots. A white Oxford shirt with the sleeves ripped off hung from his shoulders like a vest, his matted chest hair and thick beer-gut bare to the world. He strode clumsily towards Rose. "How 'bout it, eh?" His drunken baritone thundered much too loudly, even in the noisy hall.

"Fuck off," said Rose shortly, "there are two other tables open." He crouched down over the green, taking aim. "Four, corner."

"Aw, come on." The man nudged Rose in the shoulder, spoiling his shot. "No fun just playin' with myself." He stood still for a moment, thinking over what he had just said, then broke into huge peals of horse-like laughter. His highball glass dropped to the floor. "Playin' with myself," he repeated, giving Rose another friendly smack. "You get it?"

"Hilarious," Rose droned. "Now if you'd be so kind as to let me shoot..." He took aim at the four again.

"Say," the man drawled suspiciously, "you're no fun." He turned in an awkward circle, eyes searching vaguely about the room, finally settling on Knox. "Why won't that guy let me play?" he demanded.

Knox laughed down at him from his bar stool. "Maybe he's in a bad mood today." He leaned in and cupped his hands to the man's ear. "Lack of female companionship makes him irritable."

The man nodded sagely. "Maybe you could help me out," he whispered hugely. "You know, put in a good word." He jerked his thumb over his shoulder in the general direction of the table.

"Sure." Knox straightened in his stool. "Hey, Randall," he called, "why don't you play a game with this guy?" The man turned and smiled widely, revealing twin rows of yellow teeth. Rose, who had been just about to shoot, growled in exasperation. "It's my quarter," Knox reminded him.

"He's drunk," said Randall, "I'd kick his ass."

The man took a pair of bowlegged steps towards them. "Want to put money on it?"

Rose frowned. "And here I thought you were too destitute to afford your own table."

"I like easy money." Randall winked shrewdly at Rose. "How much dough, Mongo?"

The man lumbered forward, supporting himself on the edge of the pool table. He seemed to have trouble stopping, and nearly bumped into Randall. As it was, he came to a halt much too close and had to back up. His breath reeked. "The name's Jim," he bellowed, sticking out a large hairy hand.

Randall shook it once then let it drop. "How much money, Jim?" he amended.

Jim shrugged, then made an elaborate search through the pockets of his designer jeans. He pulled out a crumpled bill, unfolding it curiously. "Twenty?" he asked at last, placing the wrinkled bill on the table.

"Peanuts," said Randall. He pulled a roll of bills from his coat, peeled one off and slapped it down. "For such a low stake, you'll have to take over the game already in progress." He indicated the table with his cue. "I'm three up, and it's your shot."

"Sure, sure," Jim hollered. He made a slow circuit of the table, finally coming to rest at the opposite end from Randall. Rose handed him a cue. "Thanks." He nodded at him several times, then turned back to the green. "Four in the corner," he called.

"What a complete surprise," Rose murmured.

Jim sighted and shot, his large movements strangely graceful. The four ball rolled cleanly across the green and sank, not even touching the sides of the pocket. The cue ball spun into the middle of the table, leaving him with several open shots. "Seven in the side." He sank the maroon solid, giving the cue just the right backspin to leave it set for a shot in the opposite pocket.

"Hold the phone, gents," said Rose. "I do believe we've been hustled." Jim guffawed at this, doubling over and dropping his cue stick to the floor. His raucous laughter rang through the room, drawing the attention of the bar crowd, winding down in great hoarse gasps.

"Damn," he said meaningfully. Pulling tangles of hair away from his eyes, he rehearsed his next shot. Jim sank the five in the opposite side, then sent the cue ball racing down the green to peg the two ball into the left corner. The table shook with the impact. What few solids remained sat clustered at the opposite end of the velvet expanse. "Six in the corner," Jim called. He pulled the stick so far back the tip almost slipped out of his aiming hand. His thick arm pistoned and the cue ball flew. The six rattled against the sides of the pocket but failed to sink. "Son of a bitch," Jim swore cheerfully. "All yours, chief."

"No mercy," shouted Knox. "Remember, you have two drunkards to support." Rose saluted him with an empty beer bottle.

Several of Randall's stripes loitered near the corner pockets, the cue ball resting neatly between the two groups. He worked them back and forth, sinking the fourteen, fifteen, and twelve in rapid succession. "Nine, corner." The final stripe lay perhaps half a foot from the pocket. Randall nicked it with the cue ball, but it bounced against the edge of the rail and away. "Now or never, Jim." He stepped back from the table.

Not much remained on the green at this point, and Jim easily sank the one and the six. Next he sent the three spinning halfway down a side rail to drop in a corner pocket. Knox and Rose applauded. Jim took aim at the eight ball, which sat very near the spot at the far end of the table.

"That's a scratch shot," warned Rose. "Come at it from behind and sink it at your end."

Jim looked up at him though his drooping black bangs. "Like I'm drunk enough to take advice from you. You're just trying to sabotage my strategy, you are." He aimed carefully and gave the cue ball a relatively soft tap. The eight ball rolled straight in to its intended pocket, while the cue meandered slowly towards the left corner. It bounced once against the rim, then sank.

"Ground rule double," said Knox. "You lose."

"Nice knowing you, Jim." Randall pocketed the two twenties from the table. "See you around some time."

"Now wait a minute." Jim staggered up, cue stick in hand, his beer-gut bulging forward aggressively. "You ain't gettin' rid of me so easy. I sunk that eight ball fair and square." He swept one arm grandly around the bar, narrowly missing Randall's face. "I got witnesses."

"Yes," said Knox patiently from his stool, "but you scratched." He favored Jim with a benevolent teacher's smile. "If you scratch shooting the eight ball, whether you sink it or not, you lose automatically."

"But you cheated!" Jim blurted, still facing Randall. "Your clever friend sabotaged me." He wagged one hand behind him in Rose's direction. "Gimme my money!" Clutching the cue stick with both hands, he raised it up over his head.

"Shit!" Randall dodged back, catching the blow on his shoulder. He heard the loud slap and reeled against another table, just starting to feel the pain. Jim lurched forward, stick held like a baseball bat. He swung again, striking Randall in the side. The motley students fled from their table to the corner of the bar. Randall fell to the floor, feeling the broken ends of several ribs grinding against each other. Jim stood over him.

"We can't take him anywhere, can we?" Knox slipped lightly off his stool and grabbed a cue stick from the wall rack.

"We certainly can't." Rose pulled the pistol from his jacket pocket and leveled it at Jim's back. "Oh, laughing boy," he called, "I've got another clever trick for you." The crowd around the bar vanished, making for the door.

Jim, who had been considering where to hit Randall next, stomped slowly around to face them. When he saw Rose's pistol he laughed, supporting himself on the cue stick as he shook and chortled. "That's cute," he drawled. "Where'd you get that, a cereal box?"

"Don't fucking move," said Rose, gripping the gun with both hands and pulling the hammer back with his thumb.

The Chinese barman popped up from behind the counter. "Put that away!" he shouted in perfect, unaccented English. "You are scaring my customers." He pounded one large hand on the formica. "Put that gun away this instant, or I will call the police!" Rose held the pistol steady. Shaking with rage, the barman dropped back down out of sight.

Jim advanced, dragging the cue stick, laughing silently to himself. "I mean it, man," warned Rose. "Hold it right there or I'll blow your brains out your asshole." Jim just shook his head.

Randall hauled himself upright, hands clamped to the lip of the billiard table. His shoulder throbbed, severely bruised if not actually broken. At any rate, he could still use the arm. The shattered ribs ground at each other and poked sharply into the surrounding tissue, making it painful to breath. *Why is it,* he wondered, *that everyone I meet lately has a death wish? I should have known better than to leave my room. This obviously isn't my town.* He stood, leaning heavily against the table. Bringing one leg up he pulled the hunting knife from his boot. Rose might have things under control and he might not. Randall watched carefully.

Jim stumbled unsteadily into striking distance, one hand gripping the cue. Rose aimed the pistol at his head. "Last chance," he said. "Drop the stick."

"I ain't afraid of you!" Jim roared. He heaved the cue stick up in a wide arc, striking the underside of Rose's arms. The pistol discharged with a deafening bang, sending a hail of plaster down from the ceiling. Jim shoved Rose back against the bar with the butt end of the cue and waded after him, jabbing down savagely. Rose blocked as best could, taking the blows on the arms and legs. He had dropped the gun, and could not find it. The few people who had stayed to watch the fight fled hastily.

Knox aimed a golf swing at Jim's leg, connecting solidly with his shin. Jim staggered, then whirled towards his new opponent, more enraged than damaged. He jabbed the tip of the cue into Knox's chest, stunning him momentarily. Gripping the thin end of the stick in both fists, Jim wound up and swung. The cue snapped. Knox's head whipped back, one side of his face already livid. He fell back against the bar, slumping to the floor next to Rose. Jim towered over them, teeth bared, breathing heavily.

Randall stared at his broad back, seized with a cold rage. *God damn you,* he thought. *I've had just about enough of this kind of bullshit.* He switched his grip on the hunting knife, clutching it blade downward, then pushed himself painfully away from the table. "Oh, Mongo."

Jim turned slowly around, wobbling slightly. Seeing Randall, his eyebrows shot up and he laughed. "Ain't afraid of you either!" He brandished the broken pool cue.

"You should be." Lunging forward with all the swiftness he could muster, shutting out the pain ripping through his side, Randall rushed Jim and jammed the knife into his forearm. He felt the blade dragging against bone as he shoved the weapon as far as it would go. The cue stick clattered to the floor. Blood welled from both sides of the wound, smearing the protruding metal. Standing back, Randall had one moment of pure pleasure watching Jim tug weakly at the ivory handle. Then the police tackled him from behind.

ℜℬ

Randall sat at one end of a small table in a room without windows. Flaking off-white paint, almost lemon colored, coated the walls, ceiling, and even the floor. An empty chair sat opposite him. One metal door, again with no window, stood closed in the wall to his left. He had no doubt that it was locked. The floor sloped slightly inward towards the center of the room and a small, uncovered drain. Randall had looked, but found no water faucet of any kind.

The police had arrested them all except for Knox, who was out cold. He, Rose, and Jim were carted off in separate patrol cars. An ambulance took Knox away. Randall had not seen any of them since. First they had taken him to some sort of police infirmary. A silent doctor x-rayed his chest, set his ribs without administering any sort of anesthetic, then bandaged him thoroughly with white plastic tape. One of the arresting officers looked on the entire time, saying nothing. From there he had been led to the police station proper.

When they tried to book him, Randall refused to give his name or produce any sort of identification. They searched him, but found nothing. There was nothing to find; it had been decades since Randall had bothered to maintain the fiction of a social identity. Knox made a habit of bribing some well-placed attorney to revamp his paper self every generation or so, but he led a more public life than either of his two younger brothers. For Randall it would have been pointless; he had not held a legitimate job since the late eighteen hundreds.

After a good deal of futile cajoling-first by the arresting officers, then a desk sergeant, and finally by an unidentified man in an expensive suit-they had settled for fingerprints and mug shots, then left him in this room. The prints should produce nothing. Randall had been arrested before, several times in fact, but he always made sure that he left police custody legally dead. It was easy to do. Just pick a fight, mess himself up a little, then stop his bodily processes. Worked like a charm. The prints would be taken out of circulation, or filed as deceased at worst. Unless the local computers were outrageously meticulous they should never find the prints from his prior arrests, or the ones from his war record. Dead men commit few crimes, after all.

As soon as they put him in a regular holding cell he would go through the routine again. All he had to do was outlast the interrogation. Frankly, the prospect bored him. They would probably just shout at him a lot, try and psyche him into talking. No one had bothered to beat him since the late sixties.

The door clicked open, and the well-dressed man Randall had seen earlier stepped in. He looked tired, his expensive suit rumpled, but it might have been just a pose. Closing the door behind him, he pulled out the other chair and sat. Randall looked him over impassively. Not so tall, not so strong. Brown hair gone grey at the temples. A little bit of a spare tire. No problem at all, should it come to that, except for the gun holstered under his arm.

The man took a half pack of cigarettes from a coat pocket and tossed them onto the table. Randall shook his head. The man shrugged, then lit one for himself with a silver lighter. "Lieutenant Granger," he said, the words riding billows of smoke. Randall nodded, but said nothing in reply. Granger took another long drag. There were bruises under his eyes, and it occurred to Randall that it must be morning by now.
Perhaps Granger had not slept. Randall smiled. Maybe Granger could tell him something about his friends. He allowed the smile to remain.

"I wish I knew what this was all about," the Lieutenant began. He leaned in towards Randall, his manner earnest. "You might have been wondering how we got to you so fast. Turns out somebody called to report the fight about a half hour before it actually started. No name given. We can't be sure, but I suspect it was your friend, Mr. Sullivan."

"Who?" Randall interrupted, his voice betraying only a mild curiosity.

Lieutenant Granger sat back in his chair. "Ah, so you can speak. Good." He nodded to himself as though confirming a deeply held suspicion. "James Sullivan," he repeated, "the man you assaulted with the knife."

"Oh, I assaulted him." Randall's friendly smile twisted into a bitter parody of itself. "Never mind what he did to those other men. Never mind what he did to me."

Granger regarded him coldly. "The owner of the bar maintains that your friend Mr. Collins had a pistol, which he fired at Mr. Sullivan. We found a bullet in the ceiling, but no gun." He shrugged again, helplessly. "It's all very confusing."

Mr. Collins? Randall wondered. That must be what Rose's paper says these days. That boy has more names than a mute whore in a cathouse on Friday night. Good thing too, or there'd be a line forming just to extradite the little punk. And no gun either? Better and better. "I don't recall there being a pistol," he said.

Granger ignored him, choosing instead to resume his interrupted monologue. "As I was saying, Mr. Sullivan has taken it into his head not to prefer charges."

"I don't prefer them either," Randall interjected.

Granger pressed on, determined to say his piece. "Not to prefer charges against Mr. Collins and Mr. Knox, despite the fact that he claims both of them assaulted him. Mr. Collins, in return, has dropped all charges against Sullivan, and left the precinct without even filing a statement. Mr. Knox, I was originally given to understand, was taken from the scene unconscious, having sustained a heavy concussion and possibly even a skull fracture. But I've just been informed that he's left the hospital under his own power, and has no complaint against any of you." He slumped forward, elbows resting on the table, clearly confused.

He looked up at Randall. "That leaves you and Sullivan, who insists on charging you with assault. Considering the reports of the arresting officers, it'll probably stick. The only way we can hold Sullivan is if you file a counter-charge. And for that, we need your name." The lieutenant took a last drag on his cigarette, then dropped it to floor. It sat there, burning to a stub on the flaking paint. "So, how about it?"

This could all be a con, of course. Knox and Rose could still be in custody, despite what this fellow said. But somehow Randall did not think that was the case. There was a note of genuine desperation in Granger's voice. But still, he did not think it wise to break his silence now, even if it meant Jim's release. Randall could not legitimately identify himself. In the world of paper, he did not exist. That would cause all kinds of unpleasant questions. Besides, the other two could look out for themselves. No, he would not give his name. He might try a false one, but what good would that do? They would want corroboration of some sort, and he could provide none. Randall shook his head. "I'm sorry, Lieutenant, but I can't help you."

Granger sighed aloud. "Then could you at least tell me," he began mildly, "what it's all about?" His stare intensified, like that of threatened animal. "What's the deal between you four? What happened in that bar?" Sweat ran from his hairline down his face. "God damn it, we've found seven bodies in fourteen different places this week. That's some kind of record, even for Santa Cruz. And now you assholes show up. I swear to God, if you're in on this, if you aren't spilling something I need to know, I will personally hang you from the rafters."

Randall returned his gaze, saying nothing. At length Granger stood up, straightened his suit. "Very well then. As soon as we've established your identity, and we will eventually, you'll be facing charges of assault with a deadly weapon. The owner of the pool hall may choose to file a complaint as well." He knocked on the door, and a uniformed officer opened it. "Until then, we'll be holding you indefinitely. I'll send you the worst public defender I can find in the morning."

Granger strode out of the room. The uniformed officer led Randall away.

ᛒ

They put him in a holding tank. The single toilet stank of both urine and vomit, even from across the room. Randall put a boot on the handle and flushed. The polluted water swirled down the rusty drain, revealing porcelain stained permanently yellow-brown. Randall suppressed the urge to vomit himself. At least he would never have to use that toilet.

Though large, the cell was overcrowded. Unconscious, reeking bodies littered the floor. Many of them had shoes or clothing missing. Those on the bunks looked awake for the most part. A dozen faces stared at him with naked avarice, eyeing his coat and boots. Randall laughed quietly to himself. It should be simplicity itself to start a little trouble. He looked around at the lean faces, the strong bodies stretched out on the bunks. He might not even have to start it himself.

Randall walked slowly about the room looking everyone conscious in the eye, hoping to set somebody off. At the far end of the cell, a likely candidate sat upright in a high bunk. He wore a leather jacket a bit too large to be his, and a pair of glossy wing-tip shoes. A chord held his greasy hair back in a rat-tail. His brown eyes tracked Randall as he paced up to him. "So what do you think you looking at, man?" he said a half whisper.

"Your bunk. Get off."

The greaser laughed, then nodded. "Whatever you say, man." He slid lithely down the floor to stand poised, sizing his opponent up and grinning. Randall slapped his face, swift and hard enough to leave it red. "You son of bitch!" the greaser yelled. He punched Randall in the stomach.

Randall doubled over, but did not dodge. The greaser punched him in the face. A solid hit, sure to leave a nice bruise. Randall staggered back a little, then stood still once more. His adversary hit him again, this time with the other fist. Randall did nothing to avoid the blow. "You crazy, man!" the greaser shouted, shoving him backward.

Putting his hands to his face, Randall felt both cheeks gingerly. "Okay," he said, striding forward, "that should do." He brought a swift knee up into the greaser's crotch. The man collapsed onto the floor, moaning and cursing. "Thanks for the help."

Wearily, Randall hoisted himself onto the now vacant bunk. His bandaged ribs throbbed in complaint. A few hours of motionlessness should help. He glanced around the cell. No one looked at him any more. Randall leaned back against the wall, getting as comfortable as possible. He took one last deep breath, then flipped the mental switch that stopped his lungs. His body ached for a few moments, searching for oxygen, then went gradually numb. He listened to the sound of his heart for a while, then stopped that too.

Sitting dead on the bunk, Randall stared unblinking at a section of the bars opposite. He sighed mentally. This stasis was difficult to maintain. Slipping into the healing sleep would be much too easy. He listened to the quiet movements of the others in the cell while the blood settled into his legs. Seven bodies, he thought. In fourteen places.

He sat, and stared at the bars.

chapter eight

The cell door slid into view, its upright bars passing through those of the stationary wall, or so it seemed to Randall's blurred vision. His eyes had begun to dry out over an hour ago. He had considered closing them, but he felt he looked more dead with them open. Besides, he wanted to see. His boots and coat constituted an irresistible temptation.

Footsteps came forward into the cell. Perhaps it was mealtime. Or maybe someone had made bail. The footsteps stopped somewhere off to his left, probably in the center of the room. "Randall Springfield," a rough voice called.

Had his muscles been functioning, Randall would have flinched. His mind sent the involuntary signal, though his body remained incapable of response. As it was, he had to actively restrain himself from resuming his breathing. His whole body wanted to gasp in surprise. How in hell had they found out so soon? Any search that would have included his dead records should have taken days, if not weeks. Somebody must have told them, and recently too, after his brief interrogation. Granger must have lied to him. Either Knox or Rose must still be in custody, perhaps both. But why would they have given him away? They knew not to. He'd been through this kind of thing with both of them before. Had they been compelled in some way? What the fuck was going on?

"I'm looking for a Randall Springfield," the voice called again. Steps paced slowly about the cell. A uniformed man came striding into Randall's field of vision. His chiseled face and dusty hair swam and rippled as he looked the prisoners over. "Aw, Christ." He came forward to squint into Randall's face, sliding even further out of focus, becoming a fleshy haze with one large blue eye. "I hope it ain't this guy." He stepped back, motioning to someone outside the cell. "You, go get a doctor from the infirmary." Feet scuttled quickly down the hall. "And find Granger!" The iron door onto the cell block opened and shut, the loud metal sound echoing down the row of cages. The face swarmed closer once more. "Fuckin' Christ," the man whispered.

The old guard paced the cell up and down in a steady circuit until Lieutenant Granger arrived. He took a brief look at Randall, his tired face distorted like the reflection in a carnival mirror. He turned away, a hand held up to his temple. "God damn it!" Granger stormed out of view. Randall's brain sent half conscious, half intended signals to his eyes. Follow the motion. Keep your eye on the ball. But his oxygen-starved muscles did not obey. His eyes remained fixed, staring at the bars across the cell. "What do you know about this? Speak!" He heard the sharp slap of flesh against flesh, then the heavier sound of a body hitting the floor. Randall laughed inside his head. Granger must really be pissed.

"I don't know nothing, man," a new voice pleaded. "Honest. He picked a fight with Joey when he come in. Since then he's been sitting on that bunk all day." There was a muffled thud. The new voice grunted. "I'm telling you, that's all that happened. Ask Joey. He'll tell you."

Granger walked slowly back into view. He crouched down by the bunk below Randall, his blurred body seeming to collapse in on itself. "So Joey," he said softly, "how about it?" One suited arm telescoped out to point at the upper bunk. "Anything you want to tell me about this dead guy up here, Joey?"

"Motherfucker kneed me in the nuts, man." The greaser's voice sounded strained, like he was still in pain. "I laid on the fucking floor for an hour."

Granger's face twisted and warped. Randall decided he was frowning. "That's not what I asked you, Joey."

"I hit him a couple of times. So what? The guy was asking for it. I didn't throw nothing hard enough to kill him, big guy like that." There was a long pause. "I think he smashed my nuts, man."

"Lieutenant Granger." The old guard reappeared over his shoulder. "The doctor's here, sir."

Granger stood, springing to full size like a jack-in-the-box. One arm slithered out to point at the unseen greaser. "I'll talk to you later, Joey."

A balding man in a white coat stepped forward. He took one of Randall's limp hands. The nerves were dead, as if the arm had been slept on. All Randall felt was a ghost of pressure and a vague impression of his own movement. The doctor replaced the hand, then felt for a pulse in the neck. Randall wished he would get on with it. Shutting down like this was highly destructive on the cellular level. He would probably be sick for a week just from sitting in the tank all day. And who knew how long the rest of the formalities would take.

The doctor took an implement from his coat pocket and shined a bright light into each of Randall's drying eyes, one after the other. Randall's sight flared and washed out. Amorphous blobs of shifting color obliterated what little view he had, the static of overloaded optic nerves. "Dead as disco music," the doctor pronounced. "Have him taken over to the morgue, and I'll file the proper forms." Twin fingers pressed down on his eyelids, dragging them closed.

"Call those other two characters," Granger instructed someone. "Knox and Collins. They might know who the next of kin is. If not, they can come back in themselves." We still don't have a phone, Randall fumed. They'll have to send a car out to the mortuary. Wonder how long that'll take? Crap. Well, at least they really are free. That's something.

After a few more minutes he sensed hands grasping him, lifting him up and laying him flat on his back. Then he felt himself moving horizontally, feet first. The motion registered only as a change in balance, a phantom acceleration. On a gurney, he supposed. He found the sensation mildly unpleasant, something akin to seasickness. Had his digestive system been operating, he thought he might have felt ill. Dead in body, he experienced just a faint mental tenseness.

After several rolling jolts and the busy, shuffling sound of hallways and the combined bang of hospital doors, he felt himself lifted and then placed flat once more. Someone arranged his arms at his sides. Then he slid headlong to the sound of a file drawer being shut, only large and all around him. He stopped suddenly. There followed a metallic thud, then stillness and silence.

Well, he thought, the police station seems to be adjacent to the county morgue. Convenient, I imagine. Nice for me. Saves time, and I hate ambulances. All that speeding and rattling around, even when one's supposed to be dead. I never quite understood that. Maybe the paramedics have gotten addicted to it. Randall laughed mentally. Knox should have been a paramedic. He'd love it, altruism and reckless driving all rolled into one.

Randall quieted his mind, concentrating on the abstract patterns of light his brain insisted on drawing before his dead eyes. He floated with them, into them, swimming in a neon sea of half images. Sometimes he thought he noticed patterns, spiral geometries repeating themselves endlessly. Other times he saw pictures-faces, hands, leaves blown by a spectral wind-pulsing and fading in the false light of his imagination.

He remembered another time he had played dead this way, in Georgia. No minor bruising would suffice then. The charge had been murder. Never mind that his "victim" had vanished from the graveyard a week into his imprisonment. That only added a new perversion to his guilt. Lisel had been acting the Southern Belle, and that town wanted his head on a lance. So he had hung himself in his cell, with his bed sheet. He had been careful not to drop from too great a height, not wanting to snap his neck. But strangulation had not appealed to him either. In the end, he simply shut his body down and fell off the cot when his muscles gave. Even so, it had taken him over two months to recover fully from the experience. He still recalled how that cage had looked, the rust-rimed bars swinging gently to and fro.

Randall stirred mentally, shaking himself free of the memory. Who told them? he wondered again. Who gave them my name? I wish I knew what was going on here. And Jim? Is he just some psychotic asshole, or does he have an angle on all this? Maybe he's some new pet of Mother's. The thought disturbed him; it sat in his mouth like vinegar. But the more he thought about it the more likely it seemed. It would go a long way towards explaining his apparent disinterest in Knox and Rose. She wanted only him. Christ, he thought. I've got to get out of here.

Not much chance of that happening in a hurry, he conceded. It'll probably be hours before a medical examiner gets to me. And who knows how long until Knox and Rose show up, if they're in any condition to come at all. Thinking that, he felt the healing sleep drifting up on him, warm and intimate. That temporary oblivion would be nice just now. His body was in sad shape. No! None of that, he thought. Still, he could feel the sleep stealing over him like scented fog.

Well, he thought, if I can't go one way I'll go the other. With a mental kick he restarted his heart and his lungs, holding them to slow tempo. It would not do to look alive when the coroner came to call. The blood flowed sluggishly back into his limbs and head. A thin ration of oxygen made its rounds. Shortly he felt the pin-and-needle crawling of his nerves returning to life. His neck and back ached terribly, and the slab he lay on felt unbearably chill. Not much of an improvement, he thought glumly.

Again he let his thoughts wander. Lisel. Lisel. My wicked stepmother. You're out there somewhere. I know you are. Things will go differently this time, I promise you.

℘

The echoing clang of his little door opening brought him back to the present. Startled, he killed his heart and lungs instantly, afraid he had already gotten too warm. The slab slid out. Harsh light turned his eyelids orange. He felt suddenly vulnerable in his paralysis, like a dying man staring up at a sky filled with vultures. "Ah, Mr. Springfield!"

Randall very nearly leapt up, the jovial voice was so near. He remained still only through a violent clenching of the will. The man, whoever he was, must be standing right beside him. He could hear the fellow turning pages, flimsy paper rustling loudly. "And how are we today, sir?" What the fuck? He doesn't seriously expect me to answer that? He couldn't know, could he? Oh, hell.

"Sustained several injuries just prior to arrest. Treated at our facility. No doubt kept awake all night answering questions." Relief washed through Randall. The idiot was talking to himself. "Gets into a fight in a holding cell. Dies some time later." Had to be the medical examiner. "Well, Mr. Springfield, it sounds as if you've had a rough day." You can say that again, mister.

"Now then, let's just have a look at these injuries of yours. If we're lucky, maybe we can find a reasonable cause of death. Wouldn't that be nice?" Judas Iscariot on a pogo stick, thought Randall, this guy is truly over the edge. Guess working with corpses all day could do that to a person. He felt his coat spread open, out of the way. Something cold and metal settled onto his stomach. Oh shit. Before he could decide to make a grab for the object, he heard a long tearing of fabric. His t-shirt came away from his chest in halves, exposing him to the chill of the room.

"We'll just remove these bandages." The tape tore away from his flesh in large strips. "Exactly as I thought. Would you look at that bruising? Probably punctured a lung, if not worse. Sustained during arrest, most likely. Then that quack in the infirmary lets you go with a chest x-ray

111

and some stereo tape. After all, you're a prisoner and not a patient." He could hear the scratch of pen, then more shuffling of paper. "I hope you've got a good attorney, Mr. Springfield. An airtight case of wrongful death if ever I saw one. You could make a fortune."

Mother of God, thought Randall, I don't think I can take much more of this insanity. "But since the county's ass is on the line, we'll just have to make certain." Oh, no. What did he mean by that? Steps walked away, then wheels rolled back. Randall felt himself pulled, dropping down onto something slightly lower than the slab. The wheels squeaked again and he sensed motion, a slight wind against his chest hairs. He was pulled up onto another cold table.

Strong hands rolled him to one side, pulling his arm out of his coat and t-shirt. He was rolled to the other side and his clothing slid away. Footsteps walked around him and he felt a distant tugging at his boots. His nerves had begun to go numb again. He could no longer feel the table under him, or sense exactly how his body was placed. His boots hit the floor at his feet, one after the other. God damn, thought Randall. Autopsy.

Randall recalled a film he had seen once, some insipid piece of modern horror. One of the characters had displayed a set of autopsy tools to the audience, recounting their uses. They were not as delicate as the tools of surgeon, not as precise. A metallic half circle with teeth on the curve and a grip at the edge sufficed to crack the sternum cleanly. A sort of spring-loaded reverse clamp held the rib cage open. There were glorified pliers and saws sharp enough for bone. Siphons for blood. And gigantic shears used in the rare event that the head needed to be removed. For incisions, common kitchen knives. Nothing sterilized, of course. Why bother?

Randall could picture this fellow cheerfully removing his internal organs, scribbling something down on a clipboard, then stuffing handfuls back into the ruin of his chest. That sort of damage would take months to heal, maybe even years. He could not let it happen. The medical examiner began to whistle brightly to himself. Something Disney, Randall thought, but could not place the tune. In a minute I will sit up, he said to himself. And then I will have to kill this man. Fuck. There has to be another way out.

He considered just switching himself back on, praying that this happy fool noticed the pulse before he started carving. But then it would be back to prison, eventually if not immediately. And a hospital was just as bad. Lisel would find him as he lay immobile. Even without that threat he had no desire to remain in custody. There was no other way.

"Sorry, old man." Hands worked at Randall's belt, then whisked it away from his body. "I'm sure you'd rather have a nice juicy nurse doing this, but I'm afraid I'm all there is." Forgive me, Randall thought, and tensed himself to spring.

"Excuse me," said a familiar voice, "what are you doing?" Knox! Randall clamped down furiously on the impulses he had been about to send, not entirely sure that he had not moved already. Agonizing seconds ticked by. The hands came away from his jeans, and the medical examiner shuffled away from the table. "I'm this man's next of kin. I've been asked to identify his body."

"Sounds like you already have," the examiner returned brightly. "What relation are you to the deceased, Mister...?"

"Knox. Mr. Springfield is... was... my half brother." Three sets of steps came closer, back into the room.

"Your last names..." the examiner said vaguely. "You had the same Mother, then?"

"Yes," Knox replied dryly. Randall heard a third voice laugh.

"And you are?" the examiner inquired mildly.

"Dareck Collins, assistant director of the Redwood Mortuary." And Rose! What did Knox do, put you into a suit? Or are you pulling this bullshit in your biker jacket? Randall allowed himself to relax. These two would get him out of here if anyone could. No problem.

"Of course I'm familiar with the director," the examiner continued heartily. "I see Mr. Small professionally from time to time. You must be a relatively new development."

"Oh, yes," Rose replied just as cheerfully, "I'm quite new to the position." There followed a moment of awkward silence.

"So," Knox resumed, "what were you doing to my brother's body?"

"Ah, well." The examiner coughed. "It's rather complex. Mr. Springfield died of complications arising from the injuries he received in the, uh, fight he was in just prior to his arrest." The examiner did not seem to be aware that his two guests had been involved in the brawl as well. "Most likely a broken rib punctured one of his lungs, which filled with fluid. This resulted in a partial loss of oxygen to the body and brain. Usually this does not lead to death, but apparently Mr. Springfield was also involved in some sort of altercation in one of the holding cells."

"That's all very informative," Knox began, voice tinged with suspicion, "but you have yet to identify yourself, much less explain what you're up to." That's the way, thought Randall. Keep him off balance. "I see a great deal of ugly looking equipment laying about. Just what were you about to do when we came in?"

"My apologies," said the doctor quietly. "I am Chief Medical Examiner Wallace Brimly, and I'd be happy to explain the procedure I was about to perform."

"Then do."

Brimly cleared his throat. "Your brother's original injuries were treated by a doctor in the police infirmary. There is a question as to whether his death resulted from improper treatment by infirmary staff or from the injuries he received later in the holding cell." Isn't that interesting? Randall thought. How quickly you change your tune, Dr. Brimly.

"I see," Knox prompted.

"In order to determine the precise cause of death," the Chief Examiner continued hesitantly, "I have deemed it necessary to perform an immediate autopsy."

"I thought as much!" Knox roared. "I absolutely forbid it! I will not have my brother mutilated any further by you lot!" Randall wanted to sit up and clap. Get him Knox! Straight for the jugular.

"If I may," Brimly began mildly, "the decision is not yours to make." He played nervously with some papers. "As Chief Examiner, investigations of this sort are left entirely to my discretion. And I feel that it is my duty to determine whether or not the department is responsible in this matter."

"What do you mean 'whether or not?'" Knox replied acidly. "My brother dies in one of your holding cells after being glanced at by some prison quack and you think the department may be responsible? Don't insult my intelligence, Brimly. In what conceivable way could an autopsy be necessary to prove that?"

The Chief Examiner said nothing for some time. He set down his clipboard with soft click. "To be perfectly frank, Mr. Knox, I agree with you. The department is obviously at fault." He coughed nervously.

"However, an autopsy will be necessary to prove negligence in any, ah, legal action you may wish to take against the county."

"I'm not interested in that," Knox said casually. "A lengthy law suit isn't going to bring him back, is it?" Certainly not, thought Randall. Besides, our case would crumble the minute the county called me as a witness. "I'll tell you what," Knox continued. "In return for the immediate release of my brother's remains, I'll agree to take no action against the department." Bingo! Randall chuckled inwardly. He could almost smell Brimly's relief.

"Would you be willing to sign a statement to that effect?" The Chief Examiner's voice seemed abnormally calm.

"Certainly," Knox replied.

"I'll have it drawn up, as well as the release forms. If you'll excuse me?" Brimly shuffled quickly across the room. The hospital doors banged open. "Ah, Mr. Collins. You will be taking charge of the remains, yes?"

"That's what I'm here for," Rose declared.

"Good. Good." The doors swished closed.

Feet tapped softly over to the table where Randall lay. "Almost home," said Rose, somewhere above him.

"When we're safely out of here," said Knox, further off, "I really will kill you."

They placed him on a gurney and trundled him out into the parking lot. The wheels rattled on the pitted blacktop, and traffic hummed in the distance. Once they had stopped they transferred him onto yet another gurney and then lifted it into a vehicle of some sort. Knox and Chief Examiner Brimly exchanged a few more words. Doors slammed. An engine growled, and Randall felt the car backing out. He switched his body back on, bringing his heart rate and breathing gradually up to normal.

The noise of traffic surrounded them. "It's okay to twitch now, cousin." Rose's voice came from somewhere ahead of him.

"It'll be a few minutes before he can move much or speak," said Knox. "Has to get some oxygen to his muscles first."

"You look like shit, Randall. Do you guys do this sort of thing often? I mean, it really looks painful." Randall opened his eyes. He saw Rose staring it him, his head sticking through some sort of window. His beard was gone, leaving smooth cheeks, and his wild hair had been pulled back into a long tail. And yes, he really was wearing a suit. But his smile was the same as ever. "Hello there," he said. "So glad you could join us."

Randall clenched his fists and stretched his leg muscles, working the blood into them. His entire body felt stiff as cork. He glanced up, and saw the black velvet ceiling of the car. "Where'd you get the hearse?" he asked. His voice came out scratchy but intelligible.

Knox answered from the driver's seat. "I rented it from our landlord, Mr. Small. Told him we were going to a costume party as undertakers and wanted to arrive in style."

"Clever," croaked Randall. They might have given the Chief Examiner the name of a different mortuary, just to be safe. But then again, it made sense that Knox would call upon his landlord in his time of need. Sure. "So what's the situation, then?" he asked. "What's been happening to the both of you?"

"It's pretty simple," said Rose. "I was arrested. I gave a false name and fairly convincing driver's license. They held me for a couple hours, then let me go." He brought a hand up to caress his clean chin. "I don't understand it, really. Why they held onto you and not us, that is."

"Oh, I think I understand it," said Knox. He glanced over his shoulder quickly, then returned his attention to the road. "Jim's working for Mother, isn't he?"

"That's the way I'm figuring it," Randall confessed. "She doesn't have as much of a quarrel with you two."

"Not yet," Knox amended. "Anyway, that crack on the head Jim gave me sent me right into the sleep. I woke up in the hospital around four in the morning and insisted on being released. By dawn they had run some tests on me and agreed to let me go. The police wanted to talk to me, but they didn't take me in. I got home to find Rose sitting on the stairs. We waited around all morning, hoping to hear something from you or about you. I was on the verge of going down to the station on my own when the patrol car showed up." Knox negotiated a sharp turn. "We spent most of the afternoon organizing this nonsense."

"So what's next, Captain?" Rose inquired.

Randall frowned. "Don't call me that, please."

Rose crinkled his mouth up in puzzlement, his expression all the more clear without the additional foliage. "Why not?"

"Because," Randall replied slowly, "I used to be one."

"Oh." Rose ducked back into the cab of the hearse, then reappeared a moment later, smiling outlandishly. "So," he repeated, "what's next?"

Randall laughed in spite of himself. He thought about sitting up, but the velvet ceiling was too low. "Home," he said, "as quickly as possible."

"I'm afraid I can't do that," said Knox. He sped up through an intersection. "Mr. Small isn't expecting the car back until later. If we show up early, it'll be suspicious." Checking the mirror, he swerved into a different lane. "Any preference on where we hang out? It'll only be for a few hours."

"None," said Randall. "Park anywhere. Someplace quiet. I'll just lie in the back and rest."

Knox shrugged, his suited shoulders showing briefly above the top of his seat. "Any suggestions, Rose?"

The maniac smile stretched across his face. "We could go shoot some pool." In the seat beside him, Knox sighed.

༄

"So what happened to the gun?" Randall stood across from the bathroom mirror, examining his wounds in the unframed sheet of silvered glass. A lurid bruise, purple and swollen, spread from his left hip to his right nipple. The surrounding skin glowed an unhealthy red blending gradually into pale white, like a parody of sunset made in flesh. Bits of tape clung in random patches. His right shoulder had the yellow, diseased look of an old bruise not yet vanished. When compared with its twin it seemed somewhat misshapen. The rest of his body, even his face, looked pale and bloodless. Blue veins stood out on his white arms and legs.

Rose sat on the edge of the combination tub and shower, weary and slightly sickened. His new sport coat hung from a towel rack, though he had yet to shed the rest of his suit. "I've no idea," he replied. "I dropped it when that gorilla hit my arm and I couldn't find it again." He slipped off his polished black shoes to reveal a pair of dirty sweat-socks. "The police should have found it, but I'm not going to complain. At any rate, I thought it best not to go back and look for it."

"Probably a wise choice."

Randall stepped out into the hall to find Knox waiting. "You might want these," he said, handing over a paper grocery bag.

Randall dumped its contents out onto the hardwood floor. His coat came out in a lumpy brown wad, followed by his boots. A wooden handle stood out from one of his secret sheaths. He stooped down to remove the blade. The entire knife had been carved from a single piece of dark wood. Black age lines cut short arcs from edge to edge. "How'd you manage this?" he asked.

"I squeezed Brimly for it when we were signing the papers," Knox replied. "Made out like it was some family artifact." He shrugged dismissively. "Strictly speaking, it wasn't even evidence."

"Thanks all the same." Randall replaced the knife and forced his feet into his boots. "I would have hated to lose it."

Knox nodded. The bathroom door closed behind them. They heard water running. "You really should sleep," said Knox. "You look terrible."

"I know," said Randall, "but I can't." He walked stiffly towards his room. "She's here now, and she's watching us. I can feel it." Rifling his pack, he pulled out a clean black shirt. He shrugged into it with difficulty. "If I sleep now, she'll come for me. If I try and hide, she'll follow. I've got to stay awake until she makes her move." He sat down heavily on the blood-stained mattress.

Knox sat in the folding chair. "It'll take you a month to get over that awake." He gestured at Randall's chest. "The sleep would take a week at most. Rose and I could guard you."

Randall shook his head. "I'll hole up here, like I should have in the first place. You and Rose can hunt up that asshole Jim, if he's still around." He sat forward, wincing as his broken ribs shifted. "Maybe he can lead us to her, or give us some useful information at least. If we can find her quickly, catch her by surprise, we might just have a chance."

Knox laughed. "You make her sound like she's invulnerable."

"She's not dead yet," Randall replied.

ɋƀ

The following morning Randall heard a furtive tapping at the front door. Knox had reported to his office hours before and Rose was out buying breakfast. Reluctantly, Randall set down the history of Vietnam he had been reading and shuffled stiffly down the hall. He opened the door to find Mr. Small, the mousey funeral director and landlord. "What can I do for you?" Randall asked, grateful that he had put a shirt on earlier. "Something wrong? The hearse not returned in satisfactory condition? My brother is not the best of drivers, I admit."

"Oh, nothing like that," the mortician replied pleasantly. He held up a largish package that hung from his hand by the string. "This arrived for you yesterday. The mailman left it with us by mistake." He thrust the brown-wrapped box at Randall, who took it grudgingly. "There's no return address, otherwise I don't think they would have delivered it at all." His eyes followed the package as Randall shifted its weight from hand to hand. "My wife and I thought it ever so curious."

"Yes, thank you," Randall replied absently, "and thanks for the loan of the hearse." He closed the door.

Having set the package on his bare metal desk, he contemplated whether or not he should open it. The handwriting on the stiff brown paper was not hers, but all the same Randall knew it came from Lisel. No one else would send him anything. It was probably not a bomb. Lisel liked to watch pain, relish it in person. To her, Randall was a toy and not a true enemy. Trouble was, she had a nasty habit of pulling her toys apart.

He tested the package's weight. Not so light, not so heavy. It could have been a melon. He shook it. Something just smaller than the box rattled inside.

Randall decided to open it. He pulled the hardwood blade from his boot and cut the string. Slicing the thick tape at the seams, he pried up the top flaps. The dank aroma of decay wafted out of the box. Randall felt his stomach lurch. He up-ended the package over his dark stained mattress. Lisa Robinson's head rolled out.

Creeping grey film had grown over the charred flesh of her face. A bright shard of white bone jutted from the pulpy stub of her neck. Matted mud choked what little remained of her dark hair. She reeked of swamp. Her blistered eyes stared up at him.

Randall trudged numbly to the bathroom and vomited red bile into the toilet.

chapter nine

"She sent me a couple of Swan's fingers, too." Knox gazed into the box containing Lisa Robinson's burnt, severed head. "Little did she realize I had most of him already."

Rose leaned against the opposite wall, as far from the grisly package as he could get. "Did they come with any of that crappy cardboard bubble gum?" Both brothers turned to regard him gravely. "Sorry." He attempted a wan smile. "Just trying to lighten the mood of the situation."

Randall refolded the top flaps, sealing the box. "I just wonder when and where the rest of Lisa will show up." He sat on the stained mattress, one hand on the package. "Lisel could cause a lot of trouble with this."

Knox ran a hand through his stubble hair. "She's been watching us all this time. Hell, she might have been here before you arrived, just waiting for me to give Swan away." He paced nervously across the room, eyes fixed on the fire escape window and the alley below. "Why's she so pissed at him? What did he do?"

Randall contemplated the tarnished metal tips of his boots. "Maybe he knows something she'd rather we didn't find out."

"Like what?" Rose pushed himself from the wall, edging a bit further into the room.

Randall shrugged, resigned. "I've no idea." Unconsciously, his fingers tapped out a little tune on the cardboard lid. "But if we don't find her soon, press this to some kind of confrontation, we'll have to leave Santa Cruz. Otherwise she'll start making things hot for us. I know her. She'd rather keep us running."

Knox paused in his restless circuit of the room. "How long do you think we've got before trouble starts?"

"Maybe twenty-four hours," Randall answered. "That's being optimistic. If we were smart, we'd clear out right now."

"But that's not what you want." Knox looked down at his brother. "Is it?"

"You can leave now if you want to, and I'll hook up with you later." Randall glanced over at Rose. "That goes for you, too, Renfield." He stood up. "But tonight, I'm going hunting."

"We made a deal and I'll stick to it." Rose finally ventured into the center of the room, his face serious for a moment. "I'll stay."

Randall turned to his brother. "And you?"

Knox released a long, pent up breath. "I talked to a few of my students this morning. One of them told me a guy who looks like Jim hangs out at the Well most nights."

"What sort of place is that?" asked Randall, refusing to display his relief.

"Steam rooms. Massage parlor. Private hot tubs you rent by the hour." Knox smiled. "The kids go there to fuck."

Randall nodded. "Okay, then. We'll go there first thing after sundown. If Jim's not there, we'll spend the rest of the night prowling the booze and billiards scene. If we still come up empty, we'll clear out at first light." Gingerly, he scooped the fatal package off his bed. "You two can drive around, do some scouting. I'll get rid of this."

"Hold on a minute." Knox moved swiftly out the door and down the hall to his room. Randall and Rose stood regarding each other, faces equally puzzled. Knox returned shortly, a dusty wooden case tucked under one arm. He placed it on the desk and flipped open the tiny silver latches. Nestled in a bed of crushed velvet lay a pair of dueling pistols. They had the look of antiques-long fluted barrels, ornate trigger guards and hammers-but held the bright, oily shine of weapons well kept. Long bullets lined the sides of the case. Knox handed one butt first to Rose.

"Nice balance." He held the gun at arm's length and sighted down the polished bore. When he pulled the trigger, the graven hammer snapped dully. "Good action." Sliding out the cylinder, he began to load the weapon. "Thanks." Knox extended the second pistol toward his brother.

"No." Randall glanced down at his boot, thinking of the hardwood blade hidden there. "You'd better keep it." Knox did not protest. Bearing the package, Randall walked from the room. Behind him, he heard the snap and spin of his brother loading the second gun.

♻

Randall walked down the sunlit streets, package tucked under one arm, feeling himself sweat. The pain in his side had numbed to a dull throb which the exercise now began to reawaken. Randall could feel the pain coming, like the soft singing of air and ground that heralds a rushing train. Soon, very soon, he must give himself to the healing sleep. After tonight, no matter what the outcome. He could not continue to function this way.

Though it weighed very little, he felt intensely aware of the box under his arm and the hideous specimen it contained. Strange, he thought to himself, that all of a woman's mind-her entire being, almost-could weigh so little. Strange that her death could feel so light in his grip.

The noontime traffic was thin and hurried. People paced briskly up to restaurants and cafés, forever consulting the watches clamped to their wrists. Randall walked among them with a painful sense of conspicuousness. He felt the package under his arm attract eyes like a magnet, if only for glancing instants. Surely they could guess its terrible contents from its look, its very size. Surely they could guess his guilt from the casualness he forced into his step, from his firm grip on the nightmare box. Randall walked on, trying not to stare at everyone who passed.

What if she were watching now? he wondered. The skin of his neck went chill. Of course. Now would be the perfect time to act against him, walking the city alone. She could bring the authorities down upon him and he would never be able to explain himself, tell them how it was that he still breathed the air. Granger would lock him in cell and leave him there no matter how dead he made himself. They would watch his rot and resurrection through the bars, mystified. Or perhaps, when he left the populated avenues to dispose of his burden, she would deal with him herself. Pieces missing, Knox had said, some returned through the mail. Rose would receive his fingers, one by one, each with a brittle piece of gum.

Randall passed a narrow alley between buildings. An amazing stench of spoiled grease and ripened flesh wafted over him in a humid cloud. Randall glanced up at the business to either side. Painted letters in one window read *Dan's Fish Market, Fresh Fish Daily*. Well, that explained that. He looked at the package under his arm. If there was ever a place it would go unnoticed, this was it right here. Checking all around for suspicious eyes, he edged further into the warm darkness.

The smell intensified, making his eyes and nose run. He squinted, screwing up his face against the corrosive odor. His vision adjusted to the dimness and he saw the dumpster huddled against the concrete wall. Steam curled up from under its lid in visible waves. He stepped toward it, eyes scanning the shadows. The muscles in his back twitched, certain they were about to stabbed by hidden knives. Glancing one last time up and down the deserted alley, Randall took hold of the lid and thrust it open.

The stench rose up to blind him. He turned his head away, gasping. Inside the dumpster, flies crawled over the top layer of a yard-deep mound of fish heads, bones, entrails, oily wads of wax paper, disposable cardboard trays soaked in vinegar. Randall set the package on the ground and stripped off his coat. Bending down over the dumpster, he thrust one arm into the wet, reeking mess. He shoved aside rotting fish and disintegrating paper cups, clearing a hole. Picking up the box, he set it in the depression and began shoveling trash over it.

He paused. The box. It had his name on it, and the address of the mortuary. Did he dare leave it? They would be skipping town in the morning. The police thought he was dead, anyway. Better to leave that shriveled trophy packed away. He finished covering the box with trash and gratefully closed the dumpster.

Reeking oil coated his arm. Peering more closely at his hand, Randall noticed a fish eye clinging to his palm. He flicked it away, feeling his stomach churn. Picking a tattered page of newspaper from the alley floor, he wiped his arm as best he could. The old words rubbed black streaks of ink along his pale flesh, leaving it sticky and tainted. Slinging his coat over his shoulder, he left the alley. Until he reached the sunlight he felt watched, though whether by the blistered orbs he left behind in the trash or something in the darkness beyond, he could not say.

ℜ

They walked the night streets three abreast, weapons hidden within easy reach. They did not look at each other. They did not speak. But they walked as one, feet rising and falling in synch, arms swinging free of pockets. They strode briskly but with moderate speed, saving muscle strength and lung endurance for the long hours ahead. Their alert eyes scanned the sidewalks, the passing faces, registering and discarding all they encountered. And the people who saw them made way.

The night city swelled with men and women, voices, speeding cars, and laughter. Students swarmed the narrow sidewalks, tricked out in their most outrageous uniforms, on display for one another. A current of studded leather jackets, bleached jeans, and carefully casual hairstyles ebbed and flowed through a sea of slit skirts, loose tops, and uncomfortable heels. A thousand pairs of half-revealed breasts bobbed like buoys in the artificial moonlight. A thousand pairs of hands stirred uncertainly from pockets, then took off in pursuit.

The three men walked on, caressed by murmured prayers and seductions. They had abandoned the rooms above the mortuary. The red Barracuda sat in a municipal lot next to Rose's patchwork motorcycle, loaded down with books and bottles and three small packs of private gear. A blank envelope sat in Mr. Small's mailbox, containing only keys. They would never come back, at least not in his lifetime.

Bass guitars throbbed in open-air nightclub patios. Neon couples vibrated in time to the pulsing noise. The night swallowed individual sounds, twisting shouts and songs, lurid proposals and hot replies into one continuous, ululating roar. And the roar never changed, just shifted in volume as its component parts mixed and mingled under the glare of arc lights.

They came to a block of converted residential buildings. Boys and girls leaned out the backlit windows of a peeling three-story Victorian, chatting up the crowd passing below. A dozen stereo systems staged a dogfight from the balconies, battling for dominance. Next came the squat, weedy lair of a palmist and tarot card reader. Then the crystal-draped windows of a New Age bookstore. A hanging garden of wind chimes danced lazily from the rafters of the porch.

A long, low structure sprawled upon the corner lot. Spanish tiles armored the gently sloping roof with their dusty orange scales. Cement replicas of Fu-dog statuary stood placid watch over the gravel lawn. A wandering path of tree-stump slices led to the door, past a simple wooden sign saying only *The Well*. The three men stopped at the foot of the path, contemplating their objective.

Randall spoke. "So, do we case the place or barge right in?"

"I imagine there aren't too many windows," Knox replied. "I don't think we'd see much stalking around outside."

"Ever been in the place?" asked Rose, voice quiet.

"Of course not." Knox eyed the dimly lit porch at the end of the path. "I can't understand what Jim would be doing here if he's one of our kind."

"Well, then," said Randall, "let's find out." He stepped out onto the wooden trail. The others followed behind him.

The front door stood open, venting a warm breeze into the cool of the night. They filed into a room of dark wood, illuminated only by shaded lamps on small, carved tables. A low desk sat near the door, open guest book and closed cash box neatly arranged on the spotless blotter. The antique wooden swivel chair behind it sat empty. The faint, continuous hum of buried pipes underlined the silence, a wind-borne mantra from some distant monastery. Knox circled the desk to examine the guest book.

He flipped back through earlier pages, then returned to the current day. "No Jim Sullivan tonight, though he appears to have come quite frequently in the last month or so. Funny." He bent forward to scrutinize the book. "Either business has slacked off the last couple of nights, or whoever's been manning the desk has started getting sloppy."

"Whoever's been manning the desk isn't even here," Randall pointed out. "Something is definitely happening."

"No shit." Rose reached a hand inside his jacket to touch the dueling pistol in its pocket. "I don't like this." Knox rummaged through the desk drawer, then tossed a ring of keys to Randall.

He caught them deftly. "Okay." He pushed open the only available door. "Let's have a look around."

Steam heat filled the hallway, obscuring the dark wooden walls with clinging mist, inviting sweat to stand out on skin. Thicker wisps of smoky moisture boiled out from under unevenly spaced doorways, along with muffled trills of feminine laughter and faint snatches of Oriental music. Randall shrugged off his long brown coat, hanging it from one arm. The warmth seeped gradually into his body, coating him with a fine layer of sweat and condensation, melting the stiff pain in his side and shoulder.

Randall stopped at the fist door, listening. A woman's voice spoke, teasing. Then a man murmured in reply. Sifting through the ring,

Randall found what looked like a passkey. He inserted it into the lock and opened the door. A blond boy and a Chinese girl, both nude, looked distractedly up at him from the depths of a hot tub. "Sorry," he said, and closed the door. The languid conversation resumed after a moment. Randall opened the next door down.

A shallow pan of water sat steaming over a coal fire which burned in a concave stone upon the floor. A motionless, sexless body lay face down upon a padded massage table. Liquid beads formed on the pale skin, dripping downward. There was no one else in the room. Randall decided not to investigate and closed the door softly. In the next room, a half-seen couple made love on steam-slick tiles. They growled and moaned, passionately oblivious. The next two rooms, though locked, were empty. In one, a tape player sat next to a roiling hot tub, spilling Japanese theater music into the thick air.

A door at the end of the hall stood slightly ajar, steam boiling out like factory smoke. Randall pushed the door open wide and stepped into the room. Chest deep in a frothing Jacuzzi, head thrown back, wet skin steaming, sat Jim. His long black hair trailed into the water, the ends weaving like seaweed. Randall moved further into the room, allowing Knox and Rose to fan out behind him.

Each of Jim's hairy arms draped the shoulders of a girl. The first might have been college age, the other definitely less. Both of them drooped like wilted flowers in a vase of overheated water, eyelids at half mast. A near empty bottle of tequila rested at the lip of the tub. The girls' wet bathing suits sat in a puddle next to it. They mumbled listless questions to themselves. The wooden walls sweated, and water filmed the tiled floor. Gusts of steam billowed from the back of the room, produced by some unseen device.

"Hello, Jim," said Randall. "What are you up to?"

The raven head tilted slowly upright; the dark eyes regarded him calmly. Randall felt chill in the heat of the room. "Just entertaining some friends," Jim boomed out. He hugged the quiet girls to him. They tilted like spun tops, then stabilized once more. "Care to join us?" One dark-haired foot kicked the water, inviting.

"No thanks." Randall watched as small waves washed over the concrete lip of the Jacuzzi, stomach fluttering. "We're in something of a hurry. Truth is we're looking for someone."

"Someone specific, or just someone?" With a baritone chuckle, Jim nudged the younger of the two girls. She stretched weakly, her underdeveloped breasts bobbing briefly into view above the bubbling jet foam. Fixing Jim with an unsteady stare, she mumbled a vague complaint. "I don't think we have the same friends," he drawled.

"We think you know who we mean," said Knox. He looked down into the swirling water with undisguised revulsion. "Just what in hell are you, anyway?"

Jim stood up in the Jacuzzi. Water poured off him, dripping from his matted chest hair. "I'm old," he rumbled, "and very wild." His muscular torso bled steam into the air.

Knox snorted. "You fuck." He jabbed a finger at Jim. "I should tear you in half for what you did to me."

"Give it a try." Jim grinned a twisted half smile. Both men edged forward.

"Now, boys," a voice commanded from the mist, graceful with just a tinge of petulance, "don't fight." Randall tensed, dropped his coat to the damp floor. Rose's hand strayed automatically to his inside pocket. "At least," the voice continued with acidic sweetness, "not yet." Jim sank back into the Jacuzzi, his expression unreadable.

From the clouds of vapor emanating from the back of the room came a hollow rattle, then the splash and sizzle of water poured onto flame. Randall winced, remembering his burning arm. Slowly the mist dispersed, revealing the form of Lisel. She reclined in a wrought iron patio chair next to the extinguished coal fire. Her naked skin, white and glossy as polished bone, showed through the black bars in swaths. A heap of towels and dark clothing sat behind her on a glass topped iron table. She stood with calculated ease, seemingly oblivious to her own nudity. "Hello children," she said, smiling with mock graciousness.

Randall found himself staring. He had never seen her naked until this moment. She had never allowed that. He examined the small, tight breasts with their nut-kernel nipples, the straight gold hair plastered to her head and shoulders. Had she always been so small? She talked tall and she moved tall, and Randall always remembered her as physically impressive. Now he began to doubt. Could his fearsome image of her, the strength with which she had abused him, could it all have stemmed from her brutal personal bravado? Randall's eyes met hers, windows of pale ice fronting depthless black pits, and his fear returned. "Hello, Mother," he replied coldly.

She sauntered up to the opposite rim of the tub. "Let me make the introductions," she began, just as though they were all at tea together. "My eldest son, James." She gestured at Knox. "His younger brother, Randall. The third gentleman I am not familiar with." She let one hand fall to tickle Jim's black hair. "Boys, this is Jim Sullivan, late of London. I don't know who his friends are, but don't they look delicious?" A pink tongue caressed her pale lips. "Now isn't this a coincidence? Jim and Jim, small wonder you two get on so well." She paused, and gave Knox a look of studied concern. "Now, what's become of little Matthew? Always getting himself into trouble, that one." Knox bristled, and started to reply. She cut him off neatly. "Honestly, I don't know which of you boys is the biggest problem." Her gaze slashed at Randall, then back to Knox. "You're all so terribly ungrateful."

"You say the meanest things," said Rose, speaking for the first time. Randall spared him a glance. He looked relaxed, cheerful even, his smile wide and knowing as always. No doubt the physical fact of Lisel had fallen short of his dire visions. His hands hung at his sides, empty. Randall had felt as much himself initially. He prayed Rose would not relax too much. Lisel considered him, temporarily nonplused but covering it with a sardonic arch of one golden, laser-thin eyebrow.

Randall took advantage of her silence. "You know why I'm here," he said, "and what I want." Without looking away from her, he raised one foot and pulled the hardwood knife from its sheath. Jim tensed and Lisel's brittle blue eyes narrowed, but neither of them moved. Randall extended the blade, aiming its point at her naked breasts across the pool of roiling water. The weapon seemed to glow faintly in the heavy air, its dark whorls pulsing with hidden heat.

"You see?" Lisel glanced down at Jim, shaking her head sadly. "He's always trying to kill me." Turning her back on all of them, she resumed her seat in the iron chair. When she looked up, her expression had shifted to patient incredulity. "Now really, Randall, must we go through this again?" Her tone remained conversational. "Honestly, you just escaped the morgue. There's no reason to go back so soon."

Randall shifted the knife so that it continued to point at Lisel. "Come now, Mother," he said scathingly, "it's been well on two centuries since you raised me up, longer for Knox." His brother hovered near the lip of the Jacuzzi glaring down at Jim, the muscles of his face locked rigid. "Will you deny us maturity so long?"

"Two centuries?" Lisel spat. "Moments to me." She leaned forward to stab a finger at Randall, shivering with indignation. "Your time is nothing! Do have any idea how long I languished at half-power before the ancient one fell? Twice your years? Four times? Ten? The very pole star shifted ere I was reborn. You must learn to bide your time, child."

Knox shook his head, both in disbelief and denial. "Your eldest son was born under Cromwell," he remarked, "and yet you claim to be a daughter of the ancient one?" His eyes met hers. "You lie."

Lisel surged up, then restrained herself. She sat back in the iron chair, white hands knotted around black bars. Her ivory arms trembled. The thin ice of her blue eyes shielded a growing fury. "Besides," Randall persisted, "if you continue to deny us, word might get around." The point of the hardwood knife sliced minute circles in the air. "The great families don't generally approve of parents who refuse to step aside. It's bad for us as a race, stifles growth. But then, they're not much given to interfering." Randall forced a smile onto his face. "On the other hand, the brotherhood might just decide to have a look at you."

Lisel glanced disdainfully from one of them to the other. "They would eat your testicles raw." She gave a prim nod. "I've heard what you've been doing to some of their prospects. They aren't likely to do you any favors." One moon-silver hand searched among the dark pile of clothes on the glass tabletop, returning with a small pistol. She leveled it at Randall. "Anyway," she purred, "word isn't going to get around." Randall stared at the gun. Black metal, snub-nosed .38 revolver. Rose's. "Been looking for this? I found it just laying around. Really, you should be more careful with your toys." She thumbed back the hammer. "James?"

"My pleasure." Jim lunged across the length of the Jacuzzi. Wrapping one large hand around Knox's arm, he let himself fall back. With a shout of dismay, Knox toppled in after him. Randall tore his eyes away and started around the pool just as Lisel fired the pistol. Pain tore through his chest and he staggered into the wall. Looking down, he saw the black stain seep into his shirt from a ragged pit near his injured shoulder. His right arm refused to move. Prying the knife from his nerveless hand, he lurched forward once more.

Screaming in agony, the Jacuzzi water searing his skin to blisters, Knox grappled with Jim. The large man gripped his white-capped head and thrust it under the surface. Knox struggled, arms and legs spasming wildly. Muscles straining, Jim held him down. The two girls cowered at the far end of the tub, mewling faintly, alcohol boiling in their blood. They stared in dread fascination as a flurry of bubbles broke the surface. Knox ceased thrashing. Jim released him, and his body sank gradually to the bottom.

Randall rounded the rim of the tub and brought the knife up in a backhand slash, leaving a pair of deep red lines across each of Lisel's breasts. Reversing the motion, he jabbed the blade into her chest just below the sternum. It stuck, the wooden handle slipping from his hand. Teeth bared, she aimed the pistol at his heart, the mouth of the black bore little more than a foot away.

Jim advanced across the water. Rose backed away, his dueling pistol temporarily forgotten. What he had done to Knox… He might really be dead, destroyed. The thought filled him with horror. Jim stood at the rim of the Jacuzzi, black hair dripping. He laced his hands together and cracked his knuckles.

Lisel fired. Randall was thrown back. He found himself staring at the ceiling, the wooden rafters crawling with droplets of condensation. His right hand dangled into the Jacuzzi, skin turning red. He did not feel it. His entire body was numb. He tried to sit up, but could not. He listened for his heartbeat, feeling strangely disappointed when he heard it. Lisel stepped into view overhead. She pulled the knife from her chest and dropped it into the water. Randall heard it splash.

Knox surfaced, face and eyes red, coughing liquid pain. He raised his dueling pistol, water dripping from the silvered muzzle, and held it close to the back of Jim's head. He pulled the trigger. The gun clicked wetly. Jim turned at the sound, laughing. Knox fired again. The cylinder exploded in cloud of shrapnel, bone, and blood. Pieces of the weapon shot into the air, sizzled into the water. Jim collapsed, half his face in crimson tatters. Knox let the remains of the pistol drop from his blasted hand. He stared at the charred flesh, the stubs of his fingers. Ribbons of blood fluttered in the water.

Rose ran up and hauled Knox, unresisting, from the pool. He sprawled on the tile, coughing red fluid, nose dripping blood. Cradling his maimed hand, he curled up into a damp, quivering ball. Randall watched from the floor as Lisel leveled Rose's pistol at them. We're dead, he thought. She'll dump us all in an incinerator somewhere. "Now, what shall I do with you?" she asked. Rose stood. He took in the scene on the opposite shore of the Jacuzzi and his newly shaven face blanched.

"I don't know who you are," Lisel trilled, "but I know why you came." Distantly, Randall felt himself kicked. "This fool promised you eternal life. Youth everlasting, just as soon he dealt with one little thing." Randall's body rocked gently to another blow. "Me."

Rose stared, his mouth dry. Blood dripped from twin slashes on Lisel's breasts as well as the deep puncture in her abdomen, but she stood as though whole and free of pain. Randall lay unmoving at her feet, his chest a mass of bleeding wounds. Jim's girls cowered at the edge of the pool, the younger clutching the older, weeping. Rose swallowed. "Yeah, that was basically the idea," he managed to say at last.

"I thought so." Lisel smiled and vented a breathy sigh. "I seem to be running out of children fairly quickly these days. So I'll offer you a deal, whoever you are. You want immortality? Promise to behave yourself in the future, no embarrassing scenes like this, and I'll elevate you myself, right now."

Randall groaned, a faint sound escaping his lips. The blood seeping from his chest bubbled. God no, he thought. If Rose accepts, that's it, were finished. Last chance shot to hell. Randall closed his eyes, trying to shut out the sense of onrushing destruction. After so long a life, the thought of a pointless end was too much to bear. And to have dragged Knox, possibly even Swan, down with him... Please Rose, he thought. For us, for yourself, don't do it. Be our friend, not her slave. Please.

The silence seemed to stretch out into years. Finally, Rose spoke. "I'm sorry," he said, "but I don't think I can accept." Warm gratitude welled up into Randall, instantly replaced by cold fear. Now she would kill him.

"And why not?" Lisel asked, sounding cross.

Rose shrugged. He looked at Jim's bleeding body floating face down in the Jacuzzi, at the two girls shrinking from its touch. "I like to keep better company, I guess."

Lisel's face contorted in a sour grimace. "I'm going to enjoy shooting you," she declared.

"That's nice," Rose replied. "I don't think I'm going to particularly enjoy dodging, and I suppose at least one of us should be having a good time." Through Randall could not see it, his maniac smile had reappeared.

She laughed then. "It's a pity you won't join me. Or perhaps not. You already seem frightfully disobedient."

"I'm afraid so," Rose agreed.

She cocked her head to one side, considering. "I understand you're pretty fond of waving this thing around." She flourished his revolver. "Are you any good?"

"I'm fair," he conceded.

Lisel nodded. "You have been armed for this little adventure, I take it?"

"Yep." Rose glanced down, indicating his jacket.

"Good." She lowered Rose's pistol, holding it loosely at her side. "Since I find you entertaining, I'm going to give you a sporting chance." She smiled, a curious twist of her lips that seemed to be the first genuine expression to cross her face. "Draw!"

Rose reached into his jacket, whipped the dueling pistol free, and fired a single shot. A neat red hole appeared in Lisel's forehead, just above one eyebrow. The black .38 revolver fell to the tiled floor.

Lisel remained standing. "You..." She stuttered, voice thick. "son of a..." Bright blood leaked from both nostrils, running down her chin. "...bitch." She jerked forward, coming quickly around the lip of the pool.

Rose fired again. A crimson hole replaced one of her nipples. She continued toward him, unfazed. Rose fired once more. A chunk disappeared from one of her arms. Reaching him, she raised one hand and struck him in the face. He fell to the floor. She surged past him and out the door.

Jumping up, Rose leaned out into the hall and fired, emptying the pistol. Three red wounds appeared in her retreating back. She rounded a corner. Distant doors slammed. Rose tucked the pistol away and ducked back into the room. Unsmiling, he surveyed the carnage: the wet, bleeding bodies of his friends, Jim's floating corpse, the terrified girls. He shook his head.

Looking up from where he had fallen, Randall saw Rose's face loom into view overhead. He heaved a ragged sigh of relief. "Is everything all right?" he asked, his voice no better than a whisper.

"Sure," Rose replied, "you could say that."

Randall nodded weakly. Closing his eyes, he surrendered his grip on thought and felt himself borne away.

chapter **ten**

At first there was only darkness, wide and blank, with no awareness to trouble it. But then a light, fierce and orange, edged itself over some obstruction to pierce the mute and meaningless night. With it came pain, a general haze of complaining nerves washing up and down his body. They had been shouting at him for some time, he felt, and their voices had become weak. More insistent, in its way more agonizing, was the terrible stiffness in his arms, shoulders, chest. His muscles felt petrified, cured like strips of leather. He could not sense his hands, all feeling choked off at the wrist.

He ignored these sensations as best he could, concentrating instead on the light growing before him. The blazing orange sliver rose gradually, growing in size, becoming first a crescent then a brilliant half-circle. The space above it got gradually brighter, making the darkened territory below seem that much blacker by contrast. Must be the sun, thought Randall. He had not been sure before. The sun, rising over something I am still in the shadow of. He watched its almost imperceptible progress, contemplating the poetry of his relative position. Still in shadow. That's me all right.

For a long time, the land surrounding him remained dark. Only when the last fraction of the sun had topped the horizon, finishing the blinding sky-circle, did illumination flood into the wasteland. Randall found himself suspended above the floor of a desert valley. Indifferent, brittle scrub peppered the smooth landscape of dusty yellow sand. There were no animals to be seen, though desiccated bones lay here and there among the half dead weeds, bleached horns pointed toward the fatal sky. Nearby, the jawless skull of a human being lay in a pile of ash. In the distance sat the low hills over which the sun had risen, the broken red stone still throwing a long shadow into the valley.

Randall craned his head to one side and saw his own naked arm strapped to the green limb of a tree cactus. Suede thongs at his elbow and wrist held him against the smooth vegetable flesh. The contrast between the cool health of the cactus and the bruised, weathered look of his own arm filled him with primitive distress. He swung his head to examine the other limb. It was bound in a similar manner.

Concentrating for a moment on the constant grinding of his nerves, he discerned that some of the pain he felt came from a swarm of tiny punctures along his back and neck. Cactus needles. But most of the damage was internal. A dozen ribs smashed. Both lungs pierced in several places, filling with blood. And the weight of his body pulling downward only aggravated the problem. He felt as though both arms were being torn out at the shoulders. But with a little effort he could ignore it all. It surprised him how easy it was. He let his head fall onto his chest and looked down at the rest of his body. Naked, except for a dirty rag knotted around his waist. His feet dangled free, and for some reason he found that exceedingly funny. He kicked them a little, chuckling to himself.

How did I get here? Randall wondered eventually. And thinking about it, he could not remember anything that had come before the rising of the sun. He knew his name. Randall Springfield. Named for the place of his birth, one of the first settlements in Massachusetts. No further details presented themselves. He also recalled vaguely that he had a plan, an ultimate purpose to accomplish. Allies and enemies. Above all, he knew where he was. This valley crouched deep in the vast expanse of the Anza Borrego desert, all but inaccessible by foot. He had passed through it before, on his way somewhere. Of that he felt sure.

So what happened? he asked himself. Did my enemies win? It seemed logical, but somehow Randall did not believe it. He looked up at the sun, flash patterns burning into his eyes. Okay, he thought. What happens now?

Randall watched as the grey shadow receded toward the foothills. No matter which way he turned his eyes, he could not avoid the black smear of ash upon the sand. Wan smoke curled up from the eyes of the skull. It hurt Randall to look at the collection of bones. They marred the yellow surface of the desert. I have done this thing, he thought. Somehow, this is my fault. He wished that a strong wind would carry them all away, but the air of valley was calm as death. There was nothing he could do but wait for sundown to bury the sight in darkness.

To distract himself, Randall lifted his gaze to the broken hills at the lip of the canyon. Something moved among the red stones. He blinked, and looked again. It was still there, indistinct with distance, a sinuous twisting in the rocks. Little flashes of light reflected from it every so often. Randall wondered what it could be. He squinted. Whatever it was seemed to be progressing towards him. Who has come to visit me? He wondered.

The twisting, writhing thing came forward slowly. Time passed as Randall watched it. As the creature drew nearer, Randall saw that it was a snake. Black scales covered most of its narrow body. A pattern of copper diamonds, metal-bright as new pennies, decorated its back. It's wedge-shaped head and concentric rattle glowed pale white against the yellow sand. It wound towards him, bunching and then uncurling like a lash in the hands of a child.

Upon reaching the dead brush which dotted the valley floor the snake altered it course. It wove lazily through the dry growth, brushing each of the bones that rested there. Tongue flickering, it crawled over horns, wove through bovine ribs as though searching for something. When it had examined every specimen, the snake resumed its trek towards Randall. It reached the pile of ash just as the last shade drained away into the foothills.

Randall flinched, unable to take his eyes away. The snake wove contentedly through the gaping sockets, coiling up in the warmth of the recent fire. Its copper scales glinted in the sun. And then both the snake and the skull were gone. Lisel sat in their place, knees drawn up under her chin. She wore black jeans and a turtleneck, accented only by a necklace of copper beads. "I suppose you expect me to found a city here. At least you aren't out in the middle of a lake, though I don't expect this spot is much better, really."

"Actually," he answered, "I was expecting you to offer me an apple."

Lisel laughed, a clear and musical sound. "Honestly, my dear, don't you think all of this biblical symbolism is a bit heavy, even if you are dreaming?"

"Am I?" Randall laughed. "How ludicrous." He looked down at the woman who was his second mother, the woman who had made him immortal. They were enemies, he knew. But somehow that did not seem to matter here. All he felt was curiosity. Who was she, really? Was she as cruel as he remembered? What would she say to him now?

"You're not Jesus," she told him wryly, "and I'm certainly not Eve." Her shoulders shook with mirth. "Besides," she said, "I haven't got an apple."

"That's too bad. You'll just have to find something else to tempt me with, I suppose."

Lisel sighed. She looked up at him and shook her head. "Do you insist on following this format? Temptation and resistance. It's silly. Can't we just have a reasonable discussion?" Randall did not reply. "Very well. How about my body, then?" Her clothing ran off her like dark water then swam back up, giving him a brief glimpse of moon-pale flesh. "You seem to have rediscovered carnality lately. How about it?" She let her folded legs slide away from her chest.

"No," said Randall mildly. "I don't find you especially attractive."

"Then perhaps you'd prefer someone else." Her form flowed and rippled again, until it was no longer Lisel but Lisa Robinson who sat upon the sand. Strangely, she was soaked through with water. Drops of it hung like beads in her glossy black hair, ran down her sharp-featured face. Her white t-shirt clung to her small, loose breasts. Moisture dampened the earth around her. She shivered. Goose bumps stood out from her pale skin. She was the most beautiful thing he had ever seen. "Do you want me now?" She looked up at him through wet lashes.

Randall swallowed, and tried to speak. But his voice had gone, dried away by the heat.

"You want me. I can tell." She lay back on the sand, her body fully extended. Her lotus-petal hands caressed herself through damp cut-offs. He could see her entire body from where he hung, from her bare toes to the luminous black spill of her hair. "I always know when someone does."

Randall coughed, cleared his throat violently. "I can't," was all he managed, his voice choked and splintered. He stared down, drinking in the sight of her.

"Of course you can." She rolled over onto her side, showing him the tight curve of her buttocks beneath the wet denim. The flesh of her legs looked smooth and flawless and alive. Some of the yellow sand had stuck to her damp back, and he found it strangely attractive. She glanced up at him over her shoulder, her smile knowing and her eyes bright. "I am as she was. There is no difference."

Could it be true? She was so beautiful, sensual in a way that had nothing to do with death. "No," said Randall, his voice much clearer now. "You're lying."

Her smile expanded, her eyes became brighter still. Without looking away from him, she twisted gracefully up into a sitting position. Cheeks dimpling, she took hold of her shirt and pulled it off. The white fabric peeled away from her body like a layer of dead skin, revealing healthy pink tissue beneath. Water clung to her breasts in shining beads. "Am I?"

"You are," he said. "She's gone. I killed her. I regret that, but I won't pretend it didn't happen." Not even, he thought, for all your beauty.

She sighed, crestfallen. Her eyes dimmed, and her smile collapsed into a little pout of disappointment. "Maybe you'd like me better this way." She twisted her head from side to side, as though stretching her neck. Twin red lines appeared on either side of her throat. They gaped and expanded. Blood flowed out of them, down her chest, dripping off her breasts in tiny red waterfalls. It soaked into her cut-offs, spilled down her legs, covered her pale body. Randall stared at her, stricken. "What's the matter?" she asked. "Don't you love me anymore?" She burst into flame.

Her flawless skin blistering and charring, Lisa sat and looked steadily up at Randall. He looked back, meeting her eyes until they had gone and watching the rest until it, too, had burned. Then the ash fell away, and she was his mother once more.

"That was horrible," he said.

"Of course it was. I'm a horrible woman." She hugged her black clad legs once more. "But you never seemed to buy my image, even when you were young. The strange things is that you believed so much. You never questioned my power, my ability to harm you. I acted as though it was my right and it became my right. It amazes me the things you let me do to you. Eventually I just tortured you to see how much you would take. But even when I had gone too far and you and your brothers fled from me that first time, you still believed in my power. Since then it's just been a matter of catching you by surprise, stabbing you from behind. In a fair fight I'd probably loose." She paused, and looked up at him thoughtfully. "Do you still believe in me now, Randall Springfield? Do I still own you?"

Randall did not reply immediately. He closed his eyes, remembering how small she had seemed to him, naked in that cloud of vapor. Smaller than she had ever looked before. "All of that did occur to me," he said, "when I first saw you at the Well." He opened his eyes. She sat below him, wrapped about herself as though against a chill. "I don't believe any more, no. Not irrationally, like before. But you're older than I am. You've seen more, survived more. And you're fully mature. You may have abilities I'm not even aware of. I still think you're very dangerous."

"A fair assessment." She reached a hand up and pulled it through her straight gold hair, reminding Randall instantly of Knox. Perhaps the gesture was inherited. Strange, as none of them had any biological relation. "Still planning to let that crazy friend of yours knife you if this goes your way?"

"Yes," said Randall. "It isn't just a gesture, you know. How many children do most of us leave behind? Three? Four? Most of the great elders only have six or seven, all champing at the bit. Hell, even most members of the Brotherhood don't have many more than that. We're an endangered race. When I die I plan to leave behind dozens, maybe even a hundred mature immortals. I have to destroy you to do that. Nothing personal, that's just the way it is."

Lisel plucked a dead twig from the earth and spun it between her fingers. "Maybe we are the way we are for a reason. Did you ever think of that? Without the built in control on our population, we really would take over the Earth. Then we'd all have to feed off animals, maybe even off each other. Maybe we'd be worse off then we are now, in ways you haven't thought of. Why waste your life fighting a biological fact?"

"I'm not trying to alter what we are," Randall persisted. "I wouldn't even know how to start doing that. All I want is a community big enough to stand on its own."

Lisel snorted. "A community big enough to be discovered by human society, that's what you'll get. Not big enough to defend itself when it happens. A hundred of us couldn't stand against a fraction of an army." She broke the twig in half. "You used to be a decent strategist, Randall. Where's all your sense gone lately?"

Randall ignored the final remark. "That's why I have to die. Those hundred could make thousands if they were fully mature. The next generation will be immense."

Lisel shook her head. "The next generation will never come. You think your hundred will give up their lives as easily as you?" She laughed bitterly. "Even your lapdog is contemplating rebellion."

"Who? Rose? He wouldn't leave me."

"Don't be so sure. How much trouble can you reasonably expect him to pry you out of? How much more blood can he swallow?" She ground the split twig to splinters in her palm, then let the fragments fall to earth. "You seem to forget that when someone sticks a knife in him that he can't just pull it out and walk away. By what right do you presume so much upon his loyalty?"

What she said was true. He owed Rose his life, and had left the debt unpaid. "I always thought we were friends," he answered.

"Your brother Knox was more of a friend to him than you ever were. I'm surprised he didn't leave you long ago." She stood and dusted her hands against her jeans. "I'll give you something to think about. Why do you suppose he turned down the highly attractive offer I made him at the Well?"

"He made the only intelligent choice," Randall answered. "You're a genuinely evil person. Being one of your children is like being a slave to a sadist."

"He has only your word on that." She scrutinized her nails. "My violence towards you is no less justifiable than your attempts to destroy me. It's simply easier for you to characterize me as malignant. Maybe he doesn't want what you're selling anymore. Maybe he's having second thoughts about the entire business. Maybe when he looks at you he sees a thing that is hollow."

"This is pointless," said Randall. "If I'm dreaming I'll take it up with him when I wake up. He can go if that is his choice."

"Very well." Lisel eyed him. "Another temptation, then?"

"Tempt away."

"How about a truce? You accept that I'm dangerous, and I'd even be willing to say the same of you." She walked back and forth before him, the copper necklace flashing in the sunlight. "So why don't we cease hostilities? You agree not to come looking for me, I'll agree not to sneak up on you. Of course I realize you want maturity. That's why you started this whole thing. But you're young, and you can certainly afford to bide your time. And who knows? You might get lucky. Somebody might come along and hammer a stake into my chest one day, save you the trouble." She stopped and looked up at him from the yellow sand. "What do you say?"

Randall did not need to think to answer. "I'm sorry, but you know I can't do that. Really, I'm surprised you even bothered to ask."

Lisel threw up her hands. "I tried," she declared to the hot sand, the windless air.

"You did," Randall assured her. "Lucifer himself could have done no better."

Lisel snorted derisively. "Goodbye, Randall. The next time you see me I won't be nearly this friendly."

"I know. I'll be ready for you."

"I believe you will." Then she ran like water into the ground, leaving nothing behind.

Randall watched the ascending sun, thinking about all Lisel had said. The arguments, the doubts, had come to him before. It would be easy to live on, rather than die for his purpose. So easy, but still fatal in the end. He had no illusions, he did not expect to truly live forever. And longer life meant nothing to him. He had seen enough. Anything more would be empty of meaning if he abandoned his vision now. He laughed silently to himself. Why is all of this suddenly so important? I'm clearly not going anywhere.

He glanced at his bound arms every once in a while. The shrunken driftwood of his limbs against the vital green cactus flesh filled his animal soul with rage. He could sense the water flowing in its hidden filaments. All he had to do was pull, tear the green arm from its socket, free himself with a flood of moisture. But his muscles might just as well have been stone for all the force they could gather.

I'm dreaming, he told himself. And soon I will awaken. To what end? another part of his mind could not refrain from asking. To what end? And he thought about the death that awaited him.

The sun sank behind him, washing the wasteland with orange fire. The shadow of the tree cactus stretched out to the broken red hills, fading as the light failed. Unseen mountains cast their darkness across the valley. The sky bruised purple, deepening towards night. Randall hung by his arms, watching the land fade from view. The rim of the valley vanished into blackness, followed by the great reach of yellow sand. The dead brush near his perch surrendered next, then the ground at his feet.

He looked up, but could not find his bound limbs or the tree that held them. Perhaps he was already free. Soon there was only darkness, cold and smooth, with no awareness to trouble it.

chapter **eleven**

Randall Springfield awoke in a narrow darkness, the musk of his own sweat poisoning the stale air. Good Lord, he thought, if they've buried me again.... But in the next moment awareness of his body returned. He sat with his chin on his knees and his arms wrapped about his shins. Definitely not a coffin. He raised a tentative hand and felt rough, unsanded wood just above his head. A crate, then. But it still might be six feet under. Balling his hand into a fist, he struck the ceiling of his cubic prison. The wood vibrated with reassuring hollowness, and he thought he heard something clatter in the world beyond.

"Just a minute!" called a muffled voice, unrecognizable through the thickness of timber. A flurry of small noises followed. Grunts and rattles and a distant scraping. Then the entire crate shook with a splintery thud. A crack of light became visible under one edge of the lid, the black snout of a crowbar nosing through. With a groaning of wood and a shrieking of nails the lid tore away in successive jerks, revealing warm morning light and the beaming faces of Knox and Rose.

Randall inhaled deeply, drinking in the fresh air. Knox offered him a hand and he hoisted himself stiffly out of the big wooden box. The muscles in his back and legs felt as though they belonged to a much smaller man. His bare feet touched cool carpeting. "Where are we?" he asked, looking around at the large, unfurnished room. A row of tall windows sent the dawn light drifting down into the bare, white space. A hallway led off somewhere to his right.

"Welcome to Winton," said Knox.

"The town we're nuts about," Rose chimed in, grinning wide. Randall shook his head. He had obviously missed a joke, he could tell by the smirks twitching onto their faces. And there was something odd about Rose, something that should not be there but was. Ah yes, his beard was coming back.

"How long have I been under?"

"Almost five weeks now," said Knox, still smiling foolishly. He had on new jeans, a plain t-shirt and an unfamiliar pair of tan work boots. His dead white hair had grown another centimeter. "You just interrupted our eight-hundred and seventy-third hand of poker." He gestured at the floor.

The warped lid of the crate sat beached upon the pale carpet, twisted nails jutting from its underside like crooked teeth. A litter of cards and plastic poker chips lay strewn around it, along with a much used motel ashtray. Two lawn chairs sat on either side of the abandoned box. Their cylindrical feet had made dozens of little circles in the carpet.

"Eight-hundred and seventy-three?" said Rose incredulously. "You were counting?"

"I was kidding. Actually, it's only been four-hundred or so." Knox returned his attention to his brother. "I suppose you would like some clothes."

Randall looked down at himself. Naked except for a pair of institutional grey boxer shorts, but free of bloodstains, he noted with some surprise. "Um, yes," he said absently. They must have cleaned him up at some point. Considerate. Now he could dispense with the usual post-sleep shower. His chest had healed well. Only a strip of pink flesh indicated where his injuries had been, arcing from left hip up to right shoulder like a beauty contest ribbon.

Knox thrust a brown paper bag at him and he felt a rush of déja vu. The image of his boots spilling to the wooden floor above the mortuary played itself out behind his eyes. With acute clarity he recalled the haft of the wooden knife protruding from its sheath. He set the new bag on the floor and carefully plucked his clothes out. His jeans, miraculously clean and whole. The long brown coat. His broken boots with their tarnished metal toes. And yes, the wooden blade, retrieved from the blazing water of the jacuzzi. Finally, a bright blue t-shirt promoting Castroville, Artichoke Capital of the World. "What," he asked shortly, "is this?"

"You don't like it?" said Rose, wounded. "I chose it especially for you." He looked at Knox, terminally crestfallen except for his maniac smile. "Randall doesn't like his shirt. I just do not understand."

"You could think of it as a disguise," said Knox. He patted Rose sympathetically on the shoulder. "After all, no one would ever guess it was you in that thing."

"I also bought you an erotic postcard of the Artichoke Princess," Rose continued happily. "It's nothing too hardcore. She's still underage, after all. But she's got this artichoke, see? It's big, I mean really gigantic, and..." He trailed off when he caught the look on Randall's face.

"It must be about time to go get Swan, yes?" Randall stepped into his jeans, feeling oddly dislocated from his surroundings. It was as if Knox and Rose had developed a dialogue for his reawakening over the last month and had vowed to play it out no matter what he actually said to them. He pulled on the tacky blue t-shirt. Any complaints he might voice would be irrelevant. Plans had been made in his absence. He would just have to see where his friends had decided to lead him.

"That's right," said Knox. "Actually, we were beginning to worry that you might still be asleep when it came time to leave." He prodded the empty crate with one tan boot. "Turns out you woke up just in time."

"Is there anything holding us here?" Randall asked, jamming on his own boots, shaking out his coat.

"Not a one. As far as the house goes, we bribed a real estate agent to let us squat here. All we had to do was hide whenever she wanted to show the place to someone. The owners have already moved, but they left the power on and everything. Guess they thought it would sell better." Knox looked curiously around the room as though he were a prospective buyer. "We can take off as soon as you're ready."

"Not before I take a leak, we can't." Rose disappeared down the hallway.

"So where are we headed?" Randall asked. His brother still had not told him where Swan was hidden.

"Anaheim." Knox stooped to the floor and began gathering up the remains of the poker game, deliberately cutting off the inquisition.

Randall finished dressing while the other two retrieved their minimal possessions. They hauled the crate into the garage and left it there. Packs in hand, they moved quickly through a series of empty rooms, past a barren kitchen and out the front door. The cherry red Barracuda crouched in the driveway, a predatory monster from an alien planet. Knox locked the door and put the key under the mat. He slung their baggage into the trunk of the car while Randall looked at the front of the house.

From the outside it did not seem like much. An overhanging roof with almost no perceptible slant, a byproduct of the unchanging California climate. New paint, but of an indifferent tan and brown, calculated to offend as few potential customers as possible. A decent size lawn, now a bit overgrown. Absolutely no sign that the people who once lived here possessed any personality whatsoever. Perhaps they had taken it all with them. Randall walked around one side, half expecting to find the word "HOUSE" stenciled there in easy-to-read capitals. He had just been inside and what had he seen? A few rooms he could not recall less than five minutes later. Obscurely troubled, he trudged over to the Barracuda.

Rose had claimed the shotgun seat, relegating him to the back bench. As soon as he had sat down, Knox slammed the car into reverse and screeched out of the driveway. They jolted to a halt in the middle of the street and then shot forward, as though the sleek candy-apple behemoth was being driven by a stick shift novice. The car roared down a road lined with houses exactly like the one they had left behind. Where in hell are we? wondered Randall. This looks like a Midwest factory suburb. And how come no one in the neighborhood noticed these two lunatics knocking around? Everyone here must be brain dead. It would certainly explain the architecture.

"So, what have you guys been doing all this time?" Randall leaned forward to peer over the front seat. "Doesn't look as if this burg caters to the tourist industry."

"Oh, you'd be surprised," said Rose. He turned to face Randall, shifting instantly into chat mode. "I toured the Hershey's Chocolate factory about a dozen times. Your reclusive brother even came along once or twice."

"It was unbelievable," Knox asserted, his eyes abandoning the road ahead to join in the conversation. The streets were largely empty and Randall forced himself not to comment. "Machines like chrome elephants squeezing out thousands of Almond Kisses and Peanut-Butter Cups like an endless stream of turds. You know what the people did? Sifted through the torrent looking for deformed candy and put it on a conveyor belt leading back to the cauldron. Like panning for lead. Everything else was automated."

He glanced away just long enough to pilot his muscular whale of a car over a ramp and onto a two-lane highway. "And the smell in that place. My God. I never thought chocolate could reek, but I guess if you have enough of anything in one place it can overwhelm you. It was like someone had shot hot fudge up my nose. How those workers keep their collective gorge down I'll never know."

"I liked it," said Rose. "They give you a free candy bar after the tour." Knox glared at him disgustedly, as though he were a child who enjoyed eating worms. "Anyway, squeamish here spent most of his time in the Air Force museum."

Randall laughed. "I thought you'd gotten over the glory of war."

"Rose didn't describe the place." The Barracuda rolled serenely along, Knox's hands unconsciously keeping it between the generic road-shoulder brush on one side and the faded yellow dashes on the other. "It isn't just plaques and medals and photos of the Hindenburg going up. They've restored a couple dozen planes from the World Wars. You know the kind. Those kite-paper biplanes with machine gun mounts in the back. Fat bellied bombers with Hollywood starlets painted on the sides. We quit the army before all that came down the pike."

"Don't tell me you're getting nostalgic." Knox's possession of that pair of cavalry pistols had surprised Randall enough. This new enthusiasm for the machines of war caught him totally off guard. "I thought you were through with soldiering."

"Oh, I am," Knox replied wistfully. "Those planes were just... I don't know... a little bit of all right. So much more to them than the weapons we had."

"I'll tell you my favorite part," said Rose, bounding back into the conversation through the breach Knox had left. "There was this big fenced off rectangle full of gravel, just like where they'd parked the other planes except empty, nothing there. At one end, they had a plaque on a post that said 'Stealth Bomber.' I laughed so hard I gave myself dry heaves."

"He did," Knox agreed.

They thundered along through the growing heat. Randall looked up into the bright sky. The air seemed warmer than it should be for the time of day. Winton must be considerably inland. Randall took off his coat and stuffed it in the seat well, hoping Knox would head for the coast before turning south. "So that was all there was to do? Hershey's and the Air Corp?"

"Well, Winton isn't much of town," Rose conceded. He scratched at his returning beard. "Have you ever wondered what kind of people buy those plaster lawn ornaments they sell by the road in Tijuana? The gnomes? The deer with the huge eyes? The cute squirrels?"

"Sure," said Randall, knowing full well that Rose would finish no matter what he answered.

"Those are the people who live in Winton. Plaster of Paris gnome people, every one of them."

"Shouldn't that be Plaster of Tijuana?" Knox inquired.

"Whatever. I'm sure they all have Chia Pets, too."

"Okay, then," said Randall, "how come I didn't see any elves or pink flamingos as we were driving through town?"

"Because they keep them all in their back yards," Rose replied easily. "No one likes to admit to kitsch addiction, at least not in California anyway."

Randall snorted. "I once knew of a library in Illinois that had a circulating collection of lawn ornaments."

Rose's eyes bugged. "No bullshit?"

"No bullshit. They had to give it up when those U.P.C. scanners came into fashion. The clerks kept dropping concrete lions and such on the machines."

"And where would you hide the security strips?" Rose mused.

"Where indeed?" Randall leaned back, arms spread out over the folded and stowed convertible top, feeling happier than he had in a good long while. Ever since Texas, life had been a roller coaster of missteps and confrontations. It felt good to sit back in the sun and let the wind wash over him. And just now, joking with Rose... He looked at the blithely cheerful face staring at him over the front seat. The wide eyes with the animated brows, the wild hair... What were they if not good friends? Broken images fell into his mind. The shadow of a cactus leaning out across the sand. A night-black snake with metal-bright diamonds down its back. "You know," he said after a while, "I had the strangest dream while I was sleeping."

"Did you, now?" said Rose, his smile accelerating into Cheshire Cat territory. His bright eyes prodded Randall for details.

"I was in the desert," he began, "doing some sort of penance, I guess." Knox laughed from the driver's seat and the car swerved slightly. "Anyway, I was trapped. And Lisel came to talk to me, to convince me to give in."

"Was I there too, Dorothy?" Rose continued to grin at him over the seat.

"No," said Randall, his guilty feelings about his friend resurfacing suddenly. "But she did mention you."

"And what did Mother say?" Knox asked.

"She told me not to argue with biology."

"Sounds sensible."

"To you it does." Randall stretched, holding his hands up into the wind. "It was weird. Mother changed into Lisa at one point. Freud would have a field day with that."

"Freud is dead." Knox shook his head. "Honestly brother, you overanalyze everything that happens to you."

"Look who's talking. At least I don't mope around universities rehashing the siege of Mexico City."

Rose giggled, looking from one to the other of them. "Are you sure you two aren't blood relations?"

The Barracuda cruised through an increasingly barren landscape. To either side of the road, tangles of dry grass waited for the casual cigarette butt to send them into flames. Infrequent exits led off into the outer horizons, concrete cables linking irrigated farms. The scorched earth reminded Randall just how much of California was really desert. All the cities had been carved out of sand, coastal oases stealing moisture from the Rocky Mountain states to fight off the encroaching waste. Maybe that explained why everyone lived in apartments or condominiums. For all its bulk, civilization here had an air of impermanence. No roots could hold in this dry soil. A good wind could blow half the population away. Concrete gypsies, all of us.

They reached Monterey by noon, then transferred to the Coast Highway. "Shouldn't we stop for gas?" queried Rose as the Barracuda glided up the on-ramp.

"Nah," said Knox. "We've got enough to reach Los Angeles." Randall could not see the gas gauge from where he sat. In any case, he had no idea what sort of mileage the maraschino dinosaur got. So he let it pass.

They drove along the winding blacktop, hemmed in by shambling hills and the jagged drop to the Pacific waves. The air cooled, and the salt and seaweed smell of the ocean wafted up from below. "You got any tapes in here anywhere?" asked Rose, eyeing the cassette deck.

"Should be some in the glove box," Knox replied vaguely. His eyes were back on the road, now that it had begun to twist and curve. Out of his element, Randall thought.

"Let's see here," said Rose, sifting through a shoe box of caseless cassette tapes. "The Kingston Trio. Peter, Paul and Mary. Joni Mitchell. Don McLean." He held up a particularly dusty specimen. "The Chieftains?"

Knox shrugged. "It's bagpipe music."

Rose flung the tape out over the cliff edge, then dredged another handful out of the box. "Chicago. Supertramp. The Electric Light Orchestra. Earth, Wind and Fire. The Moody Blues. Foreigner. Cheap Trick."

"Spare me," said Randall.

"Gladly." Rose cast the cassette out to sea. "The Eagles. Beethoven.

Carly Simon. Honestly, Knox, did you buy these with a blindfold on or what? I know, they came with the car. Okay… Styx. The Steve Miller Band. Ah-ha!" He clutched suddenly at a prize cassette.

"I don't remember buying their albums."

"Not Ah-ha the group," Rose said acidly, "Ah-ha the exclamation." His eyes rolled.

"So what is it, then?"

Rose brandished the tape proudly. "The Doors. Morrison Hotel." Whistling a short fanfare he slapped it into the cassette deck.

"I don't remember buying that either," puzzled Knox.

"You didn't," said Randall. "I gave it to you."

The dormant speakers crackled into life and a four-four blues riff came pumping out. "Keep your eye on the road," Jim Morrison cautioned, "and keep your hands up on the wheel."

"Cute," said Knox. "Real cute."

ℜ

Several tapes later the Barracuda's quietly purring engine coughed and stuttered, gasped, then died. Knox shifted the car into neutral and let it coast along the shoulder, frustrated confusion crumpling his brow like a concertina. The rolling auto lost speed gradually, grinding to stop nearly two minutes after the motor quit. "What's wrong?" asked Randall, leaning over the front seat.

Rose smirked sourly. "Ran out of gas." He tapped a finger on the gauge.

"I don't understand it," Knox exclaimed. "I swear the tank was three quarters full this morning." He slumped behind the wheel. "There must be a leak or something. It's a miracle we weren't all blown to pieces."

"Don't be ridiculous," snapped Randall. "Sure, the tank might have been full this morning, but we've driven non-stop since then. I don't know what kind of otherworldly mileage you imagine this brontosaur gets, but it's only natural that it should run out of gas at some point. Normal people refill their tanks occasionally to avoid this sort of thing."

Randall hoisted himself out of the car and went around to the trunk. The lock was a fragmented ruin. A twist of stiff wire held the lid down.

Randall unwound the knot, then jumped back as the lid sprang up. A dark stain coated the litter of tools, caked and dry like rust. Is that her blood or mine? Randall wondered, fumbling blindly for the gas can. He slammed the lid back down and retied the wire, furious.

Rose climbed out of the inert Barracuda to join him. "Which way do you think, north or south?" They had left the Coast Highway an hour ago to join the 101. Southern sections of the ancient, shore-hugging road were still buried under the mud of winter. Rose looked up and down the lanes of tarmac as if anxious to cross. Cars sped by in roaring blurs.

"South, I think," said Randall. "I believe the last sign we passed said the exit for Solvang wasn't too far ahead."

"Oh, God," moaned Rose. "Little Denmark? Kitsch capital of the universe? Just setting foot in that burg makes me want to strangle small children in Lederhosen." He turned resolutely north. "Let's walk back to Winton."

"Nope. South it is." Gas can in hand, Randall strode off down the margin of the road. Rose sighed histrionically, then fell in behind him. "You coming, Captain Nemo, or going down with the narwhal?"

Knox stood up in his seat, leapt to the back, then over the trunk and onto the pavement. "Sorry about this, guys." They walked single file down the shoulder, the afternoon sun a bright mote in the corner of the sky. Cars rushed by like predators in chase, the jet-wash of their passing pushing against their shoulders.

"So where's the motorcycle?" Randall asked after a moment.

"In that long-term garage in Santa Cruz," Rose replied. "Both you and Knox were in the big sleep after your family reunion. I wanted to blow town immediately, so there was no way I could take it. Lucky thing for you two I remember how to drive a car."

"Yeah," said Randall, staring at the dusty stretch of highway leading off toward the horizon. "Real lucky." He looked west, beyond the broken lip of the road. Brown waste choked with dead weeds. Darker hills farther off, crusted with half-baked ice plant abandoned there by uncaring landscapers a thousand years ago. It would never catch fire, so who cared how it looked? "Did I imagine it, or did you really shoot Mother in the forehead?"

"Yep. Actually, I missed. I was aiming right between her eyes." Behind them, Knox gave a staccato laugh. Rose flushed slightly, then grinned his crazy grin. "Didn't seem to bother her too much, though. Just made her mad, as they say. She knocked me on my ass and ran. I put five more holes in her and she didn't miss a step. That's one tough bitch, your mom."

"No doubt," said Randall. "I didn't think any of us could take a header like that and still keep walking. Turns my bowels to water just to think about it. But she'll still need sleep after a hit like that. Months of it, probably. If we could find her, if we knew where she holed up, then we could finish her off easy as you please. We might start looking in London. I don't know. We could waste a decade prowling around that place, it's so spread out. And odds are she isn't even there. Shit. This is the best chance we've had so far. I don't want to waste it."

"We'll get Swan," Knox said earnestly. "If he says Lisel was in London, we'll go. She may not be there, but we could probably get a lead. A couple of the bigger families live there."

Randall turned to regard his brother. Knox's face was set into grim lines. "So you're finally with me, then?"

"Yes." He ran a hand through his dead white hair, scratched his neck. "I didn't appreciate Mother ordering that orangutan to drown me, not one little bit." His lips curled, and he spat upon the ground. "I'm with you."

The margin of road began to narrow. Cars shot past less than half a yard to their left. Randall watched his footing carefully. "So you got us out of Santa Cruz without any trouble?" he asked Rose, not looking at him. "No police? No landlord? No demons gibbering at your heels?"

"The touchiest part was getting you two into the car. We parked it halfway across town, if you remember." A red Jaguar flashed past, engine screaming. It disappeared instantly into the distance. The sudden wind made all three men stagger. "I took the keys to the Well off you, locked the place up, and ran. There were still some people in there and I was terrified they might have heard the shooting and called the cops. When I got back with the Barracuda the place was empty except for you two. The Doublemint twins were gone. So was Jim."

"You're kidding." Randall felt his stomach lurch.

"Even his clothes were missing," Rose continued. "Don't know what the hell happened to him. Didn't stick around to find out. I dragged the two of you out back, stuffed you in the trunk and got the fuck out of

Dodge. Stayed a few nights in a hotel in Atwater. Heard Knox banging on the lid about a week later. We drove into Winton, cooked up that deal with the realtor. That's about it. We spent the next month playing poker and reading *Spy* magazine."

Randall stopped abruptly. Rose nearly walked into him. A temporary wall began just ahead of them, linked sections of molded concrete. It closed off the shoulder, protecting an abandoned strip of construction. Apparently, a new lane was being added. The margin disappeared behind the wall, broken into fragments by jackhammers. Traffic rushed by, inches from the barrier. "Well, shit." Reluctantly, Randall stepped down off the tarmac into the shin-high brush. He walked quickly, staring ahead. The construction went on as far as he could see. The others followed.

"Actually, we were a bit more productive than that," Knox said. He stepped up to walk beside his brother. Rose moved to the other side, and they trooped through the weeds three abreast. "I phoned my pet lawyers and made myself legally dead. Nonexistent hit and run accident in Berkeley. They informed the cops and the University. Apparently, some of my students held a memorial service at Cheap Saké Billiards."

"Touching." Randall grinned humorlessly.

Knox pressed blithely on. "Rose got in touch with those biker friends of his. I figured they could help us get Swan out. Close to a dozen of them are interested in joining up with us. We can call them when we get into L.A. County."

"*If* we get into L.A. County." Randall pointed ahead into the waste. Just shy of the horizon, the highway spanned a narrow chasm. "If we can't get across that, we're screwed. We'll have to turn back, go north."

"Maybe there's a shoulder on the bridge," Knox said hopefully. "Anyway, it doesn't look that deep." Randall gritted his teeth. They walked on, eyes fixed on the dark gap.

"If nothing else," said Rose, "your brother and I got to know each other better." His eyebrows twitched. "He even saw my tattoo."

"You have a tattoo?" Randall asked, properly incredulous. Since Rose was trying to entertain him, he thought he might as well go along with it. "You'll be sure to go over big with Swan. He thinks sitting under the buzzing needle for five or six hours at a stretch is the ultimate Zen experience."

"So I've heard."

"What is it?" asked Randall, now genuinely curious. "For that matter, where it?"

"Not saying. In fact, I wouldn't have shown it to your brother, except I lost a bet."

"You have only yourself to blame," said Knox. "It's not my fault if you can't pick roller-hockey teams."

Randall laughed. "Sounds like I missed a lot."

"Sure did," said Rose. He looked sideways at Knox. "For example, you ever wonder what the reluctant vampire here does for his daily blood?" Knox emitted a warning growl, but Rose ignored him. "Birds!" he exclaimed. "Pigeons. Sparrows. Crows. God damn birds!" Rose began to giggle. "He kills them with a little brass letter opener." Rose stumbled on clod of fractured asphalt, twitching with mirth. Knox turned and gave him a couple of light kicks. Rose toppled over, writhing in the bushes, great cackles bursting out of him.

"On second thought," said Randall, "I'm glad I wasn't awake." Knox grunted his assent. They walked away leaving Rose sprawled in the weeds, laughing madly.

Soon they reached the chasm. Its dirt walls were steep and sheer, but it did not appear to be more than eight or nine feet deep. Dried brush lined the bottom, which was only a few yards across. There was no shoulder of any kind on the bridge. "Looks passable," Knox said at length. "We might have to scramble to get up the other side, but we won't break our necks or anything." He looked from the ditch to Randall. "What do you think?"

Randall pitched the gas can across to the other side. It hit with a spray of dust. "Let's do it." Rose joined them, staring down into the trench. Randall sat on the edge, then pushed himself off. He crashed through a deep layer of brittle foliage, landing on his side in a tangle of twigs. He stood up. Thorns plucked at his clothing. The dry brush reached up past his chest. "It's a bit deeper than it looks," he called up. Knox and Rose merely stared. "Well, come on."

The other two climbed carefully down, clinging to the chasm wall. Rose slipped half way through and plunged into the weeds. He came up sputtering, coughing up dirt and fragments of dry grass. "Who's brilliant idea was this?" he inquired mildly.

Knox dropped the last foot and a half to the plant-strewn floor. "All complaints must be submitted in triplicate to the officer in charge of company morale," he proclaimed. Randall began to shove his way through the brush to the opposite wall.

The bushes to their right rustled. Something growled faintly.

Randall froze. "Probably just a fox or a possum or some such," he said quietly. "We're disturbing its home, most likely."

Whatever it was growled again, this time louder. "Well," said Rose, "let's get out of here before it decides to disturb back." He resumed his trek to the far rim, breasting through the bushes.

The creature roared. It came charging forward, shaking the entire mountain of brush. The three men yelped in unison, plunging wildly through the weeds in the opposite direction. Randall could hear the animal's footsteps as he struggled through the encumbering plants. Branches grabbed at his arms and hair. Roots tripped his feet. The beast bellowed behind him, snorting and stamping and uprooting dead shrubs. Randall lunged forward, scrambling over rocks and tearing through matted manes of grass. He struck the opposite wall before he saw it.

Randall clawed at the embankment, holds disintegrating even as he found them. He climbed and fell and climbed again, blinded by dirt, the creature's labored breathing all around him. Clutching at roots and half-buried stones he hauled himself out of the chasm. Randall collapsed on the level ground, gasping for breath. Knox and Rose sat beside him, wheezing. He rubbed at his eyes. The beast sniffed and snorted below, quieting. "What was that?" Randall breathed hoarsely.

"Well," said Rose, "It wasn't any God damn sparrow."

❧

"Civilization!" Randall exclaimed. "Sort of."

They reached Solvang at dusk, limping stiffly past china shops and doll boutiques disguised as Danish cottages. Planked roofs and elaborately carved shutters abounded, giving the town a decidedly fairy tale look. Blooming vines covered the white pillars of the arcade. Wrought iron benches sat in secluded nooks, cozy with vacationing lovers. "I think I may vomit," said Knox.

They passed a fountain sporting a replica of the Little Mermaid, and a toy store housed in a windmill. The scents of breads and jellies wafted from a dozen bakery windows. Even the gas station was not immune. The cashier's box was round and plastered with artificial bricks. A Danish flag flew limply amid the miniature crenellations. "I'll pay," said Rose. "I still have most of Randall's money." He wandered off towards Rapunzel's tiny prison.

The brothers stood by the only leaded gas pump, waiting for it to come to life. "We'll get a cab to take us back to the Barracuda," Randall said. "I don't feel like braving the wrath of that mutant wildebeest after dark."

"Sure," said Knox. He glanced over at Rose, who was still trying to convince the cashier that they only needed a single gallon of gas. "You want to crash here for a little while, or just keep on going to Anaheim?"

Randall leaned back against the pump. "Why don't you just tell me where you've hidden Swan?" he demanded. "The suspense is starting to irritate me."

Knox grinned wickedly. "You're going to love it," he said, eyes flashing. "After all, it is the happiest place on Earth."

Randall groaned.

chapter

"The Tragic Kingdom. God, I hate that place." Randall and Rose stood on a condominium balcony at the border of Garden Grove and Anaheim, watching the nightly fireworks burst over the peak of the Matterhorn. Rosettes of pink and orange fire tinged the eternally snowy peaks with sunset colors. The sound waves reached them a second later, rattling the French doors like a sonic boom. A raucous laugh went up from inside. The bikers had been feeding Knox margaritas all evening, and he was telling them about the burning of Washington, D.C. during the War of 1812, which he had seen firsthand.

Randall turned his back on the explosions to look at Rose, who was sipping from a champagne bottle. "Is there anywhere in So Cal that you do like?"

"Sure." Rose belched fiercely. "The Madonna Inn, that baroque hotel I had you stop at on the way down. I make it a point of honor to piss there whenever I get the chance."

Randall winced at the memory. "I thought Solvang was bad... Jesus.

All those Cupids and pink carpet. And grape vines growing on the stair railing! I can't imagine what you see in the place."

"I'll concede that the lobby is a bit much, even for me. But the men's room has the only functioning waterfall urinal in the entire state. You just missed it, is all."

"I saw postcards at the front desk." The fireworks display boomed its way into the finale, bright constellations of color bursting over top of each other in a chaotic cloud of fairy light. A series of concussions shook the doors in their frames and pressed uncomfortably at the two men's ears. Car alarms in the lot below them wailed into life. As the last fire died in the sky, they heard a scattering of applause borne on the night wind. "How does this crap affect the property values?" Randall wondered aloud.

"You'd have to ask Toad-Eater," Rose replied. "But I would imagine it lowers them, if he can afford this place." In the distance, toboggan cars on rails ran up and down the artificial mountain, jammed with screaming passengers. Below it and to the right, the white ribbed roof of Space Mountain gleamed in the flood lamps like a displaced Mormon temple. Rose gestured at the scene with his bottle. "I used to work there, you know. Summers when I was still in high school."

"You're kidding."

"Nope." Rose shook his head with alcoholic exaggeration. "That's how I earned my fun money. Bought me gas and cigarettes, the occasional Queen album. It was hell, though." He drained the last of his bottle and set it carefully at his feet. "Hair above both ears and collar. No facial growth, no side burns. Earrings no larger than a quarter of an inch in diameter, on ladies only if you please. Never point when directing a guest to the nearest shitter. Gesture with the whole hand." He demonstrated, aiming all five fingers at Randall in a polite karate chop. "Wouldn't want to accidentally flip anybody the bird, now would we?" He slumped forward against the railing. "Shit howdy. The Marine Corps has nothing on Walt."

"The last time I was there, Monsanto Chemical was sponsoring the Journey Into Inner Space."

"They tore that out a few years ago," said Rose. "Lucasfilm has sort of taken over Tomorrow Land lately."

"*Jaws* was never my scene, and I don't like *Star Wars*."

"Wait, I know that one." Rose turned away from the view, knocking over the empty bottle. His eyebrows sunk and merged in concentration. "I'll remember it when I'm sober, I'm sure of it." He tapped at his temple.

They leaned against the rail, simply looking up at the sky for a few minutes. The lights from the park washed out the stars, leaving a luminous blue haze shaded somewhere between daylight and darkness. They heard another burst of laughter from inside. Long after it subsided, Toad-Eater's distinctive wheeze sawed the air. "Look's like the show's over," Randall said. "How long until the park closes, do you figure?"

"What is it, ten o'clock now?" Rose consulted his bare wrist, seemingly surprised by the lack of a watch. "They close at midnight. Figure an hour or two for trash detail. After that it's just security and maintenance. Should be safest around three, I guess."

"We've got a bit of a wait then. Shall we?" Randall gestured at the crowd inside.

"Sure." They pulled open the twin glass doors and stepped inside. The condominium looked as though a woman of taste had furnished it. Framed prints hung from the light yellow walls, mostly early impressionist garden scenes. The sofa and a pair of large stuffed chairs had been upholstered to complement the decor. A low, antique coffee table filled much of the main room. An array of porcelain coasters sat on it, largely ignored. The tiny open kitchen had been tiled and papered in coordinating patterns as well.

This had confused Randall at first, as Toad-Eater did not appear to be with anyone in particular, and none of the biker women seemed the type for it anyway. But searching for the bathroom he had come upon a locked door. Listening carefully, he thought he had heard movement within. No doubt some disapproving schoolmarm lurked beyond. Randall had wondered what sort of professional woman would put up with that asthmatic ball of leather and his cronies, and what had drawn them together in the first place. He briefly considered asking Rose, but decided it was none of his business. Hell, maybe Toad-Eater lived with his mother.

Because of the furnishings the biker gang looked distinctly out of place, as though they had broken into someone's home and were living it up. And to a certain extent they had, Randall reflected. At the moment they were crowded around Knox, who sat blocking the television in a yellow kitchen chair. There was Toad-Eater, of course, wheezing hysterically and slapping his knees. Randall had also met Silverfish, a greying lady who wore glasses and had to be in her middle fifties at least. She had introduced her adolescent daughter-the lovely gatekeeper at the last biker party he had attended-as Corrodencia, or Corrie for short. A number of unfamiliar men stood around in their leathers drinking cold beers or shots of whiskey from the kitchen counter. Bad Bob sat in a chair in one corner, sober as a stone. He nodded at Rose and Randall as they came inside.

"The government was different in 1845," Knox was saying. "None of this War Powers Act, National Security Council, finger on the big red button bullshit. No C.I.A. No Federal Bureau of Investigation. And the Department of the Treasury was just that and only that, not some paramilitary anti-gangster squad." He paused to take a sip from his latest margarita. "Congress still held the power to deploy troops, not the President. Nowadays technology has made that separation obsolete. But believe you me, a century and a half ago it took a hellish lot of back slapping and palm greasing to start a decent war."

"I didn't think there'd even been as many wars as you say there have," breathed Corrie. She looked much less arousing in jeans and a baggy sweatshirt than she had in her chaps. "There was World War One, World War Two, then Vietnam. All the rest were just little ones, right?"

Knox shook his head sadly, looking at Silverfish. "Is this the sort of brainwashing they perform in public schools these days? There are some books I can lend you." He returned his attention to the girl. "There was the French and Indian War, while we were still a crown colony. And what do think the revolution was, a bunch of guys in wigs writing pretty speeches and heaving tea off of boats? The fighting dragged on for years-decades, really, if you count the political maneuvering. Britain might have recognized our independence in 1783, but they didn't mean it until after the War of 1812." Knox paused momentarily, counting silently on his fingers. "My little tiff with Mexico came next. The Civil War, of course. Then the Spanish American war. Teddy at San Juan hill, and all that. Now we get to the biggies. You forgot Korea, of course. Everyone your age assumes Alan Alda conquered the communists. Vietnam. There's the Cuban Missile Crisis, if you'd care to count that. Smiling Jack very nearly got us all vaporized. Panama, though they called that a police action. And have you forgotten Desert Storm already?"

"And those are only the public wars," he continued relentlessly. "We've had soldiers all over the world, unofficially, in secret. Timor. Cambodia. El Salvador. Nicaragua. That business with the Shah of Iran. We've suppressed several revolutions in the Philippines. And don't think we didn't have a hand in the Argentine atrocities. The Palestinians would kick the rug out from under Israel if we didn't send them weapons and money. And now Bosnia. Wherever the U.N. decides to go, there we are at the head of the line. Peace keeping forces. What a subtle phrase that is."

"You've forgotten Laos," said Randall, coming up beside him. "And Somalia. Then there was the Navy's whistle-stop tour of the Pacific. Another of Teddy's ideas, I think. You also neglected to mention all the expatriates who went to fight in Spain. Mustn't omit Papa Hemmingway." He pulled another chair from the kitchen and sat. "We're probably still missing a few. There are more than I can remember. And Lord knows what's going on now. I'm sure wherever there's trouble in the world some American military advisor is out there stirring the pot."

Corrie had gone pale. Even Silverfish looked disturbed. The rest of the crowd talked over them, oblivious. Rose sashayed in from the kitchen, a can of beer in each hand. "Don't tell me you're watching *Easy Rider* again," he cried, pointing at the television. "What did you do, buy the tape? You guys are such pussies." A chorus of shouts and protests greeted this remark, along with one or two raspberries. Rose wagged his tongue at the crowd. He dropped one beer in Randall's lap, popped the other, and waded into the fray. Someone reached around Knox to turn up the volume on the TV.

Bad Bob appeared at Randall's side, his lean face taut with annoyance. "You want me to cut the boys off?" he asked. "They're already pretty drunk."

Randall chewed his lower lip, considering. "Drunk is fine, I guess," he said at last. "After all, you guys are supposed to be loud and obnoxious when the time comes." He scanned the crowd. Aside from Bob and Corrie, everyone had a drink in hand. Several of them looked rather unsteady. One woman had even passed out on the couch. Randall frowned. "You might lock up the hard stuff, though. Obnoxious is one thing, comatose is another."

Bob moved off into the kitchen. Randall looked at the can of beer Rose had delivered. After a moment's hesitation, he popped it open and settled down to wait.

⁂

"Here, try these on." Knox hauled a pair of rubber hip boots from the trunk of the Barracuda and handed them to his brother.

Randall stared at them for a long moment. "If it's not asking too much, what the fuck for?"

"We'll need them when we get inside." He took out another pair and slung them over his shoulders. "Come on now, try them out."

"You expect me to climb a fence in these?" Randall held the boots out at arms length, their dangling ends bumping together.

"Don't be an idiot. We'll put them on inside when we need them. I just want to know if they fit." Knox slammed down the lid of the trunk and retied the wire catch. "God, but you're dense."

"Sorry." Randall sat on the bumper and pulled off his own leather boots. "Where did you get these things, anyway?"

"Oh, I've had them for four or five years now. They're generally useful when you're allergic to water." Knox boosted himself up to sit on the trunk. The rear of the car sagged. "Besides, I like to go fly fishing every once in a while." Randall gave his brother a long look, then resumed his struggle with the rubber boots.

A pack of Harleys rounded the building, pipes booming. Bob headed the charge, riding a surprisingly small bike with extended front forks. Most of the others had big distance cruisers, 1000 ccs or more. Silverfish sat astride a retooled 550. A windscreen had been added, along with a straight-back cruising seat. She wore an open-face crash helmet and a Marine Corps night camouflage jacket. Corrie clung to her waist, virtually unrecognizable in leathers and a full helmet.

They growled to a halt surrounding the beached Barracuda. Toad-Eater drew along side the car, his gigantic monster bike the largest of the bunch. Rose, who had been riding sidesaddle behind him, pitched off the back of the cycle and stumbled over to Randall. "The regiment is assembled, Captain, and awaiting your orders." He snapped off a clumsy salute.

Randall ignored him. Slinging the hip boots into the back of the car, he walked over to Bob in his socks. "Give us about ten minutes to get to the back fence. Then get into the parking lot and make as much noise as you can. The more security you draw off the easier we'll have it."

"How long do you want us to keep it up?" Bob revved his engine, anxious to be on the move.

"As long as you can." Randall looked Bob in the eye. "Don't go getting arrested or anything. Leave before it comes to that. We're going to be in there at least an hour, but I don't really expect you to cover us that long."

Bob nodded once, curtly. "See you boys back here, then." They shook hands.

Randall jumped into the Barracuda's passenger seat. Knox was already behind the wheel. Rose lounged on the backbench, toying with the octopus muddle of boots. They rolled out of the parking lot in a cloud of exhaust and engine thunder. The bikers turned left, waving and shouting as they passed. Knox drove straight ahead.

After two blocks packed solid with hotels they reached the fence. It rose over ten feet into the air, tightly woven chain-link supported by frequent poles and topped with barbed wire. They drove parallel to it for a while, Knox watching the buildings behind it closely. They drew abreast of a large warehouse with no windows. He slowed the car, then parked in an alley just across the street. Rose hauled himself out of the car and wandered over to the fence. Randall followed while Knox rummaged around in the back seat. They walked right up to the wall of metal mesh. "Think it's electrified?" Rose asked, squinting at it suspiciously.

Randall reached out a hand and grabbed hold of the fence. He shook it, then let go. "My guess would be no." Rose stared at him, mouth open.

"Wait for me, guys." Knox trotted up with a duffel bag in one hand and a pair of wire cutters in the other.

"You're not going to get through that fence with those puny things," said Rose.

"I wasn't planning on it." Knox threw the bag up over the fence, put the clippers in his mouth and started climbing. The stiff metal clattered like a tambourine. Reaching the top, Knox took the cutters and sniped carefully at the barbed wire. The severed ends sprang back from each other, coiling up at opposite poles. Knox hoisted himself around and clambered down the other side.

"Last one over's a girl!" crowed Rose, and flung himself at the fence. Randall leapt up after him, jamming his socked feet into the tight mesh with difficulty. Rose reached the top ahead of him and began to descend. Randall hoisted both legs over and simply dropped to the ground, landing in loose crouch. "Cheater," said Rose, jumping down the final yard.

Knox held a finger to his lips for silence. Shouldering his bag, he led them around the side of the warehouse. They came out onto a narrow street lined with stark, utilitarian buildings. "What part of the park is this," Randall whispered, "Industrial Park Land?"

"Nah," said Rose. "This is backstage. Props and equipment storage, most likely." Knox halted them with a raised hand, peering up and down the darkened lane. After a moment he motioned them forward. They dashed across the street and between the buildings opposite, empty offices of some kind.

"Ever been here before?" Randall whispered to Rose.

"Afraid not. I mostly worked in Fantasy Land, in the center of the park. I loaded children into lion cages on the Casey Junior railroad ride." He grinned through his beard.

They worked their way cautiously to the back of the office buildings. A high stone wall separated this area from the park proper. Behind it, they could see the dim outline of a Victorian house. "Up and over," said Knox. They scrambled up the wall and dropped down into a pet cemetery.

Tiny headstones dotted the small lawn, sporting names like Rex and Fluffy. A marble frog sat on low pedestal, eyes closed with dignity. There was a sculpture of a mouse, perched atop a minuscule crypt. One particularly large stone had grown a set of antlers. "Jesus H. Christ on a popsicle stick," exclaimed Randall, "where are we?"

"Back of the Haunted Mansion," said Rose, crouching down to pat the frog. The cemetery lawn was raised about a yard above the concrete walk ringing the house. They hopped down and walked furtively around the dark, ivy covered bulk. Coming around the front of the building, they gazed out onto New Orleans.

Stately plantation houses lined one side of the gently sloping street, their verandahs dark and widow's walks untrodden. A wide, slowly running river lapped at the shore across the road. Moonlight glittered on the black Mississippi waters. Tom Sawyer's island floated in the distance, a rough and tumble playground washed all the way downstream from Missouri. Ornate street lamps lined the scenic boulevard, their oil or electricity extinguished.

"Oh, there's a moon… over Bourbon Street… tonight," Rose sang, horribly off-key. Randall elbowed him into silence.

"Two houses down the slope," Knox whispered. "The Pirates of the Caribbean." He jogged down the street, hunched over as if fearful of incoming artillery fire, his movements plainly visible in the moonlight. Randall snorted and strolled after him, upright and unhurried. The buildings seemed peculiar to him in some way he could not place, and he stared at them intently. It was only when he approached the house Knox had indicated that he realized what it was. Though perfectly formed, the artificial Victorians were slightly small, perhaps three quarters the size they should have been. The doors and windows were necessarily large, marring the illusion if one happened to concentrate on them.

When they had all gathered at the front of the house, Rose tested the door. It swung slowly inward on silent hinges. "That's odd," said Knox. "I had to pick the lock the last time."

"There's probably a maintenance crew inside," Rose answered. "We'll have to be careful." Knox unzipped his duffel bag and handed out flashlights. He looked at each of his companions once, then slipped inside. Rose switched on his light and followed. Randall brought up the rear.

Their flashlight beams played upon walls of dark, rough lumber. To the left these planks rose all the way to the low ceiling, but to the right they stopped about a yard from the floor. Randall aimed his light into the darkness beyond. The half wall sheltered a sizable pool of murky water, filled almost level with the rim. In its middle was a tiny island. The small circle of illumination crawled up the sandy shore, encountering a wooden chest overflowing with wax doubloons and plastic jewels. "Good grief," said Rose, "it's Neptune's something-or-other all over again."

Knox shushed him, holding his flashlight just under his face. Lit from below, his sunken eyes and pale hair looked truly sinister. He motioned them to continue. The passageway narrowed. A rough wooden banister divided it in two. After a few more yards they came to a pair of turnstiles. Knox handed Rose his flashlight and jumped over. The others did likewise. They descended a short flight of plank stairs, turned a corner, and halted in a flat, open area. A faint glow seeped up from the water before them, and as Randall's eyes adjusted he was startled to find himself on a wharf.

The walls were gone. Behind them was a dense barrier of trees and brush, clearly fake. Across the lake of luminous water was what appeared to be a riverfront café, closed for the evening. Chairs rested upside-down on tables. Awnings and umbrellas were folded shut. The furthest reaches of the strange pool lay in hazy darkness. If there was a ceiling, Randall could not see it. He pointed his flashlight straight up, illuminating a patch of egg-shell dome forty or fifty feet above them.

"Where's the sky?" asked Rose, aiming his beam up beside Randall's. "I remember this part of the ride had the most fantastic artificial sky. Always deep blue, lighter to the west. Just after sunset. There were clouds, even. And I could never tell how far away the ceiling really was."

"Projectors," said Knox shortly. He gestured them over with his flashlight. "Come on, Randall. Fly fishing time." He unzipped his duffel and dumped the hip boots out onto the wharf. Randall sat and began to pull his on.

"How come I don't get any?" Rose whined. He looked from one to the other of them with a pouting frown.

"Because, dear boy," Knox replied, "I only have two pair and your flesh doesn't sizzle in the bath tub." He wrenched one rubber boot up past his knee. "Randall and I are taking a big enough risk as it is. One false step and we'll be poached like lobsters. You saw what happened to me when I got yanked into that hot tub."

"You looked deep-fried when I pulled you out," Rose agreed. He kicked off his own boots. "Still, I wish you would have mentioned this a bit earlier. I would have worn my swim trunks or something." He stepped out of his jeans, revealing peppermint-striped bikini briefs. He shoved his clothes into the duffel bag. "Well, what are you staring at?"

"Nothing," Knox mumbled, smothering a laugh. He began battling with his second boot.

A fleet of low plastic boats moored at the wharf, held motionless by some unseen mechanism. They were rudderless, had no oars or sails, and seemed to be composed entirely of seating and safety handles. "Why don't we take one of those?" asked Randall.

"They're propelled uphill by rollers at a couple of points in the ride," said Knox. "Those won't be running now. Besides, I'm not sure we could even get one loose." He slipped off the dock and into the dimly glowing water. It only reached his knees. "This way's better." Randall stepped cautiously off the dock, holding onto a post until his feet touched bottom. The floor of the pool was level, but unnaturally slick. He could slip all too easily.

Rose dipped one foot in, then laughed. "It's warm," he said, astonished. He hopped easily into the water, Knox's duffel bag tucked under one arm. "Why would they heat it?" he wondered aloud.

Knox led them away from both the wharf and the café, into the hazy territory beyond. They stuck close to the narrow strip of wooded shore, which hid the dome wall. Though shallow, the pool looked as though it might deepen further out. When they had gone perhaps thirty yards they came to a miniature swamp shack, perched on stilts above the water. Randall aimed his flashlight at the rickety porch. A withered grandfather sat dead in his rocking chair. Just a robot, Randall told himself, peering at the wrinkled face. He hastened to catch up with his brother.

The other two had reached a cave mouth, which gaped from the edge of the shore. Water poured down into it in a steady stream. The cave must pass through the dome, Randall reasoned, and something must pump water back up here. Rose examined the entrance with his flashlight. A skull and crossbones had been "carved" into the stone-like surface, along with an inscription below. "Abandon all hope, ye who enter here," Rose read. "Well, that's encouraging." He took a couple of steps into the cave, then tumbled into the darkness. There was muffled splash, followed by a prolonged thrashing sound. "God damn!" They heard Rose spit and sputter. "Son of a pedigree bitch."

"Be careful," Knox said with perfect seriousness. "There's a bit of a slope inside." He ducked into the cave.

The brothers descended the slippery incline, clutching at the walls to either side. The "rock" felt a bit like paper, or so it seemed to Randall. The slope leveled out quickly enough, becoming a close tunnel just wide enough for the boats they had seen earlier. Rose stood before them in the knee-deep water, his curly mop of hair plastered to his head and face. Drops clung to his beard. His damp shirt hung down to his thighs. The flashlight he had been carrying bobbed up and down in the miniature waves, casting odd shadows on the root-woven ceiling. "Did you know that was coming?" he asked, wet hands poised to flick droplets of liquid pain.

"You charged inside before I could warn you," Knox said reasonably. He edged past Rose, careful not to brush against him.

Randall walked cautiously down the tunnel, rubber boots squeaking. He had difficulty sensing the floor beneath him, the soles were so thick. "Come on, Renfield," he said, "fall in." Rose gave him an evil look, then sighed and scooped up his flashlight and bag.

They walked on in silence, except for the occasional drip. Randall thought they might be on a slight downward slope. The water level rose gradually, confirming his suspicion. He stepped even more cautiously, afraid of another drop. Knox was only just visible in the gloom ahead.

Eventually the tunnel grew wider. The left wall receded, creating a pocket cave above the waterline. Randall played his flashlight about the dark recess. Cobwebs hung thick from the stone roof, catching the light like mist. He swung the beam down. A skull grinned at him with rotten teeth. Randall jumped back in surprise, nearly falling over. "Just Hollywood," he muttered under his breath. "Nothing real. Christ, I'm a fool." Cursing, he stabbed the light back into the alcove. The skeleton rested in a gigantic bed of rotting wood, a dusty nightcap on his time-gnawed head. Ancient riches sat about him on the floor: moldering paintings, clouded crystal goblets, a rusted suit of armor. Randall shivered. "Hollywood," he repeated aloud.

"Up here," called Knox, somewhere in the distance. "Second diorama." Randall turned away from the scene of grey desolation. With Rose beside him, he trudged through the deepening water.

The next alcove was more glamorous than gloomy. Bright gold trinkets lined the walls, reflecting Knox's flashlight like a lighthouse lens. Giant chalices. Jewel-studded scimitars. Royal crowns. Brassy shields and gleaming spears. Thick rings and enormous bracelets. Entire ropes of pearls. Heaps of coins spilled across the floor. In the middle of it all stood two skeletons, collapsed against one another, each impaled on the other's sword.

Knox sat on the edge of this treasure trove, booted feet dangling into the water. He helped first one and then the other boost themselves onto the ledge. Randall laughed, then kicked lightly at a drift of glittering coins. They did not move. Each one of them was fixed in place. "Over there," said Knox, pointing to a half-buried pirate chest lurking behind the eternally greedy skeletons.

A clunky old padlock held it shut. Knox produced an equally ancient looking key and opened it. He pried up the rounded lid, careful not to disturb the blanket of dust. Inside was a small body bent in half, swathed completely in plastic garbage bags.

Randall reeled. He staggered back, eyes riveted to the chest. At any moment he expected the shrouded corpse to sit up and tear the black veil away from a burned and ruined face. Then Lisa Robinson would stand, and a dozen white hands would point at him in accusation.

Knox and Rose began to haul the body out of the chest. "Give us a hand, will you?" said Knox. "He's gotten rather stiff."

Reluctantly, Randall stepped up and took hold of the black plastic. The flesh beneath felt hard, unyielding as wood. It can't be Lisa, Randall told himself. She was so soft to the touch, even dead. I wonder what Mother did with the rest of her? He shuddered. The three of them finally succeeded in pulling Swan from the chest. They set him down on the carpet of fool's-gold coins, a curled fetus trapped inside a punctured womb. "Why's he all wrapped up like that?" Randall asked quietly.

Knox stared at him as though astonished by his sudden stupidity. "You'd rather we wake him up by scalding him? How the hell else do you expect us to get him out of here?"

"I'm sorry," Randall murmured. "I'm not thinking too clearly just now."

"Well, snap out of it," Knox ordered. "We still have to sneak back out of here you know." He dragged Swan's cocooned form to the edge of the alcove, then rolled him into the water. The body sunk with a splash, then bobbed to the surface once more. "I just hope those bags don't start to leak. Give me my flashlight, will you, Rose?"

The three men slipped quietly back into the water. Knox continued down the tunnel, pushing the floating corpse before him. "Wouldn't it be better to turn back?" asked Rose.

"I don't think Randall and I could climb up that slide, not with water running down it all the time. There are roller ramps further on and they're relatively dry. Besides, we've gone about half way as it is." Knox paused at the end of the tunnel. A slope composed of narrow rubber cylinders led out of the water and up into a hole in the ceiling. "See?" He gestured at them as if showing his friends into an exclusive restaurant.

"It's lovely," said Rose, and began to ascend the ramp, walking in a crouch so as not to slip. The brothers followed, dragging the body between them. A thin film of water on the plastic bag burned Randall's fingers painfully. He gritted his teeth. "Should have brought gloves," said Knox.

"You can't think of everything," Randall replied. "Just imagine how long it would take." Fingers smoking visibly, they passed through the hole in the ceiling and crested the top of the ramp. The rollers leveled out and then dipped down into a new pool of water. Gratefully releasing their burden, the brothers pushed him the rest of the way with their booted feet.

They were in another large chamber. Randall could sense the free movement of the air immediately. To one side a stone fort perched on the edge of a rocky shore. Silent cannons lined its battlements and protruded from open windows, black mouths pointing out to sea. Randall traced the line of fire with his eyes. A darkened ship sat opposite, perhaps twenty yards away across the water. He aimed his flashlight at the rigging. The sails were in tatters, and two of the smaller masts had splintered. But a pirate flag still few above the crow's nest, a white skull on a black field. Randall brought his light down to the motionless deck. A dozen sailors stood frozen at their battle stations, turned to stone by some fey creature of the deep.

"Hey," said Rose, "why don't we just go out there?" He pointed with his flashlight. Across the water a small red sign glowed: EXIT. "Hell, we probably could have come in there."

"That's an emergency exit," Knox said calmly. "We would have set off all kinds of alarms."

Rose grimaced. "How did I know you'd have a plausible explanation? Crap."

The battle came to life around them.

Steam shot from the mouths of the cannons, tinged orange by a light within. Suddenly illuminated, the pirate ship returned fire. A sunset sky appeared on the dome above, dark clouds boiling rapidly across. The pirates chopped the air with their swords, or set torches to endless fuses. Coarse shouts and loud explosions rang from concealed speakers. Pumps hidden within the pool shot water into the air, counterfeiting splashes for invisible cannon balls.

Randall looked around wildly. The water before him boiled and sprang up at him. He brought an arm up to shield his face, already blinded. His rubber boots slid on the slick floor and he narrowly avoided tumbling in completely. Eyes burning, he struggled in the direction of the fort. "All right, who's in here?" called a voice from the battlements.

chapter thirteen

Randall collided with the fortress wall. A window cannon belched steam at him. Hands and face blazing with pain, he stumbled up the tiny shore of foam-rubber rocks. He rounded the corner of the stone wall. His rubber boots slipped out from under him and he fell. Something hard knocked the air from his chest. Gasping for breath, he forced his eyes open. His vision was red, smeared with patches of haze and sightlessness.

He had fallen on a stair. His chest ached, bruised in a series of horizontal bars. Concrete steps led up behind the battlements. Randall dragged himself forward, crawling on hands and knees. He reached the top and stood, swaying dizzily. Below the crenellations was a concrete walkway. Plastic hoses led from the floor to the backs of the frothing cannons. A man stood on the walkway, staring intently over the waist high wall. He wore a yellow rain slicker and a pair of fireman's boots, thick soled and bristling with straps and buckles. Condensation dripped from his hatchet face. A control console glowed in the wall at his side.

"Hold it right there, you two," the man shouted over the prerecorded din of splintering wood and growling pirates. "Don't twitch a muscle. You're in a shit-load of trouble, sneaking in here." He turned suddenly, just noticing Randall. "That goes double for you mister," he sputtered, face red. "All of you stay put or else." He reached for the radio hanging from his belt.

Randall lunged forward. He punched the man in the jaw, grabbing the front of his slicker as he jerked back. Reaching down, Randall wrapped his free hand around the thick tool belt. A horrible grimace contorted his face, part pain, part fury. With a double-handed shove he sent his victim toppling over the battlements. The man struck the shallow plastic sea bottom with a wet smack. For a moment he hung below the water, then bobbed to the surface, unmoving.

"Motherfucker," Randall whispered to himself. Below, Knox thrashed about wildly, one hand pressed tightly over his eyes while the other clawed at the surrounding air. Rose walked methodically towards him, carefully avoiding the sudden fountains of spray. The bag containing Swan's body drifted toward the pirate ship. Steam blasted from the cannons. G-rated cursing punctuated the clashing of swords.

"Enough," Randall shouted. His voice vanished into the motley din. "Enough! Enough! Enough!" He kicked savagely at the control panel. The toe of his molded rubber boot shattered plastic buttons, dented wire gratings. "Fuck! Fuck! Fuck!" The sheet metal cover fell away under the assault. Randall jammed his heel down into a tangled nest of wires and analog circuit boards. "Fuck!"

Sparks flew. And then, abruptly, silence. Randall stood there for a moment, his own breathing filling his ears. Patches of his face were painfully wet. "You two okay?" he called, looking down at the still-churning water.

"Never better," yelled Rose. He was leading a blinded Knox towards the fortress wall. "I love being attacked by animatronic pirates in the middle of the night, soaking wet in my underwear. In fact, it turns me on." They reached the shore. Knox crawled out of the water and onto the stairs, shuddering.

"Wonderful. In that case, why don't you swim out to the ship and retrieve our package?" Rose snapped off a quick salute and trudged through the waist-deep water. The black plastic bundle bobbed near the pirate prow. Groaning, Randall descended the stairs. Knox lay huddled on the bottom steps, his balled fists pressed into his eye sockets. Randall put a hand on each arm. "Hey, are you all right?"

Slowly the fists unclenched, the arms lowered. Knox's eyes were swollen red balls. He coughed, and fluid streamed from his nose. "I am really beginning to hate water," he said.

Randall held his brother's head, peered closely into his eyes. "Can you see at all?"

A tremor shook Knox's body. "Enough to know you look like a piss-dipped rat."

"Look who's talking."

Rose returned, Swan's garbage-bagged body floating behind him. He shoved the bundle up onto the narrow shore. "What do you want to do with this other cat?" The technician hung in the water, limbs waving loosely.

"Depends," Randall replied. "Is he unconscious or dead?"

Rose waded over to the man and peeled back an eyelid. "Beats me." He shrugged. "What do I look like, C. Everett Koop?"

"Then to hell with him," said Randall. "We really should be getting out of here." He helped Knox to his feet.

"Hang on a minute," said Rose. "At least let me get him out of the water." Gripping the technician by his slicker, he hauled him towards the stairs.

Randall stepped carefully onto the slippery bottom of the pool. Knox came after him, a hand clamped to his brother's shoulder. "Which way should we go?" Randall asked. "You said we were about the same distance from either end of this fun house."

Knox shook his head. "We can't go back the way we came. Remember that slide?"

"Damn, that's right. I guess we'll just have to press on."

"Fuck that," said Rose. He dragged the limp technician up onto the stairs. "Let's take the emergency exit. We've probably set off a dozen alarms already." He leaned the man back against the railing, then plucked the radio off his belt. It was rubberized, waterproof. Voices chattered from the tiny speaker.

The brothers looked at each other with bloodshot eyes. "He may have a point," Knox said.

The door made no sound when they opened it. No alarm. No siren. Nothing. "Now I'm really scared," said Rose. "Walt sees all, you know."

"Probably a red light at some security desk," Knox agreed.

"Then let's get the hell out of here," said Randall. A flight of metal stairs led upwards. Holding the dripping bundle between them, they climbed to the top, free hands tugging at the cold railing. Randall pushed open a final door, and they moved out into the hazy, arc-lit air. Mist rose from their bodies, leaving gooseflesh behind. The Matterhorn loomed in the distance.

Randall turned to shut the door and found himself staring at a wooden outhouse. He blinked and shook his head. Clever that, he thought. No wonder Knox didn't find this way in. Looking around in the half-light, he saw that all of the nearby buildings were made of split planks, or at least appeared to be. "Anybody know where we are?"

"I think so," said Rose, squinting into the gloom. "The perimeter should be in that direction." He pointed down the street, gesturing with his whole hand.

The plastic bundle swung back and forth, banging into their legs. A thin film of remaining water caused the brothers' hands to steam and smart. Knox staggered as the package bumped his knee. "Hold up a minute," he said. He motioned them towards the nearest building. "Over here. Let's see if we can wake him up." They set their burden down on the wooden arcade fronting a shooting gallery. Repeating rifles hung limp at their mounts. Against the far wall, plastic mallards froze in mid-flight.

Knox tore at the garbage bags. Beneath the wrapping was a corpse in rags, thin as famine. Dry blood matted his hair and uneven beard, speckled his chalk-pale skin. He had curled into a ball, arms clasped around drawn-up knees. "Hold his shoulders, would you?" With an effort, Knox pried the stiff hands apart, unfolded the wooden legs. Black ink glowed upon the pale flesh. An intricate pattern of Celtic knots wove up both Swan's legs, disappearing into a pair of cut-off jeans. A spray of old blood crusted the faded denim. The sharp silhouette of a dragon in profile covered most of the chest, its tail merging with the knot designs near the lower abdomen. Circuit diagrams webbed one entire arm, wrist to shoulder. The remains of a t-shirt clung to the other.

Just over the heart, three thick white lines interrupted the sweep of the dragon's wing. Scars. They faded into the tattoo, only to reappear over the ribs. A network of similar lines flawed one leg, narrow erasures in the flesh. Randall counted a dozen sets of three parallel lines. He shifted position and noticed a ragged blob of white between the elbow and shoulder of the digital arm. "Pieces missing," Randall mumbled to himself. "Christ."

"Seems to have healed well," Knox announced. He ran a hand through his hair, unconscious of the gesture. "Rose, would you get the smelling salts out of my duffel bag? It's a small glass bottle with a rubber cap."

"Oh, shit." Rose looked rapidly about the arcade. "I must have dropped it during the attack of the Spanish Armada." He stood up and looked back over the ground they had covered. "Damn it, my boots were in there."

"Great," said Knox. "Now what am I supposed to use?"

"I'm not sure smelling salts would have worked anyway," said Randall. "Usually we just wake up when it's time."

"It was going to be an experiment."

"Here," said Rose, "let me try." He stood directly over Swan's head. Taking hold of his soggy t-shirt, he wrung out a thin dribble of water. The droplets hissed and boiled on the white skin. Rose gave the shirt another twist. Water dripped onto Swan's cheeks, singeing his tangled beard.

"Hey man, cut that out." Swan blinked in annoyance, put a hand over his face. "God, I feel like I've been varnished." He rubbed at his eyes for a moment, then stopped suddenly. "Where am I?" Fear edged his voice.

Knox crouched down beside him. "It's okay, Matt. You're safe now. And we're both here with you, me and Randall."

"That must be you, Knox. Nobody else calls me Matt." Swan's eyes swam vaguely. "I'm having a little trouble seeing."

"That's normal," Knox assured him. "It'll come back once your blood gets going."

"You said Randall was with you?"

"Right here," Randall answered, feeling strangely embarrassed.

"Been a long time, brother." Swan turned his head towards the sound of Randall's voice. "You still fighting that bitch?"

"Always." There it is, Randall thought. I didn't even have to bring it up. Swan always was more sympathetic than Knox, more eager for the power. Of course, he went his own way, too. But he's young, not even past his human years. I can remember when all I wanted to do was see the world, kick around the planet forever. But once you've seen enough, you realize it's all the same. "Some things don't ever change," he said.

Swan squeezed his eyes shut, then opened them again. He looked up at Randall. "Hey, there you are." His eyes focused visibly, pupils expanding into the surrounding green. "Jesus shit, you're livid."

Randall frowned wryly. "We've been swimming," he explained.

"Can you stand yet?" asked Knox. "We need to get moving. No telling when security's going to show up."

Swan pushed himself into a sitting position. "Why?" He stared at the silent shooting gallery. "For fuck sake, where are we?"

"Frontier Land."

"You're kidding."

"Afraid not." The elder brothers hauled Swan to his feet. He dangled between them, arms draped over their shoulders. "Watch your step." They lowered him to the pavement, then followed Rose down the street.

Swan craned his neck as they passed a deserted saloon. No horses stood at the hitching post. Inside the bat-wing doors, racks of souvenir sweatshirts hung motionless from chrome gallows. "We in L.A. or Orlando?"

"Anaheim," said Knox. "I figured you'd be hard enough to find in here without going out of state."

"Good," Swan replied. "Florida gives me bad vibes. Too many old farts and alligators."

"Watch your tongue, young man. Your brother and I were both close personal friends of Methuselah, remember?"

"Speak for yourself," said Randall. "I only wanted his autograph."

"Sorry I brought it up." They shuffled past another store, this one disguised as a trading post. An expanding gate covered the open front. Beyond, a barrel of Davey Crocket imitation coonskin hats sat next to a rack of cap rifles. "So who's the five-pint?" Swan asked, pointing over Randall's shoulder. "I can feel his heart from here."

"Sorry, Swan. Hands off."

"Damn right," said Rose. "I may only be human, but I'm not deaf." His right hand moved to where his pistol would have been. "And I'm not lunch, either."

Randall sighed wearily. "Swan, this is my boon companion and partner in warfare, Rose. Rose, this is my younger brother, Swan. Now that I have introduced you socially, I forbid either of you to eat, shoot, or otherwise mangle the other. Understood?"

"A pleasure, sir." Rose smiled instantly and stuck out a hand.

Swan glanced dubiously at his own supported arms, shrugged. "You look like a used dishrag," he said.

Rose's smile only intensified. "And you look like you survived a Nazi war experiment designed to turn prisoners into blotter paper." Swan strained forward, the chords in his neck pulsing. The brothers tightened their hold on his arms.

"Wait a minute," said Knox. "Wait a minute!" Swan sagged. His head dropped to his chest. "Listen." A faint electric whine floated towards them, getting louder. Twin lights flashed in the distance, low to the ground. The noise and the lights approached as one, skimming towards them through the streets.

"Heads up," said Rose. "It's security." A golf cart slid into view. Four men in navy blue jumpsuits sat cramped together. "How nice, one for each of us."

The cart hummed to a stop just up the street, headlights glaring like interrogation lamps. Randall realized how ridiculous they must look. Two damp men in hip boots, one of them with bone-white hair, supporting a carnival freak. Then there was Rose, a drenched weasel in a knee length shirt, his peppermint stripe bikini briefs showing through the wet fabric. There would be no talking their way out of this. "Let's see if we can get us some wheels."

The security guards clambered out of the cart, their movements hidden behind the glowing headlamps. As they stepped forward into the beams they transformed into stark silhouettes, bodies black and faces invisible. Each man carried a riot baton in a loose, familiar grip. A single figure detached himself from the rest, came forward. "I'm placing you all under citizen's arrest," he said. "Remain where you are and please keep your hands where I can see them."

Randall tensed. He cast a quick look at his companions. "Gentleman?" Rose nodded wordlessly. Swan unhooked his arms from his brothers' shoulders, stood poised on the balls of his feet. Knox assented with a barely perceptible dip of the head.

The leader took another pair of casual steps forward. A military stubble of blond hair covered the top of his head like dead sod. "I'm going to have to ask you not move, or speak amongst yourselves." His riot baton swished at his side, the tail of a peevish cat. "You'll be transferred to police custody shortly."

Randall smiled. "Now." His hand was on the leader's throat before the word was finished. Knox and Swan flew past them in a blur. Rose followed at a more human speed, his wet t-shirt flapping. The baton swept upward toward Randall's head. He grabbed it with his free hand, taking the force of the blow on his palm, bringing the weapon to a dead stop. The color drained from the leader's face. Randall wrenched the baton from his grip with a laugh.

A scream sounded from somewhere ahead, but Randall paid no attention. The leader's eyes tried to look through the back of his skull. Randall shook him, hard. The eyes snapped back. Randall flipped the baton over and caught it by the handle. He held the weapon up between them. "Now where," he asked with infinite seriousness, "would you like it first?" The man fainted.

Randall let him drop, staring intently into the headlights. The other three security guards were down, but the fight continued. Rose hung from Swan's back, a riot baton clenched around the young immortal's neck. Swan twisted wildly, face crimson, trying to shake him off. Knox had Rose by one leg. "God damn it! Cut it out, both of you!" Rose's foot caught him in the face and he fell backward, tripping over an unmoving guard.

Randall waded into the light, stepping over uniformed bodies. He waited until Swan's thrashing brought them face-to-face, then sent the liberated baton smashing into his brother's chest. The linked adversaries slammed against the front end of the golf cart. Swan slumped to the ground. Rose remained where he was, halfway through the shattered windshield. "What is this shit?" Randall yelled. "Damn you both, I told you no fighting. Now what the fuck is going on?"

Neither of the combatants answered. Swan glared up at him from the pavement, green eyes smoldering. Rose lay on the hood, moaning faintly. "Look," said Knox. He gestured at one of the fallen guards. A black puddle spread outward from his neck, creeping gradually down hill.

"I was just having a little refreshment," Swan said, "when this five-pint friend of yours jumped me." He crossed his arms over the dragon on his chest.

"How did you expect him to react? He's human too, remember?"

"But you said he was with us."

"And so he is," Randall replied. "And so you should have a little more respect for your companions."

"This is bullshit." Swan stood rapidly, unwinding like a whipcord. "What am I supposed to do, pretend I'm a vegetarian? Look at me, Randall. I haven't fed in months. I need blood." Randall met his stare, said nothing. Swan laughed hollowly. "What was I thinking? What more could I expect from a dried up half-blood like you? Tell me Randall, when's the last time you drank from the deep, deep well?"

Swan's body smashed into the golf cart. His elbow shattered one of the headlights. When he looked up, Randall did not appear to have moved. "I drank a pretty young thing in Santa Cruz a few weeks ago," he hissed. "Though we tried to hide it, her body led our mother right to us. She nearly destroyed us both. My five-pint friend here saved our ass." Then Randall's face was an inch away, red-veined eyes bright with anger. "You do whatever the fuck you like, but not in front of him." Swan looked away.

Randall stood up slowly. Rose sat with his legs dangling over the hood. Blood seeped from a cut across his forehead. "Get in," said Randall. "We're leaving."

"We can't go yet," Swan protested. "I haven't finished."

"Get in!" The look on Randall's face promised agony. Swan scrambled to his feet and leapt into the back of the cart. "Knox, drive." Rose slid through the empty windshield frame and into the passenger seat. Knox sat down beside him. Randall took the remaining space. "Go," he said.

Knox peered up the narrow street, getting his bearings. "I'll have to turn this thing around."

"No time," said Rose, looking over his shoulder. "The cavalry's already here." Another golf cart coasted out of the darkness behind them, engine humming.

"Great," Knox muttered, "just perfect." He pushed the accelerator to the floor. The cart bounced over the dead man's body. "Shit." They gained speed slowly, topping out at thirty miles per hour. The speedometer went no higher. "Christ," said Knox. "We could run more quickly than this."

"It's okay," Randall answered. "Our friends back there can't go any faster." The intercepting cart had gained on them somewhat, but now the distance between them held constant. Their pursuers passed the scene of the fight without slowing. One of the victims was on his feet, waving them on. "We'll have to lose these guys before we jump the fence, otherwise it'll be another rumpus."

"I don't even know where the hell I'm going," Knox snapped. They approached a desert mesa, a hill of sculpted sandstone jutting out of the asphalt, the red soil thick with weeds and the half buried bones of animals. Narrow gauge train tracks ran along its perimeter, snaking in and out of buttressed tunnels. A string of mine cars rested in the shadow of the hill.

"Drive around this thing and then through the big gate," Rose directed. "We're pretty close to the main entrance." They circled around the bluff to the right, climbing steadily. The cart lost speed, lurching to one side on the steep curve. "Hang on to your seats," Rose crowed, his voice caked with Old West grit. "This here's the fastest ride west of the Pecos!"

They topped the rise and left the mesa behind. The pursuing cart climbed slowly after them. They sped past a darkened corral, no horses in sight. A wrought iron arch spanned the road ahead. They passed underneath it and into another world.

Cartoon images passed one after the other in a senseless parade. Lewis Carroll's caterpillar looked disdainfully down from a mushroom, the business end of a hookah held in a pensive claw. A dozen flying elephants sat tied to an octopus of metal hoists, like slave labor used to turn some giant cog. Monstro the whale lay beached in a shallow stream, fanged mouth frozen in a final roar. A silent merry-go-round loomed before them, impaled horses straining at the bit.

"Wow, man," Swan called from the back seat, "I feel like I'm having a bad flashback."

Rose laughed. "Glad I'm not the only one." He pointed to the left of the carousel. "Turn here. Once we get through the castle we're home free."

They rounded the corner. A pair of parked golf carts blocked their path. "Oh, shit!" Knox jerked the wheel to the left. The cart plowed through a net of velvet ropes and brass poles, then skidded onto a spinning pastel disk. Technicians leaped out of their way. A neon orange teacup the size of a porcelain bath tub swung towards them, spinning on its axis. Knox screamed in terror and wrenched the wheel to the right. The cup drifted by them, its handle smacking the side of the cart. The pursuing cart crashed onto the disk behind them.

A giant pink teacup whipped across their path, the saucer no more than a foot away. Rose gripped the windshield frame with bloodless fingers. "Jane," he hollered, "stop this crazy thing!" Knox twisted and jerked the wheel. Day-glow china spun past them like alien invaders from a surrealist nightmare. The cart behind them ran headlong into a great blue cup. Security guards spilled out, scattering as a whizzing green beverage swooped in for the kill. With a terrible crunch their cart was demolished. The spinning platter slammed to a stop beneath them.

Knox dodged a now motionless red cup, tore through a hedge and back onto the pavement. The pinnacles of a fairy tale castle rose up before them. They drove over a drawbridge, under a raised portcullis, and out onto Main Street U.S.A. "God damn," Swan yelled. "That was fun!" He vented a delirious shriek.

"Can we do it again?" asked Rose. "Can we?"

"Good work, Knox," said Randall breathlessly. "Remind me not to bitch about your driving anymore." Knox merely grunted, keeping his eyes on the road ahead.

They left their golf cart at the main gate and jumped the turnstiles. "You'd think they'd make it harder to get in this way," Swan mused.

"Why bother?" asked Rose. "They probably figure security can handle whatever lunatics decide to try it."

Swan hoisted his starved, tattooed legs over the barrier. "So much for that theory."

They walked past the ticket booths and onto the parking lot. A wrecked golf cart lay on its side a few yards away. All of the glass on the vehicle had been shattered. Black boot marks dotted the cracked plastic chassis. Three of the tires had been slashed. The fourth hung from a nearby tree. A hail of broken bottles and dented cans littered the surrounding blacktop. Further on, a flashlight sat in a pool of congealing vomit, light shining weakly. There was nobody in sight, and no other cars visible on the lot.

"Well," said Randall, "it looks like Bob and the boys did a thorough job." He prodded a shard of glass with a toe. "Pity they left already, we could have used the lift. I only hope they didn't land themselves in the slam."

"It's only a mile or so to the street," said Knox. "Then maybe another half to the car. We can walk it."

"Like we have a choice."

"Jesus, Wormwood, what happened? You look like you had a bad weekend in Vegas." Wheezing hysterically, Toad-Eater held open the condominium door. Inside, the party raged as though it had only just begun.

"Give me a dry jockstrap and a nice warm beer and I'll be fine." Rose edged past the enormous biker. Cheers and laughter greeted his entrance, followed by applause.

"And greetings to the rest of you fine gentlemen." Still chuckling, Toad-Eater looked Swan up and down. "That's some impressive paint you've got there, if I do say so myself." He pulled up one of his own sleeves, revealing a faded blue hula-hula girl. "Now this I got in '75 up in Frisco. Funny story, that. Me and this girl named Jasmine..."

"Is Bad Bob inside?" Randall interrupted, his patience worn through.

"He certainly is," Toad-Eater replied. "I do apologize. Didn't mean to keep you out on the porch all night." He backed out of the doorway with a grin. "Make yourselves at home."

They found Bob reclining in an overstuffed chair. Though a bottle of Corona balanced on his knee, he still looked sober as granite. When he saw the brothers Bob grinned, saluting them with a nod and a sip of beer. "Well, hail to the conquering heroes," he drawled. "Everything go as planned?"

"Pretty much," said Randall. He shrugged off his coat, noticing a few damp patches near the hem. "There any of that left?"

"In the fridge." Bob hooked a thumb in the general direction of the kitchen.

"We saw a bit of your handiwork in the parking lot. Things didn't get too out of hand, I hope." Randall rummaged around in the refrigerator until he found the six-pack of Corona. There were three bottles remaining. He grabbed the carton and carried it back to the living room.

"You would've loved it," said Bob, sitting forward in his chair. "We're there about five minutes, yelling and throwing bottles at the ticket booths before security shows up. There were three carts, twelve guys total. Puny thugs, every one of 'em. We got twice as many guys, and everybody's on his own bike. So we rode out a little, let 'em chase us onto the blacktop. Then bingo, they're surrounded. Just like Indians on a wagon train."

"Sounds cool," said Swan. He popped a beer open on the edge of the hardwood coffee table. Randall winced, thinking of the woman locked behind the bedroom door.

"We played with them for a while," Bob continued. "A guy driving one of the carts got brave, decided to rush us. We cut him out, surrounded him in his own little ring. That one turned into a stand-up fight. The other two carts didn't try anything after that."

"I would imagine not." Randall sat on an arm of the sofa. A knot of bikers jammed the cushions, each holding part of a long, narrow snake. One woman was trying to stuff its tail into an empty tequila bottle. Randall twisted open a beer and took a big hit.

"We kept that up for maybe twenty minutes." Bob settled back into his chair with an air of contentment. In that moment he looked like nothing so much as a middle-aged bachelor, pleasantly tired after a long day at the office. Only when Randall looked at the heavy motorcycle boots and torn jeans did the impression fade. "We split when reinforcements arrived. They might have gotten some license numbers, but no big deal. Most of us have an outstanding warrant or two already. Anyway, I figured you were over the wall by then."

The captive snake writhed and hissed in aggravation. Laughing and shrieking, the bikers tumbled to the floor, feigning a desperate struggle. In the tangle of bodies the snake slithered loose and bolted under the couch. Knox snagged the reptile, then draped it over his shoulders. He caressed its head with a gentle finger. The bright tongue flickered. "Is Silverfish still here?" he asked suddenly.

"No, she took Corrie home right after the raid." Bob shrugged. "You know, school night." Knox nodded absently.

Swan drained his beer and slammed the bottle down on the coffee table. "So, Randall," he began, "you said something about your little human friend wounding our dearest Mum." He pulled the last Corona from the carton and snapped off the cap. "How bad was it? I mean, would she still be under by now?"

"I imagine so," said Randall. "She took a slug in the head and three or four to the body. That kind of damage takes forever to heal." Randall sat up straight on the arm of the sofa and looked his younger brother in the eye. "Why?"

Swan took a swallow from his bottle and grinned from ear to ear. "Because I found out where the bitch sleeps."

chapter **fourteen**

"You know man, this is a trip," said Swan. "I mean, when's the last time we were all together like this, walking down the street? Got to be, what, twenty or thirty years?"

"And such a marvelous choice of streets for a reunion," said Knox, looking up and down the length of Harbor Boulevard. Theme motels and family restaurants sat interspersed between dive bars and pink-roofed strip joints. Well-heeled conventioneers shared the pavement with bums and swaggering teenage gangsters. Dawn was over an hour away, but cars cruised the street in heavy waves. "What is this affinity you have for whores, anyway?"

Swan shrugged. He had picked a leather jacket off the floor at random before leaving the condo. It hung loosely from his narrow shoulders. "They're safe targets. I mean think about it, if I wandered around tearing the tits off dental hygienists on a regular basis, people would start to get pissed. Then I got to worry about the cops, maybe leave for a new city. It's a monster hassle. But if I stick to whores, who gives a fuck? That's great, people think, one less hooker walking the streets. They're a hassle-free meal."

"Pretty clever," said Randall.

"People got basically the same attitude towards tourists," Swan continued. "But with whores the approach is so easy. All you got to do is walk up and say hello." Swan stretched, making circles with his arms. The dragon silhouette flexed its wings. "In fact, that's sort of how I met Shannon."

"You never told me she was a prostitute," said Knox

"She wasn't," Swan replied, "not really." A black BMW cruised by, overamplified bass shaking the tinted windows. Swan glared at it, giving the unseen driver the finger. "Anyway, I was hunting for a good looking snack," he continued. "I'd been bumming around Blackfriars and the

City. A lot of the younger whores hang there, working the businessmen. So I go to this pub I know, start checking out the crowd. And there she was, pulling cigarettes out of the ashtrays and drinking from leftover glasses."

"Sounds alluring," said Randall.

"You know it, man. She had this blue-black mohawk, but her hair had started to grow out again so there was this blond stubble too. Reminded me of peach fuzz. She had six studs going up one ear and three in the other. Her jacket looked pretty solid, but the rest of her clothes were thrashed. Turned out she'd been wearing them for months. Her toes were starting to come through her shoes. I tell you brother, she was cute."

"I knew it was love," Knox said to Randall.

"Might've been," Swan conceded. "Anyway, I bought her a pint and we talked for a while. She named her price and I took her to this by-the-hour flop house. I got her clothes off and it turns out she has this great labial pierce, I mean truly professional. So I showed her my tattoos. And then we're fucking. And it's, you know, pretty good. And then she's crying. Not just tears, either. She's like sobbing and shit. Turns out I'm only her third paying customer. What can I say? I couldn't kill her, not after all that."

A station wagon pulled out of a motel parking lot ahead of them. Four small, genderless children pressed their faces to the foggy windows. Each of them wore a set of stylized mouse ears. The three brothers paused at the corner, waiting for the light. "Amazing," said Randall as they crossed the street. "I never suspected you were a man of such tender sensibilities, Swan."

"Up yours." They neared a squat, squarish restaurant. Pink signs painted on the glass front advertised *Foot High Pies* and *Big Big Portions*. The place was packed, every seat taken. A marquee jutted from the roof, reading *5 out of 4 eat here 24 hrs.* Below that hung a bench swing supported by a set of wrought iron struts. Pink paint clung to the metal in patches. "Would you get a load of that sign?" asked Swan. "What the hell do you think that's supposed to mean?"

"Beats me," Knox answered. "Must have made sense to somebody at some point."

"In theory," said Randall. He scrutinized the marquee for a moment longer, then proceeded down the street. "So where does Lisel come into this?"

"Well," Swan replied, "the whole thing started when we met this acid dealer."

"That's what Timothy Leary said."

"Don't start," said Swan, "okay?"

"Sorry."

Swan padded the pockets of the borrowed jacket and pulled out crumpled pack of cigarettes. His other hand found a disposable lighter. "Cool." He jogged a cigarette, lit it, then took a deep drag. "Shannon and I were playing our game." Smoke drifted out with his words. "Knox tell you about our little pastime?"

"You mean your stoned and obnoxious tour of the sights of London?"

"That's the one." Swan took another drag, shunting the smoke out his nose. "We were drunk off our ass at the Kew Botanical Gardens. Boring place, really. No good flowers even, just a hundred different species of fern. But we were having a blast reading all those scientific plant names. A lot of them sounded like rock bands. Kaput Medusa. Morel Fungi. Eventually we got tired of walking, crashed on a bench. This old guy's already sitting there. He's got on a baggy purple sweatshirt and old jeans. Long grey hair in a tail. Beatnik survivor, you could tell just by looking at him. We got to talking with this dude. After a while he says, 'You two seem pretty cool. How'd you like me turn you on to a good trip?'"

Swan took a final drag off his cigarette then pitched it into the gutter. "We take the Underground to this guy's pad in Kensington. Nice place. White wool carpet. Killer stereo. Turns out the guy's some kind of chemist, makes the shit himself. 'First of the batch,' he says, and he hands me an eyedropper. Not even a blotter yet, man. This is straight fucking acid. I squeeze a little on my tongue, do the same for Shannon. Stoner, that's the dude's name if you can believe it, he takes a hit too. We popped a couple of beers and waited for the shit to hit us."

The street lamps stopped at the end of the block. Beyond the zone of illumination the bars became more numerous while the restaurants dwindled. Fewer tourists strayed this far down the boulevard. The occasional street walker loitered on the pavement. "So what's Stoner's angle?" Randall asked. "What's he getting out of this deal?"

"Fuck if I know. Maybe he just wanted a couple of bodies to test the batch on. Beats me." Swan eyed one of the hookers but kept on walking. "Didn't matter anyway. The shit was good. About twenty minutes after the hit the walls started breathing in and out, rippling like mercury or something. Shannon was talking and this sort of vibrating light came out of her mouth instead of sound. But I could still understand her."

"And this was a good trip?" Randall said dubiously.

"That's nothing," said Knox. "The time I did peyote I thought I was plucking stars out of the sky." He lifted a hand and made a little tweezer motion with his thumb and forefinger.

"Cool," said Swan. "I thought everyone in the world had turned into reptiles once. But that was a mescaline trip, and you know what crazy shit that is."

"Sure," said Randall. "Always makes me see lizards."

"Cherry." Swan lit another cigarette. "After it kicked in I started thinking we ought to go out and play the game. No sense spending the whole trip staring at the ceiling, not with such a long crash to look forward to. I asked Shannon if there were any high traffic places we hadn't hit yet. 'Yeah, sure,' she said, 'the British Museum.' We'd told Stoner about the game and he decided to come along. The tube station was right near his place, so we hopped back on the Underground."

Swan flicked ash off his cigarette, exhaling smoke. "We must have gone there on a weekend, because the museum was jammed full of humans. I thought beautiful, more limey bluebloods to annoy. Less chance of security spotting us right off. We were keeping up the appearance pretty well, acting straight. Except for Shannon. She had this permanently startled look on her face, like she'd just had her first orgasm or something. And she kept waving her hands around, trying to grab shit that wasn't there."

They came to a dirt lot. A temporary fence surrounded piles of lumber and bags of cement, mounds of transferred earth. Graffiti covered the plywood barrier, scrawled initials and crude murals. A line-drawn woman bent over receptively, a knothole where her sex would be. "We started small, pushing our way to the front of crowds, getting in the way. There was a withered old gal in a straw hat and this God-awful flowery dress. I stared at her real ugly, but she just ignored me. The Brits will swallow a lot of shit before they complain, you know. More than Americans would."

"True," Knox agreed.

"I coughed up a few beer belches. That earned me some titters of disapproval, nothing else. It got harder and harder to think of shit to do. The trip was really strong and I kept getting distracted. We went into this room filled with nothing but clocks and watches. Fucking hundreds of them. Pocket watches. Wrist watches. Mantel clocks with built in match dispensers. Wall clocks. Grandfather clocks. Little watches set in lockets and rings. All of them antiques and most of them still running. The air was ticking man, every bit of every second. It was so physical I could see it. After a while I could hear time passing around me, only it was like I wasn't inside it any more. I thought I'd stepped through a hole in the universe or something, and I could watch time rolling by without going along for the ride. I don't know how long we were standing there. We might have been there all day, except the clocks struck. Not all at once, but in layers. It must've lasted well on ten minutes. All this chiming and bonging and crashing."

"Sounds like a Pink Floyd album I heard once," Randall interjected.

"Yeah, sort of." Swan nodded. "It woke me up, though. When all the noise had stopped, I looked around. There were different people in the room, so it must have been a while. Shannon was completely out of it. She looked like a statue, except for the little line of drool on her chin. Stoner must've been having the trip of his life. You couldn't have cut the smile off his face with a razor. I tugged on his arm and he turns to look at me. 'Sarcophagi,' he says, 'we have to see the sarcophagi.' And he starts off down the hall. I grabbed Shannon and chased after him."

"That Egyptian collection is incredible," Knox commented. "I'm just surprised the archaeologists didn't try to import one of the pyramids. The English were cocky as hell before the empire collapsed."

"You would know." Swan snuffed his cigarette on the sleeve of the leather jacket. "So we climb up to the top floor. The room's filled with humans shuffling about, gawking. There's coffins lining all four walls, standing, and a few on their backs in the middle. We get in line, file along looking at each one for a minute or two. Most of them are wood, the paint faded and powdery. But the symbols are really cool. Snakes and eyes and guys with dog heads, all that King Tut-type shit. One had the lid taken off and you could look at the mummy inside. The bandages were crumbling, yellow. You could see strips of shriveled skin between the gaps. Looked like clay, dry clay. One of its fingers was exposed, all gnawed bone and dead meat clinging like dirt. But the fingernail was perfect, cut in a smooth crescent. Man, it was spooky."

"I turn around and standing right there is this huge golden sarcophagus. Looks like a woman, a queen maybe. She's wearing this gigantic headdress striped with gold and some kind of deep blue metal, snakes and moons all over. Same deal with her clothes. She had a toga or veils or something, one tit hanging out. Her skin is gold, her face too. Her eyes are flat silver. I start getting this very bad feeling looking at her, like some mean little animal just woke up in my stomach. And this black vibe starts pulsing from her eyes, dripping off her fingers. I see it seeping out from under the lid, misty liquid hate pooling on the marble floor. It's glowing, beating like a heart. The black stuff spills across the ground, creeping and sniffing. I know it's hunting for me. I know it wants to kill me. And all the time it's pulsing, beating, calling. It sprays out of the sarcophagus in fountains, infecting the walls."

"I take a step back and almost trip over Stoner. One glance at his face and I know he sees it too. Shannon's staring at the coffin, eyes bugging. She looks like she's about to piss herself. Stoner and I each grab an arm and drag her out of the room, shoving people out of the way, practically running. We caromed down the stairs, tripping and stumbling. I slammed into this guy and knocked him flat. Then people really started bitching, pointing fingers. Security came after us, but we didn't give a shit. We ran for the doors and out into the street, Shannon yelling something about karma. Stoner led us to the tube station, jammed us into a train. I just stood in the middle of the car gasping and shaking, trying not to freak out completely. We made it back to Kensington and took the longest, meanest crash I've ever lived through."

The three brothers stood at a street corner. They had stopped walking. A middle-aged hooker stared at them with a mixture of incredulity and loathing, her painted mouth hanging slack. "So," Randall said at length, "you think Lisel was in the sarcophagus."

"I don't think it, man." Swan looked his older brother in the eye, gaze firm. "I know it."

Randall smiled crookedly. "How?"

Swan flicked a glance at the hooker. "Business first." He stepped up to the woman. She wore a young girl's clothes, a short striped skirt and a stringy mesh sweater over an old black bra. Blue veins stood out in her bare legs. Swaths of makeup failed to hide the lines at the corners of her eyes or the slight twist of a nose broken long ago, thinning hair. "You look cheap," Swan said.

"That's good," she replied, "'cause you look poor."

Swan grinned wickedly. "You've got quite a mouth."

"And I know how to use it." She jerked a thumb towards a rundown apartment across the dark street. "Want a demonstration?"

"Why not?" They walked off together, leaving Randall and Knox standing on the corner.

The woman led Swan up a flight of stairs at the side of the brown stucco building. A fat man with a drooping mustache sat on the landing, reading a newspaper by the pale glow of a florescent tube set into the wall. An aluminum baseball bat rested on his knees. "You give the lady any trouble," he said, "I come fuck you up."

"No problem, man." The hooker pushed open a second story door. Swan followed her inside, pulling it closed. A light snapped on behind limp curtains.

Randall stared at the window for a moment, then laughed. He paced back and forth a few steps. "How long you figure this is going to take?"

"Depends on whether he's hungry or horny." Knox glanced up at the building. "My guess is he won't be long."

"Probably not." Randall continued to pace a slow circuit of the corner, the hem of his trench coat swinging to the rhythm of his steps. Several minutes passed in relative silence, punctuated only by the tap of his boots and the occasional rush of a passing car. "There's something I always wanted to ask you," he said abruptly.

Knox looked up, frowned. "Okay, shoot."

"Who was it fired that first shot across the Rio Grande? You were in D.C. just then, if memory serves. And I know it wasn't me."

"All smoke and mirrors, my brother." Knox replied. "I gave one of the enlisted men thirty pieces of silver to make trouble. Damn good thing I did, too. If I'd left it up to Taylor the Tory we'd have had a beach picnic instead of a war. I'm afraid the gentleman's name escapes me now."

"Guess I'll never know."

"Sorry." Knox chuckled to himself. "Then there's the nameless Mexican who shot Old Zack in the nuts at San Pasqual. Him I owe a bottle of champagne. Guess I'd leave it on his grave, if I knew who the fellow was."

Randall ceased pacing. "You can break it over my tombstone when this caper is over."

"It was you?" Knox gaped. "Jesus, Randall, how come you never told me?"

"Well, when you first joined me out here in California you had other things on your mind. After that, I guess it just never came up until now."

Knox's face fell. "I always regretted leaving Sarah. But what else could I do? Mother would have killed her if I hadn't. She wanted to eviscerate me when she found out I'd become President. The families and the Brotherhood weren't too pleased with the idea, either. I had to run. There was no other way."

"You could have told her," Randall said. "She suspected, I think. You could have taken her with you."

Knox shook his head. "One way or another I would have been her death." He looked vaguely at the street, eyes unfocused. "She lived to be eighty-eight, you know. That's forty-six years, thinking I had died."

"I was surprised you didn't throw in with me right then and there. It disgusted me that you didn't." Old anger rasped in Randall's voice.

Knox looked up, met Randall's stare. "It disgusted me, too," he said. "It still does."

"God, I'm sorry." Randall took his brother by the shoulders, embraced him. "I didn't mean to dig all that up." He clapped Knox on the back, then held him out at arms length. "You had more than most of us ever get. You had years. A marriage. You know me; since the change I haven't made love to a woman without killing her." Randall let his arms drop, then resumed his rhythmic pacing. "Why don't you find yourself another girl? Maybe a witch. They're still around, you know. More of them than ever."

"Please..." Knox shook his head. "Have you ever been to a Wicca meeting? It's not so much a cult as a fashion trend."

"I see." Randall glanced up at the apartment window, the weak light behind the dead curtains. "What did you think of Swan's little story?

Sounded like drug induced paranoia to me."

"Those scars on his chest aren't paranoia," Knox said. "Somebody got to him, all right."

"Okay, I'll give you that." Randall sunk his hands into his coat pockets. "But is there really a connection? Outside his imagination, I mean."

Knox shrugged. "We haven't heard the whole story yet."

"True." Randall completed another lap of the corner, looked up at the window again. "Taking his God damn time, isn't he?"

The woman's figure passed behind the dim curtain, followed by Swan's lean shadow. A moment later something heavy crashed to the floor, a musical explosion of glass clearly audible across the empty street. The fat man glanced up in annoyance. He folded his newspaper neatly and set it on the stair. Hefting the aluminum bat, he trudged up to the apartment door. "Think we should nail him?" Knox asked.

"Swan can take care of himself."

The fat man tried the door. Locked. He set his shoulder against it and heaved. Nothing. Gripping the bat in two thick hands, the man wound up and smashed the lock. The door swung slowly inward, revealing only a bare bulb hanging from a long cord, grey walls. Bat held up and ready, the fat man stepped into the room. Total silence followed, lasting a full minute.

A loud thud echoed through the open door, followed by a series of sharp cracks. This grew into a flurry of crashes and grunts, the hard slap of blows landing. The baseball bat flew out the door, rolling down the stairs with a hollow clatter. It came to rest a pair of steps down from the newspaper. The sounds of battle gradually diminished, then ceased altogether. Swan exited the apartment and descended the stairs, his bare feet moon-pale in the fluorescent glow. The leather jacket hung from his thin shoulders.

"Satisfied?" asked Randall as he approached. Swan smiled red. "Lovely. Listen, we better split before somebody calls the cops."

Swan licked his lips. "Don't sweat it, man. Just walk away like you don't know nothing about it."

They hiked back the way they had come, towards the illuminated end of Harbor Boulevard. The asphalt gleamed under the distant lamps, a frozen sea trapped between concrete shores. People scurried along the flat grey banks, talking with wide gestures, hailing taxis to ferry them away.

"Say, Randall," Swan began, "you ever run across an immortal that could change shape?" He caressed the parallel scars above his heart. "A mature one, I mean. I know we can't do anything cool like that. But do you think it's something we might learn when we get the power?"

"Change shape." Randall thought back over the years. "You mean green mist, flying rodents, that sort of thing?" Swan nodded. "Nope, can't say as I've ever seen anything like that. Then again, I've met damn few full-fledged immortals. Most of them don't care to show off, either. How about you, Knox? You've been around longer than I have."

The eldest brother ran a hand through his short, white hair. "I'm pretty sure that's all apocryphal. You wouldn't believe how most of this peasant lore got started. Some fellow living in a Romanian dung heap would steal his neighbor's goat and blame it on his dead cousin. Next thing you know the whole village would be digging up old relatives, hacking them to bits with scimitars and stuffing garlic up their assess. Parts of Britain were just as bad, not so long ago." He scrutinized Swan for a moment. "Why do you ask? You know something about this we don't?"

"Maybe." Swan pulled the crumpled cigarette wrapper from his pocket. It was empty. He wadded the glossy paper and pitched it over his shoulder. "Well, it's like this. I woke up from the crash first, of course. The sleep is great for that kind of shit. No hangovers. No burnout. It even cures the clap. Shannon and Stoner were out of it, completely zoned. I checked the old guy's fridge, but there wasn't much inside. Just a rack of test tubes and some stale bagels."

"You still eat regular food?" Randall asked, incredulous.

"Sure," said Swan, looking puzzled. "Don't you?"

"No. Gave it up a long time ago. It doesn't do anything for me anymore."

"I don't know," said Knox. "Every once in while I like to have a little something. There was this Chinese place in Santa Cruz that served the most wonderful squid in oyster sauce. I used to go there two or three times a year."

Swan grimaced. "And you guys think I'm disgusting." He spat a blob of crimson saliva onto the sidewalk. "Kensington is a weird neighborhood, mostly middle aged Indians and old Irish. They seem to get along okay, though. I went to this grocery across from the tube station, a real mom-and-pop-type place. There was a counter up front and you told this ancient Irish dude what you wanted and he got it down from the shelves for you and bagged it up. I swear, he must have been at least as old as I am. Anyway, I got some fresh bread and some cheese and couple of six packs then headed back to Stoner's place."

Swan dug into a pocket of the borrowed jacket and pulled out the disposable lighter. He twisted the fuel feed up as high as it would go, then jammed the striking mechanism down in on itself. Holding the lighter head downward, he flung it forcefully at the street. The red plastic trinket exploded in a miniature ball of flame. "I had left the door unlocked, so I just sauntered right in. Stoner's dead on the living room floor, blood all over the fucking place. He wasn't far from the couch where he crashed. I doubt he ever woke up, the poor bastard. There's this gigantic dog standing over him. I mean it, man, this mother is huge, built like a God damn bulldozer. It's bristling and snarling, digging its claws into Stoner's corpse. Shannon's crouched in the far corner, shivering like crazy, holding a kitchen knife with both hands."

"I drop the shit and go for my own blade. The dog hears me and whips around. The weird thing is, it didn't jump me instantly. The fucker turned around and just looked at me for a cold five seconds. I even had my knife up by the time it sprang. Sucker ran straight at me, knocked me down, then started ripping up my leg with its front claws. I stuck the beast in the shoulder a couple times, but it didn't do much good. Just pissed it off. The bastard jumped on top of me and tore into my chest. Motherfucker practically disemboweled me. I stabbed at its face, but I couldn't see shit from the pain. Thought I was going to pass out for sure. I was screwed."

The brothers reached the first street lamp. People walked blithely up and down as though the feeble yellow light protected them from any harm, as though the adjacent vice and darkness were truly a world apart. "Shannon must've nailed the bastard right between the shoulder blades," Swan continued. "The dog dropped like a sack, which actually didn't make me feel much better. Its front legs twitched and jerked, and I could look right into its eyes. They were blue, and bright as bicycle reflectors. More like a cat's eyes than a dog's. I tell you, it was strange. But you should've seen Shannon, man. She stood over both of us, legs apart, stabbing that kitchen knife into the dog's back like fucking

Norman Bates. There were tears in her eyes, running down her face. She pistoned the knife up and down, cussing a blue streak. Must have stabbed it ten or twelve times."

"The dog finally managed to get up. It gave Shannon a kick with a back leg, sent her sprawling. The beast tensed, then sprang off me and out the door. So I'm lying there, wondering what the fuck happened. I'm not thinking too well, and I can't figure it out. Then it hits me. The golden sarcophagus."

"I still don't see how you're reading Lisel into this," Randall said. "It could have been anyone in that casket. Somebody from another family. One of the Brotherhood's little creations. Maybe something we never ever heard of."

"Would you hold your water for a minute?" Swan growled, "I'm getting to that." The black BMW they had seen earlier rolled slowly past, bass notes pulsing out from behind the tinted windows. Swan stared after it, jaw clenched, then forced himself to relax. "Shannon wanted to take me to the hospital, if you can believe that. There I am, lying on the carpet with my intestines spread out around me and a third of my ribcage exposed and she wants to call a fucking ambulance. I explained to her that if I had been human I would be severely dead at this point, and if I showed up at a hospital somebody would start asking a lot of unanswerable questions. She hadn't really believed I was immortal, you know. I finally convinced her to tube back to our motel and get my important shit, my stash and my cash. She didn't want to leave, but I told her if she didn't go get the stuff I'd do it myself."

"That would have been interesting," said Knox.

"Tell me about it. When Shannon had gone I dragged myself a little further into the room. I wanted a view of the door in case that damn dog decided to come back. My body was shutting down, I had to fight off the sleep. I'd been alone not ten minutes when Mother came strolling past the window. She opened the door and stood there for a while just looking at me, smiling that superior smile of hers. She had on this grey business suit, real smart and new, but it was her all right. Blond hair straight as an arrow, eyes like fucking ice water. I didn't move a millimeter, probably couldn't have if I'd wanted to. She stepped into the room, stood over me. I thought I was dead. She stooped down, dipped a finger into my chest wound and licked it clean. The bitch grinned again, then turned around and strolled out. I tell you man, I couldn't fucking believe it."

They paused at a corner, waiting for the light. Randall pumped the pedestrian crossing button. "I don't get it either," he said. "Sure, she likes to play around with the three of us, but I would've thought she'd have finished you off. She had to know this information would get back to me eventually."

"So you believe me now?"

"Yeah, I believe you found Lisel's hidey-hole. I just wonder why she didn't seem to care. That worries me."

"And what about this dog creature?" said Knox. "Mother didn't look wounded when she came to gloat?"

"Not in the least." Swan frowned. "Why? You think the beast was somebody else, some new friend of hers?"

"I think I know exactly who the beast is," Knox answered.

Randall slapped his forehead with his palm. "Of course. That bastard."

"Would you guys mind clueing me in here?" Swan asked. "Who the fuck are you talking about?"

"It's kind of a long story," said Randall.

"I'm immortal, take your time."

"It can wait until we get back to the condo." The light had changed. Randall stepped out into the road. The others followed. A thin wisp of dawn had just begun to show in the east, a soft orange glow between the buildings. The brothers walked side by side through the dim streets of morning.

The black BMW crept up behind them, music throbbing. The car paced them for a moment, tinted windows revealing only their own warped reflections, then accelerated. Swan scooped a beer bottle from the gutter and hurled it at the vehicle. The brown glass shattered against the rear window, leaving a web of cracks. The car jerked to a stop. Swan walked briskly towards it.

After a moment's hesitation, the car sped up and disappeared into the distance. The music faded. "Best move you made all night," Swan said.

chapter **fifteen**

By midmorning the condominium looked as though a plague had hit it. Motionless bikers littered the plush carpet and coordinating furniture, sprawled in a variety of unlikely positions. Empty bottles and crushed cans dotted the room like the droppings of several large animals. Toad-Eater lay beached in front of the television, hands folded angelically under one cheek. The narrow snake that had escaped earlier coiled contentedly around one of his meaty arms. Rose had crashed face down across the sofa just after dawn. A trio of women dozed on his back and legs, their hair in tangles, eyes shut and jaws loose. One male hand dangled between a pair of female legs, the fingers just brushing the lip of a half-empty tequila bottle standing miraculously upright on the floor.

"Reminds me of a photograph I saw once," said Randall, seated at the cramped kitchen table. "Aftermath of a chlorine gas canister, World War Two."

"Except for the snoring," Knox amended.

"Yes, but the vomit's there."

"True."

Inspired by their previous discussion, the brothers were eating breakfast. Swan had fried up eggs and bacon while Knox burned several slices of toast. Bob, still alert and lucid as ever, discovered a pitcher of orange juice and a tub of butter. Despite the presence of the snoozing bikers and the occasional whiff of bile, Randall found himself enjoying the meal immensely. It had been such a long time that the novelty of taste and texture had returned. He found the salty flesh of the bacon especially appealing.

"You didn't fight in the World Wars, did you?" Swan had finished his food and sat shaving, unaided by any mirror, with the curved blade of a Japanese punch dagger.

Randall took a sip of juice. "No, I gave up soldiering before the turn of the century. When the guns got big enough to completely obliterate a human target, I decided it was time to get out of the army."

"Sounds like a wise choice." Swan drew the dry knife-edge carefully down the slope of his neck. His jugular vein pulsed visibly beneath taut skin. "Mother and I were in Berlin when Adolph invaded Poland. She seemed to get off on the scene there, sick twist that she is."

Bob mopped his plate with an over-crisp piece of toast. He bit into the bread with an audible crunch, chewed once, then let the remainder drop to the table, swallowing with difficulty. "Seems to me you've just replaced one kind of war with another," he said, then coughed into a napkin.

"I'll admit to that." Randall pushed his plate away. "But I think I can legitimately expect Mother not to use artillery on us."

A door creaked open down the hall and a woman stepped into the living room, a full-length flannel nightgown sheathing her body. Small, smooth hands blossomed from the gathered sleeves. White feet poked out from under the hem like the clappers of a large, plaid bell. A twist of elastic gathered her brown hair into a thick rope. She looked to be in her early thirties, though the set of her eyes suggested a deeper maturity. Swan set down his knife and tapped Bob's arm. "Who's the gash?"

"That's Gwendolyn," Bob murmured in reply. "She's Toad-Eater's old lady." He shifted in his seat to observe her.

"Gwendolyn?" Randall stifled a laugh. "Toad-Eater's ball and chain is a Gwendolyn? Where did they find each other, in line at the DMV, waiting for vanity plates?"

"She's some kind of lawyer. The story is they met in court the time Toad-Eater went to the slam." The woman walked gingerly among the sleeping bikers, plucking up empty beer bottles and tucking them under one arm. When she reached maximum capacity, she made for the French doors leading onto the balcony. Passing behind the couch, she stopped suddenly, scowling with distaste. She stepped over or around something, then pushed through the twin glass doors.

"Probably the vomit," said Swan. Bob laughed silently, lips clamped together, pounding a fist on the table. They looked at each other, then dissolved into a fit of snickering.

"Lawyer, you say?" Knox stood up from the table and began loading plates into the dishwasher. "Was she his defense attorney?"

Bob shrugged. "I've spoken to the lady all of twice and Toad-Eater never says a word about her. She could have been the prosecutor for all I know."

Knox gathered the silverware and dropped it into the bin. "I love these things," he said, shutting the metal door. "Before they invented the dishwasher I had to wear elbow length rubber gloves to keep my skin dry."

"And what did you do before rubber gloves?" Randall asked.

The French doors swung open and Gwendolyn reappeared. She negotiated the maze of bodies and leaned into kitchen. "Good morning, Robert."

Bad Bob acknowledged his pajama clad hostess with a nod. "Morning, Gwendolyn."

She explored the kitchen with her eyes, noting the remains of breakfast. "You're up early."

"No, late." Bob poured the last of the orange juice into his glass and downed it, deliberately turning away.

Gwendolyn frowned silently at him for a moment. "I have to leave soon," she said at length. "Would you be so good as to clean up behind the sofa before you go?"

"Sure. No problem."

She continued to look at them for a few seconds, then nodded absently to herself. Returning to the living room she retrieved another load of bottles, picking them from nerveless hands like a detective at a bomb site. She deposited them on the balcony, then retreated down the hall. Doors closed, and shortly the localized patter of shower water could be heard.

"Weird," said Randall, contemplating his fingernails. "They actually married?"

Bob spread his hands. "Living in sin, so far as I can tell."

Swan picked up his knife and pointed it accusingly at Knox. "You told me this was Anaheim."

"Same difference."

Swan grinned and resumed shaving, passing the blade down his neck just under the ear. He had removed all of his beard except for the elongated sideburns.

Rose moaned from the sofa. "Could you turn the television down?" he mumbled petulantly. "Trying to sleep here."

Randall hauled his seat around to look at his friend. Rose's face was flushed red, almost as though sunburned. A little puddle of drool darkened the peach upholstery under his chin. "The television is off, actually." Randall informed him.

"Really?" Rose's dangling hand crept gradually up to his face, then peeled his eyes open one at a time. Veins shot through the whites like cracks in glass, and large dry crystals clung to his lashes. "I could have sworn I heard Regis and Kathy Lee talking about feline diabetes." He rubbed at the inner corners of his eyes with a thumb and forefinger. "Must have been a nightmare."

"Quite likely."

Rose braced his hand on the edge of the sofa and attempted to push himself upright. The weight of the women asleep on his back held him flat. "My God," he said, neck twisting frantically, "I'm paralyzed!" He pushed and strained, his socked feet twitching at the opposite end of the sofa, then went limp. "I didn't think I'd had that much to drink."

"Calm down," said Randall, smirking faintly. "There are couple of ladies using you as a futon, is all."

"Christ, no wonder I'm numb." Rose stretched to look over his shoulder. "Are they naked?" he asked hopefully.

Randall glanced at the three women, snoring audibly in their spiked jackets and motorcycle boots. "Hardly," he said.

Rose slumped. "Well, that explains it. All that gear weighs a fucking ton." He flinched suddenly, then stared suspiciously at the drool stain.

"I don't suppose you could persuade them to move?"

"I'll see what I can do." Randall stood and went to the side of the couch. Gripping the first woman by the arms, he pulled her forward off Rose's legs and let her slip to the floor. She grumbled incoherently, then curled up against the side of the coffee table. Randall performed a similar procedure on the woman at the opposite end, then paused to consider the remaining sleeper. "Have to come up with a new tactic," he said. "Can't very well send her smacking head first into the mahogany."

"That's okay," said Rose, "I think I can manage now." Gripping the arm of the sofa with both hands he pulled himself forward, worming his legs out from under the unconscious woman. She bounced and jostled as he squirmed, finally listing sideways onto the cushions. Rose stood stiffly, borrowed jeans and Harley t-shirt skewed across his body. He paced slowly up and down, wincing intermittently. "You know," he said, "there's only one thing worse than losing circulation to your penis."

"And what might that be?" Randall asked dutifully.

"Getting it back."

"Glad to have you back among the living," said Knox. "Or the unliving. Or whatever."

"Swell," Rose replied, his voice tired. "Somebody give the prodigal son an aspirin."

"Sorry," said Bob. "All we have is warm beer."

Rose sighed, bringing a hand to his forehead in a gesture of infinite pathos. "Guess that'll have to do." Bob grabbed a can from the kitchen counter and tossed it at him.

"Well," said Randall, "Now that we're all assembled, I think it's time to discuss passports."

"Passports?" Rose repeated, blinking in confusion.

"You know, those little legal documents in simulated leather covers that allow you to move from country to country. You must have heard of them."

"Sounds vaguely familiar." Rose popped open his beer and took a healthy swallow. "Where are we going?"

"London."

Rose glanced over at Swan, then nodded slowly. "I get it. The human lithograph brought you a lead."

Swan bristled, and started to rise. Randall stopped him with look. "Just don't call me human," he growled, sinking back into his chair.

"At any rate," Randall continued, "I've got a valid U.S. passport." He sat down on the edge of the coffee table. "It's not in my name, so my supposed demise in Santa Cruz won't give us any trouble. How about the rest of you?"

"Mine's current," said Knox. "Unused and almost expired, but current."

"What about you, Bob?" Randall asked. "I'd be willing to pay your way if you want to come along. I have the feeling we're going to need all the help we can get."

Bob chewed his lower lip thoughtfully. "I'm pretty sure mine's still good," he said. "I'd have go back to the house and dig it up. Might even be in my bank box." He scratched at his receding hairline. "I'll have to find somebody to keep an eye on the lot, too."

"Just what is it you do for a living, anyway?" Randall asked.

"Oh, these days I run a Harley dealership."

"Figures." Randall shook his head. "In that case, you can buy your own airline ticket. I've got enough deadbeats to support." He turned to Swan. "How about it? I don't suppose you have a valid passport?"

"Several. How do you think I got to England in the first place? I don't mail myself in fucking packing crates unless I have to."

"Sounds plausible." Randall held out a hand for Rose's beer, took a good hit, then passed it back. "Maybe you could doctor one up for the convenience store bandito, here."

"I've got an old Canadian passport I bought when I got out of the lock-up," said Rose. "It's not beautiful, but it'll probably pass."

"You ever use it before?" Knox asked.

"Yeah, once."

"Well that settles that," said Randall. He stood up and clapped his hands together. "Bob, why don't you go see to your business? The rest of us'll do some travel shopping. Knox, is my pack still in your car?" The eldest brother nodded. "Good. I'd like to leave today, so why don't we meet at the British Air counter at LAX in a couple of hours."

"I think I can manage that," said Bob. He got up from the table and walked around to the television. Stooping down, he shook Toad-Eater awake. The big biker opened his eyes, then groaned and clapped a hand across his face. The narrow snake slithered away behind the TV cabinet.

"Come on, now," Bob said, "time to get up." He helped Toad-Eater gradually to his feet. One arm draped over broad shoulders, Bob walked him slowly across the living room and around behind the couch. "There's a little something here I'd like you to take care of."

⚜

The combined murmur of a hundred conversations vibrated in the air, rising to the vaulted ceiling like the tuning of an orchestra. A thousand shoes rang cathedral echoes from the tile, while unintelligible announcements droned continuously over the P.A. Following the back-lit signs and television monitors, the travelers made their way towards their gate.

"You know," Rose said to Randall, "I always thought Heathrow was British slang for puking."

"You're kidding."

"Nope." Rose toyed with the strap adjust on his newly purchased satchel. "It sounds right, doesn't it? 'Stop the car, Angus! I'm going to Heathrow!' Or something like that."

Randall checked over his shoulder to make sure the others were following. Bob had lent Swan a pair of grey slacks and a cream-colored dress shirt. The spiked jacket he had lifted complemented the outfit strangely well. Bad Bob himself looked even more respectable, and somehow more dangerous, in a gunmetal blue business suit. Knox still wore his habitual jeans and work boots, but his tie-dye shirt had reappeared. The vortex of color contrasted sharply with his dead white hair. Randall returned his attention to Rose. "Let me see this passport of yours."

Rose whisked the document from his satchel with a magician's flourish. Randall scrutinized the photo, then read over the particulars. "Geddy Lee?" He arched a dubious eyebrow.

Rose batted his lashes winningly. "Did I mention how inexpensive this passport was?"

Randall snapped the document closed and handed it back. "You just better pray the customs officer isn't a fan of progressive rock."

They walked down a long, carpeted hall towards the departing gates. A moving conveyor belt propelled the tired and the elderly forward at just above a crawl. Regularly spaced windows provided overhead views of waiting aircraft. Fuel trucks and maintenance crews surround the planes like insects feeding on a larger carcass. They approached the black arch of the metal detector.

"Hold on a minute." Randall halted Rose with a hand against his chest. "You did remember to leave your pistol in the car, didn't you?"

Rose slipped a hand inside his leather jacket. "Oops." He flashed his maniacal grin. "Silly me."

৭৬

"Hey! How come he gets the window seat?"

"Luck of the draw, five-pint." Swan flopped down into the overstuffed chair. "You lose." He kicked his duffel bag underneath the seat in front of him.

Rose brandished his ticket, waving it under Randall's nose. "It says quite clearly on my boarding pass that I get seat J, which is the window seat."

Randall sighed in exasperation. "Come on, Swan, let him have the window."

Swan folded his arms across his chest and settled deeper into the cushions. "Like hell."

"All right," Randall said, glaring down, "but if I have to listen to him complain for the next eleven hours I'm going to rip out your spine with my teeth."

Swan scowled, but stood up. A flight attendant walked briskly between the rows, her skirt swishing. "On second thought," said Rose, "maybe I'll take the aisle seat." His eyes followed the woman until she disappeared behind the curtain to first class. "That way I'll be able to get up whenever I want."

"Whatever," said Randall. "I just don't want to hear you bitching later." He nodded fractionally to Swan, who sat back down.

Knox and Bob had settled in across the aisle, to one side of the middle section of seats. "Who needs children with them around?" said Bob. "I feel like I'm on a family vacation."

"You are," Knox replied quietly. "Just feel lucky we're sitting over here." He hunched down to unzip his pack, pulling out a softbound book and a leather spectacle case. Settling the wire framed half-lenses onto his nose, he leafed through the glossy pages. A creased grocery receipt held his place.

"You need glasses?" Bob asked incredulously.

"My near vision has always been bad, even before I was elevated." Knox plucked the bookmark from its place and tucked it under the front cover. "It hasn't gotten any worse in the last three centuries, but it hasn't gotten any better either."

Bob chewed on that for a moment. "What's that you're reading?" he asked, glancing curiously at the text.

"*Finnegan's Wake*. I've been at it for a couple of decades now, off and on."

The seatbelt sign chimed on, and a moment later the plane lurched forward. Tarmac crawled by outside the widow as the plane executed a wide turn. During the interminable taxi, the flight attendants mutely demonstrated flotation devices and oxygen masks while an instruction video played on the tiny screen at the front of the cabin. They finished by indicating the emergency exits, then strapped themselves into the folding seat in the galley.

The plane sat motionless at the foot of the runway for nearly a quarter of an hour, waiting for air traffic to clear. Without prelude, the engines powered up, turbines wailing hollowly. The concrete outside the window began to move, sliding away with increasing speed. With a stomach-wrenching lift, the plane left the ground. The land dropped away, buildings and highways becoming small and unrealistic, receding into harmlessness. They continued to climb, gravity pulling insistently at Randall's guts. The plane banked slightly, and the view of the city disappeared, replaced with the rippling blue ocean.

When they completed the turn and leveled out, Randall forced his hands to unclench. His fingernails had made long scratches in the metallic armrests. With an effort, Randall relaxed his jaw, then his shoulders. His whole body ached as though bruised. He stared past Swan and out to sea for a while, allowing himself to go totally limp. "I hate flying."

"Why's that?" asked Swan, looking contentedly out the window.

"It's like artillery fire." Randall sat up straight and rubbed at the back of his neck, persuading the muscles there to relax. "There's a small but very real chance that this plane will crash and we'll be destroyed outright, regeneration or no. I hate putting myself in that kind of position now, when things are finally starting to go my way. It's like Russian roulette."

"You need to learn to relax, man." As if setting an example, Swan tucked his arms behind his head and slumped down in his seat. "We could just as easily be killed in car wreck, especially the way Knox fucking drives. Our kind faces the same risks that everyone else does. You just feel it more, 'cause you expect to be around longer. Forever isn't really forever. You got to accept that."

"I have accepted death," Randall answered. "Think about where all this is leading me. I don't want to go meaninglessly. I want to finish what I've started."

"How noble of you." Swan yawned.

The seatbelt sign chimed off. Rose immediately unbuckled his restraint and stood up. He swung his arms in a pair of wide loops, turned in a circle, then sat back down. Randall stared. "Just exercising my options."

Two flight attendants appeared shortly, trundling drink carts down the twin aisles. Rose rubbed his hands together in anticipation. The woman arrived in due course, shoving the over-laden cart before her. She leaned familiarly forward, addressing a space somewhere over the three of them. "Would you care for something to drink?"

Rose stared rapturously at her face. "Oh, coffee, I suppose." He vented an airy sigh.

"I really don't think you need any stimulants," Randall warned. "After all, we're going to be basically immobile for the next half a day or so."

"Put some whiskey in it, then."

"Anything else?" the attendant asked. "Cream? Sugar?"

"How about a teaspoon of the radiance from your luminous blue eyes?" The woman barked out a laugh, then clamped her mouth shut, struggling to maintain her professional demeanor. She busied herself mixing the drink. "Half a teaspoon," Rose pleaded, "I'm really hurting."

The flight attendant set the coffee down without looking at him. "You'll have to excuse my friend," said Randall. "He hasn't had his lithium today." She muscled her cart forward.

The first of the in-flight movies began. Everyone pulled down their shades, and theater darkness enveloped the plane. Knox refused to abandon his book, reading with only the overhead lamp illuminating the pages. Rose squinted at the far-off video screen, sipping furtively at his coffee and stirring it occasionally with a finger.

Randall ignored the film as best he could. Instead, he repeated in his mind the story Swan had told him. Could the vicious dog-creature really be some sort of immortal? Very little struck Randall as incredible any more, but in two-hundred-plus years of living he had never seen or heard of anything quite like it. Maybe it was unique in the world of the night. Randall hoped so. The mere idea that there might be other, similar beings out there filled him with a dark uneasiness. You would think, Randall told himself, that after so long one might at least know what to expect from reality.

Other memories returned. Once again he felt Lisa's throat collapse between his jaws, tasted her jetting blood. Once again he saw her burning face, boiling eyes fixed on his. He felt the bullet rip through his chest, slam him to the damp tiles. He heard his ceremonial knife splash into the water. At the thought of the hardwood blade, Randall smiled faintly. He had not lost it after all. First Knox, and then Rose, had retrieved it for him. It rested in his pack even now, wrapped in a spare shirt. With any luck, the knife would soon fulfill its purpose.

Once the movie ended and the lights came up, the flight attendants distributed lunch. Bad Bob and all three of the brothers declined. Only Rose accepted the plastic tray, wolfing down the colorless fruit and oil-drenched pasta as though abandoning a hunger strike. Once he had eaten all the food, including three packets of crackers and a mint, he punched a hole in the foil top of his orange juice carton and sucked it dry. Randall looked on in disgust. "Now I remember why I stopped eating."

"Actually," said Swan, "I'm getting kind of hungry myself." He looked casually around at the other passengers. "They sure cram an awful lot of people into coach class, don't they?"

Randall winced. "Could you wait until we touch ground, at least? I don't want be trapped twelve thousand feet in the air with a lynch mob."

"Don't sweat it," Swan answered sharply. "I know how to control myself."

"Glad to hear it."

Now that he thought about it, Randall felt rather hungry himself. In fact, he had not fed at all since awakening in Winton over twenty-four hours ago. That was not good. The healing sleep had burned all the fuel in his body, converting his dead flesh into new muscle and bone. Breakfast at the condominium had fooled his system temporarily, but the red lust would assert itself soon enough. Well, he thought, I can take care of that as soon as we arrive. I just hope I can last that long.

An elderly woman two rows ahead of them shuffled out into the aisle, hefting an animal carrier. She set the plastic box down, then opened the cage door. A small white dog emerged, eyes totally obscured by overhanging tufts of fur. It sniffed the air with a damp nose. The animal trotted down the aisle, its scruffy head turning this way and that. Coming abreast of the brothers, it stopped, growling low in its throat. "He's usually very friendly," the woman said. "Perhaps flying doesn't agree with him."

"That must be it," Randall agreed politely.

The dog yiped a couple of times, then launched an attack on Rose's boots, raking the leather with ineffectual claws. The old woman smiled warmly. "You don't mind if I leave him out a while? His carrier is so cramped, you know."

"That's fine," said Rose, bending down to scratch the animal's furry head. The woman nodded, then sat back down in her seat.

Randall looked at the dog, which sat chewing at the hem of Rose's jeans, then looked at Swan. "Care to join me?"

"Not my thing, thanks."

Unzipping his pack, Randall searched inside for the knife.

ॐ

The tunnel mouth exhaled a ghostly breeze onto the platform, and the blackened rails moaned in their trench. A dot of light appeared in the circular maw, expanding rapidly. With a blast of air the train hurtled into the station, sealing over the tracks with its sleek metallic segments. It stopped with surprising abruptness, screaming brakes murdering the momentum. A dozen sets of twin doors opened simultaneously, sliding back into the body of the beast.

Randall slid into a seat beside a large window. The glass bowed outward slightly, giving it an aquarium look. Swan sat down beside him. It had been the youngest brother's idea to take the tube from Heathrow. Knox had not even known there was a station in the airport, he had been in America so long. The humans were tired, especially Bob, who had been awake for almost two days. The train began to move, accelerating so smoothly that for a second Randall thought the white tile walls of the station were receding. They sped into the oncoming tunnel and the illusion vanished. Fluorescent lights flashed by at smaller and smaller intervals. "So," said Swan, "How did you get rid of the evidence?"

"The dog, you mean?"

"Yeah. Who else?"

"Well, you know how those vacuum toilets work."

Swan chuckled. "Spoken like a true junkie." His eyes, normally so immediate, stared off into the dimness of the car.

Amazing, Randall thought. He's actually worried about this Shannon of his. I've never been so preoccupied with a woman. I didn't think we could be. Maybe Knox was right. Maybe the rules don't apply to him. Maybe there are no rules, except in our own minds.

Daylight filled the train car, quick as the flip of a switch. A wall of concrete flew by outside the window, graffiti blurred into a chaotic dance of color. Random hunks of twisted metal jutted up from the gravel. The wall descended, then vanished. The weedy strip of land narrowed, transforming suddenly into a bridge. Ancient beams blinked by the fishbowl glass, barnacled with orange rust. Dark clouds hung low in the sky, menacing the shingle roofs of close packed houses, clotheslines strung between windows.

Droplets of water appeared on the outside surface of the window, dragged backward by the force of the wind, leaving snail streaks across the glass. It took Randall a moment to realize they were rain.

chapter sixteen

"Big, isn't it?" Rose's voice sounded absurdly loud in the otherwise silent chamber.

A barrier of velvet ropes surrounded the Rosetta Stone. The man-high slab of rock loomed above them on a dais, its dark surface the texture of coarse sandpaper. Three sets of ancient script covered the stone. Egyptian hieroglyphs, the pictographic shorthand that evolved from them as a business language, and the more familiar symbols of the Greek alphabet. Each figure had been carved half an inch deep.

"Made the damn thing to last, didn't they?" said Bob, glancing nervously towards the arched entryway.

Knox edged closer, brushing up against the barrier. "It amazes me that some experts still think its translation value is incidental. How could you look at that monster as anything other than a time capsule?"

"What's it say?" asked Swan, eyes scanning the text.

"Something about bushels of wheat and casks of wine," Knox answered. "There was a good deal of speculation when they first dug it up. One popular theory held that it was a piece of a contract."

Bob snorted. "The entire original would've been big as a highrise. You know how lawyers get."

Knox pointed at the bottom rows of script. "Notice how nearly every Greek character gets used, even the obscure ones. Granted, with a truly alphabetic system that's less of a coincidence, but it still seems too convenient." He cocked his head to one side, looking from language to language. "Reminds me of those mnemonics they teach in typing classes."

Bob nodded. "Now is the time for all good men to come to the aid of their city-state."

"Exactly." Knox continued to stare raptly at the stone.

Randall squinted at the graven figures. If he concentrated his attention on one particular character, the surrounding script seemed to blur and writhe in his peripheral vision. The pictographs disturbed him the most. Stylized eyes blinked open and shut while bird caricatures flapped in broken agony. Good thing I'm not on acid, he decided. This place is bad enough without it. "Well," he said, "fascinating as this is, we have business to attend to. Where do we go from here?"

"Upstairs," Swan answered. "Top floor."

They turned away and walked back through the archway leading to the foyer. Twin sphinxes, chipped feet and faces restored with plaster, stood guard to either side. Randall stepped carefully over the body of the man whose neck he had broken.

They had arrived at Heathrow just after eight in the morning, not exactly prime time for cruising London's nightspots. Bob was exhausted, though grimly determined to remain alert. He had been unable to sleep on the plane. Blue bruises underlined his eyes, and wrinkles veined his expensive suit. Even Rose was beginning to wilt. His incessant banter had dropped off three quarters of the way through the flight. By the time they landed, he had even given up propositioning the flight attendants.

The underground carried them to Bayswater. After a futile hour of wandering the quaint residential streets, the rain tapping insistently on the brothers' oversized umbrellas, they succeeded in finding an off-license boarding house. The weathered old landlady had been reluctant to let the five men beyond the wrought iron fence encircling her three-story home. She disliked their appearance, she disliked their accents, and she did not care the least bit if they knew it. The only thing she seemed to like was the thick wad of pound notes that Randall pulled from his coat pocket. In the end, they had been forced to pay a week's board in advance. Randall did not really mind. It was worth it just to get out from under the rain. The unavoidable closeness of so much potential pain set his nerves on edge.

They were given the entire top floor, which consisted of four closet-sized bedrooms and a slightly larger sitting area. The nearest toilet lurked under the stairs a flight below. Randall suspected the whole floor had been added to accommodate siblings grown old enough to dislike one another. The humans were in no mood to complain. Bob and Rose vanished immediately into their respective rooms and were not heard from again for some hours.

The brothers stowed their gear and settled into the sitting room. Swan paced back and forth before the storm windows, his bare feet noiseless on the hardwood floor. Seated at a rickety card table, Randall reviewed his finances. The short-notice airline tickets had drained him considerably. What remained amounted to less than a thousand pounds. If something went wrong, prevented them from putting an end to Lisel here and now, then he would have to spend some time accumulating new funds. Then again, he reflected, if something went that far wrong, money would not help.

Knox had kicked off his boots and sprawled across the ancient sofa that took up nearly a quarter of the room. Though it sat low and legless on the floor, it sagged like a swaybacked horse under his weight. The upholstery was truly hideous, broad orange and yellow stripes that must have been painfully bright a decade ago. Since there were only four rooms, the landlady must have intended one of them to sleep on it. Knox retrieved the book he had been reading on the flight, becoming quickly absorbed in its pages.

Once Randall had finished his accounting, he tried to talk to Swan. The young immortal made no response, pacing the floor with his head down as though no one had spoken. Randall let him brood. He borrowed a day-old copy of the *L.A. Times* from Knox and took it back to the card table to read. It had been a long while since he had allowed himself time to review current events. The recent increase in multiple homicides caught his attention right away. Perhaps the Brotherhood was up to something.

Randall briefly considered taking the paper into one of the empty rooms. After the cramped intimacy of the flight, he wanted to be alone. But he stayed, just in case Swan decided he wanted to talk. It proved to be a poor decision. The youngest of the brothers said nothing for the next eight hours, and he did not stop moving for an instant. Randall grew sick of the sight of him. As the shrouded sun rose higher, his restless shadow passed back and forth across the surface of the newspaper, descending the page in pendulum fractions. Rain pattered on the roof like static from a distant room, half noticed. Water poured down the windows in grey, syrupy waves.

At six o'clock Swan stopped pacing. "Guess it's late enough," he said, then sat against the arm of the sofa to tug on pair of socks. He stood up immediately, stepping into the oxblood loafers Bob had lent him. "You guys coming?"

Randall felt both relieved and annoyed. He finished the paragraph he had been reading, then folded up the newspaper.

�

Water ran down the concrete steps leading out of the Blackfriars tube station, pooling around a small drain. "It's just across the street," Swan said.

"Good." Randall watched his boots as he climbed the stairs, one gloved hand sliding along the railing. "I want to be outside in this slop as little as possible." He opened his umbrella on the landing, well before the waterfall's origin.

Knox did the same. "I moved to California to get away from weather like this," he said. "I'm beginning to think I should have stayed there."

"I thought you were a native Londoner."

"Just because I was born here doesn't mean I'm married to the place."

They reached the top of the stairs and stepped out onto the sidewalk. The roar of the rain filled Randall's ears. Water flowed through the street in a shallow river, pitted with an infinity of tiny impact craters, pouring into the gutters. It hammered at the dome of his umbrella, wind driven. The damp air stung his face like aftershave. "Over there," said Swan, pointing at a low building almost totally obscured by veils of rain. "Let's go." He jumped out into the street, against the light, sprinting forward with his umbrella held like a shield.

"Fuck." Randall leapt after him. The spray from his boots lashed against his legs, sending spikes of pain straight to the top of his head. A horn sounded to his right. Headlights transformed the mist into a twisting halo of brilliance. Rainbows flickered among the suspended droplets. Randall stumbled but did not stop, running blind in the direction he had begun. He reached the opposite shore with Knox a pair of steps behind. Swan, who stood waiting under the awning, pushed open the tall wooden door.

Heat billowed out at them, carrying the smell of wood smoke. They filed quickly inside, folding their umbrellas. A cluster of shaded lamps hung over the bar. The dark wood drank in the warm light, exhaling only a dim glow. A ring of moisture shone with unnatural clarity on the polished surface, while the couples at distant tables sat in private pools of shadow. Coals radiated orange from the stone fireplace set in the far wall of the dining area, tingeing the paneled walls with sunset flame. The door swung closed behind them, shutting off the noise of the rain.

"Nice place," said Knox. "You say whores hustle in here?"

"See for yourself." Swan strolled past the bar into the dining room, examining the patrons as he went. The elder brothers followed curiously. Nearly all of the men wore office clothes, ties pulled loose and blazers draped over the backs of chairs. They hunkered down over their drinks, talking quietly or not at all. The women looked comparatively young, most of them in their late teens. They wore the practical garb of runaways and impoverished students. Rugged slacks or jeans, a modest blouse, ugly indestructible shoes, and the mandatory giant handbag. They talked and drank with equal speed, signaling the barmen the moment their empties touched the table.

Must be new to the game, Randall thought, not desperate yet. I'd guess three quarters of them leech a mark dry and then send him home alone. Look at them. Faces scrubbed clean, makeup deftly applied. Just paying the rent until a secretarial job comes along. Christ, I bet they all have boyfriends.

"I don't see Shannon," said Swan, facing them as they neared the fire.

"Why don't you ask one of the barmen?" asked Randall. "See if she's been in lately."

"Right." The hanging lamps threw overlapping shadows across the bar top as they approached. A white-shirted man hovered behind the counter, drying the inside of a pint glass with a pristine rag. "Hey, man," Swan began, "there was an Irish girl used to hang out here. Nineteen, a little shorter than me. She had a black mohawk, blond hair growing back out, lots of earrings. You seen her around lately?"

The barman looked at Swan for a moment, taking in the spike-studded jacket and silk shirt, the two men loitering behind him. His expression went gradually sour, narrowing towards hostility. "We get a lot of folk in here," he said eventually. "I don't remember the girl you're talking about." He turned away.

"You got to be joking, man," Swan persisted. "She was in here hustling five nights a week. She had a mohawk. How could you not remember a girl with a shaved head?"

"What do you mean 'hustling?'" The barman leaned forward again, placing the dry glass carefully between them on the counter. "We run a nice, clean establishment. Nice clean gentleman, nice young ladies. Nobody hustles nobody in here. Now either order up or shove off, your choice."

Swan took a deep breath, then let it out slowly. His facial expression had not changed, but his hands clenched into fists at his sides. "Listen man, I'm just trying to find my friend. She used to come here a lot and I want to know if she's been in lately."

The barman leveled a finger at Swan's chest. "Look, you little sod, I already told you I don't remember your fucking friend. She doesn't sound like the kind of girl we let in here." The finger stabbed Swan's leather lapel. "Now shove off."

Swan's jaw clenched shut, the muscles in his neck twitching. His balled fists shrunk tighter, knuckles blanched white. After a grim pause, he forced his face to relax. "If you see my friend," he said, "tell her I'm looking for her." He spun on his heel and headed for the door. Randall hefted his umbrella and started after him.

"Fucking nutter," the barman muttered, just loud enough to be heard. Swan stopped, his back rigid. A second later he stood atop the bar, poised delicately on the toes his oxblood loafers, the empty pint glass resting between his feet. He looked down at the uncomprehending barman for an instant, then whip-kicked him in the face. The man flew backward, smashing into a shelf of bottles. He slid to the floor, blood flowing from his face onto his white shirt, shards of glass protruding from his neck and shoulders. The hospital aroma of spilled alcohol filled the room.

The force of the kick brought Swan around. He leapt nimbly from the bar, the empty pint glass undisturbed. Yanking open the tall wooden door, he walked out into the rain.

Randall watched the door as it swung closed. Knox grabbed him by his trench coat and pulled him out of the pub. The rain lashed down, searing his face like hot solder. He fumbled desperately with his umbrella, practically breaking it as he wrenched it open. Stinging droplets clung to his hair. He dried his face with the edge of his shirt, then set out after Swan. They caught up with him halfway down the block, walking away from both the pub and the tube station. Water steamed from his hands and face, but he had not yet opened his umbrella. "Was that wise?" Randall asked, shouting to be heard over the incessant drumming of the rain.

"Maybe not," Swan conceded. "But if Shannon ever shows up there she'll sure as shit know I'm back in town."

The rest of their search proved equally productive. Swan led them through every upscale bar and public house in Blackfriars and Temple, scanning the patrons and interrogating the staff. Everywhere it was the same, no sign of Shannon.

The rain continued to pour down. They trudged up and over steep sidewalks, past the unlit fronts of venerable banks and spruce office supply stores, under a darkening sky. Windblown water soaked Randall's jeans in spite of his umbrella. His boots protected his feet and ankles well enough, but wide fetters of liquid agony encircled his shins, working their way towards his knees. Below the twin circles of pain his feet went gradually numb. The hand clutching the umbrella became stiff and immobile, dead meat wrapped around the aluminum rod. Swan's searches became more brief, almost preemptory, a quick once-through to look at the customers then a word with the barman and out.

Meanwhile, the distance between pubs grew and grew until Randall had almost become accustomed to the all-encompassing howl of falling water.

By nightfall they had been inside every drinking establishment within a twenty-block radius of St. Paul's cathedral, including a short jaunt across the Southwark bridge to the other side of the Thames, without obtaining a single lead. Sunset was a pathetic thing, a slight rusty tinge to the westernmost clouds, then darkness. They took the tube from the Cannon Street rail station to Regent's Park.

Randall felt grateful for the break. He sat in the padded seat of the subway car, the cuffs of his pants pulled up past his knees, drying his legs as best he could with coarse paper towels from the station men's room. Knox sat beside him, doing the same. Swan's borrowed dress slacks were plastered to his skin from mid-thigh down, but he did not seem to notice. He merely stared out the window into the blackness of the tunnel. People in the car were looking at them with obvious amusement, but Randall could not bring himself to care. Rain continued to hammer the pavement unabated. His jeans soaked through within moments of exiting the station.

From the vestigial tail of Park Square, they made a systematic search of Camden's nightspots, starting with those catering to tourists and the after-theater crowd then moving east into the territory of London University. Closer to the college the pubs became student oriented, with cheap beer and cheap furniture, dartboards and stacks of small-press poetry magazines. It was in one of these that they heard their first news of Shannon. The barman remembered her quite clearly. She had been in with a group of girls, all of them varying degrees of punk, six or seven weeks ago. They came in before dark and stayed until closing, drinking gallons of beer, talking nonstop, and fending off suitors with curses and laughter. Some of the girls had been back since, individually and together, but Shannon had not returned.

Swan seemed more frustrated than relieved. He strode down the rain-slick pavement at a walk so brisk it was almost a run. His conversations with barmen and hostesses became less polite at each new stop, questions terse and hostile. In a pub across from the University, he knocked out a young man in a rowing club sweatshirt who tried to shoulder him aside to order a beer. Swan kicked the unconscious body in the ribs three times before Knox and Randall grabbed him. The brothers had to drag him out of two more places, once for throwing a glass at the barman and later for chasing a waitress into the ladies' room when she fled there for cover. After that he regained a modicum of control, and they investigated several more bars without incident. They found no further word of Shannon.

It was well past last call with the rain still showing no sign of letting up when Randall gently suggested they return to the boarding house. Swan's entire body tensed momentarily, muscles taut as drawn bowstrings, then went suddenly limp. He nodded mutely. The underground had shut down for the night, so they took a cab to Bayswater. Randall barely noticed the expense, glad to be out of the rain for more than five minutes at a stretch. Once back in the sitting room, he and Knox changed immediately out of their wet clothes, drying off with hand towels borrowed from the bathroom under the stairs.

Swan paced restlessly, damp cuffs flapping. After a quarter of an hour, he left to investigate a flat in Islington where some of Shannon's friends had lived. Randall watched him through the storm windows, a lone figure walking through the steady rain, all but hidden by a black umbrella.

He returned just after dawn. The humans were already awake. Bob lounged on the sofa next to Knox, back in his biker garb, reading the paper Randall had abandoned. Rose stood in the doorway of his room, dressed only in an undershirt and boxers, brushing his teeth with feral intensity. "Stopped raining," said Swan as he entered the already crowded sitting room. Though basically dry, his clothes hung limp from his thin body, designer creases totally erased.

Randall looked up from the layer of dead skin he had been peeling off his leg. "Yes," he said, glancing out the window. "I guess they finally ran out." He pulled the cuff of his jeans back down and straightened in the folding chair. "Any luck?"

Swan shook his head. "Shannon's friends have moved. The two dykes living in the apartment didn't appreciate me leaning on their buzzer at four a.m." He pulled out a chair and sat down opposite Randall. "Man, that was stupid. I don't know why I went out there."

"Hey, it was worth a try."

"One of them almost brained me with a cricket bat."

"We all have our problems."

Rose yanked the toothbrush from his mouth and darted to the window. He thrust up the inner pane, then the outer one. Leaning over the lawn, he spat out a mouthful of foamy saliva. White tendrils dripped from his chin, joining the mass below. He pulled his head in and closed the window. Both Swan and Randall stared at him, stunned mute. "What?" he asked through lathered lips.

Randall shook himself. "Nothing, I guess. Wipe your mouth." He returned his attention to Swan. "I know finding Shannon's important to you, but I'd like to do something about the museum. Once Mother's out of the way for certain, then we can hunt around as long as you want. But I don't feel safe putting it off, especially if we have to keep shaking down nightclubs. I'm sure Lisel has friends in this city."

"You don't have to convince me," Swan replied. "I want the power as much as you do."

Bob lowered the paper. "How are you planning on getting into this joint? I imagine security's pretty tight."

"It has to be do-able," said Randall. "Mother obviously gets inside somehow."

Swan pulled off his leather jacket and deposited it on an empty folding chair. "The Egyptian room is in the center of the top floor," he said. "The whole damn ceiling is one big skylight. I was thinking we could scale the building and drop down through there. That puts us in the room we want with a minimum of hassle."

"There's bound to be alarms," Bob replied. "Not to mention guards. This is one of the richest museums in the world, you know. They got shit in there that's irreplaceable."

"That's just it," said Knox, sitting forward abruptly. "The majority of the security systems will be designed to prevent theft, not entry. We don't want to steal anything, so we don't have to touch anything. All we have to do is get inside."

"But that's our problem," answered Randall. "We need a surefire way to get in, or else it won't matter what we do or don't touch."

Rose sat down on the edge of the card table, the foam flecked toothbrush still clutched in one hand. The table sagged under his weight, listing slightly towards the door. "I say we should walk into the museum while it's open for business and hide in the John when they shoo everybody out. Once they've locked up for the night we head for the top floor, taking out the guards as we go." The maniac grin shone pearly white.

Randall looked up at his friend, chin in hand. "That has got to be the single stupidest plan I have ever heard. Let's do it."

❧

"Shouldn't we tie him up?"

Randall glanced over his shoulder at the corpse. "Don't bother."

"What?" Rose stooped down to take a closer look at the limp body. "You mean he's dead?"

"Unless you believe in reincarnation."

Rose felt for a pulse, then noticed the unlikely angle of the man's neck. He jumped back. "Christ, you killed him."

Randall shrugged. "It was an accident."

An intense frown creased Rose's beard. "You always say that."

"It's usually true."

The plan had worked remarkably well at first. They had entered the museum separately, about a half an hour before closing. After meeting up in the gift shop they headed for the men's room, which turned out to be in its very own subbasement, down an obscure flight of stairs. Crouched on the toilet seat, his knees aching, Randall had felt rather juvenile. Almost as though he was a boy again, spying on the women of Springfield as they bathed and sported in the river.

They had waited a surprisingly long time. Nearly an hour went by before someone entered the restroom. Randall tensed, expecting immediate action. But whoever it was unzipped his fly and urinated into the long steel basin that lined the opposite wall. Only when he had finished did he turn to inspect the stalls. The doors swung both ways, and Swan kicked his into the man before he could open it. They bound the unconscious body with duct tape, sealed his mouth, and hefted him into a stall. The guard had been unarmed, carrying nothing more dangerous than a flashlight and ring of keys.

After such an easy victory, the man in the foyer had surprised them. Randall saw him, of course, as the five invaders topped the stairs from the basement. But he had not expected the man to charge, or the billy club clenched in his fist. Randall met him with a punch to the solar plexus which should have floored him. It didn't. They wound up grappling in the archway to the next room, struggling for control of the club. Randall shoved the man against the wall, backing off to gain some distance. The guard's head struck the arch where it began to curve, and he collapsed to the floor. Randall straightened his clothes, startled, and found himself staring into the featureless eyes of a stone sphinx.

"Well," said Swan, "No sense letting him coagulate." He crouched down beside the body, licking his teeth.

Rose kicked him in ribs. "Don't you dare," he said coldly.

Swan gave him a weary look. "What the fuck's the matter with you, five pint?" He gestured at the corpse. "The son of a bitch is already as dead as he's ever gonna get."

Rose shook his head. "Just don't."

"Let is slide," said Randall, placing a hand on Swan's shoulder. "We don't have time for this shit now, anyway."

Swan glared up at him for a hard moment. "All right." He brushed off Randall's hand and stood. "For now, but not forever."

They walked quickly across the marble floor, its squares dulled and grey like a faded game board. A wide glass cylinder stood on a pedestal in the center of the foyer, a foot-deep layer of coins glinting from within. As they passed, Knox pulled some change from his pocket and dropped it into the donation slot. "Karma," he said to no one in particular.

Broad stairs of the same scuffed marble led up one flight, then split at the landing. Swan led them up the left fork, down the railed balcony, and up to a narrow arch. The light dimmed beyond. Curious shadows fell across hardwood floor. Swan strode through without hesitation. Rose followed, then jumped back with a yelp. A hulking figure stood just inside the doorway, thick arms and heavy shoulders scarcely visible in the gloom. Swan turned at the noise, then grinned. He stepped up to the tall, motionless figure and rapped it on the chest. Hollow metal rang. "Nervous, five pint?"

Rose put a hand to his heart, fingers splayed. *"Moi?"* He batted his lashes. Bob chuckled, and ushered him into the room.

Randall peered at the suit of armor. When his eyes adjusted he could see the lion of Tudor England, still faintly gilded on the breastplate. A fine mesh of chain links joined each plate to the next, protecting every joint. The gloves, woven metal with studded knuckles, appeared to be fully flexible. An iron crown sat atop the helm. Randall stared into the eye sockets of the lowered visor. Impenetrable darkness stared back.

Weapons lined the hallway. Swords of every length hung from pegs, blades downward. A king's mace, a plain steel version of the royal scepter, rested on a pillow of crushed velvet in a display case all its own. Pole axes stood at attention along the wall. A collection of ornamental rods and double-pronged sword breakers dangled from what could only be a coat rack, counterbalancing a five-chained flail. A second suit of armor lurked at the opposite door, a ragged puncture folding the metal of the breastplate inward just below the shoulder.

The hall opened out into a larger chamber. Battered shields and ragged standards hung grouped like paintings in a gallery. A single flight of stairs led up to a surprisingly large landing, a mid-level loft that ran the entire length of the room before the second stairway. A dozen display cases lined the narrow walk, entirely devoted to baroque snuffboxes and ladies' hand mirrors. The five men mounted the second set of stairs. Randall looked down on the room from the balcony above, the battle flags draped flush with the wall, tapestries of mutilated glory. A queer serenity, like the approach of certain death, settled over him.

They confronted three sets of open doors, heavy wood with large brass hinges. Swan chose the middle passage. A short, empty hall led them to spacious archway. Twin statues of Anubis leered at them from either side, cruel jackal heads atop muscular human bodies. "This is it," said Swan, stopping short.

"Abandon all hope ye who enter here," Rose muttered.

They advanced into the tomb. Sarcophagi lined the walls, elbow to elbow, celestial travelers awaiting passage down the river and into the land beyond. Withered corpses slept curled upon the floor, winding cloth pulled tight about them, some without the comfort of a coffin. Pinprick stars beamed down through the immense central skylight, destinations on the map of Heaven. "Which one is it?" Randall asked, studying the faces of cold silver.

Swan raised his arms, encompassing the assembled dead. "Guess," he said, his own face a mask. Only three or four of the dozens looked at all female. Remembering the tale of the evil black vibe, Randall selected the most sinister.

The sarcophagus stood seven feet tall, golden skin swathed in robes of indigo. One breast hung bare, an Eye of Osirus centered on the tiny silver nipple. A asp reared from her headdress, fangs revealed, its metallic hood fanned. The face beneath looked smooth and natural, lips small yet full, with the faintest suggestion of a smile. Flat silver eyes reflected nothing at all. Randall advanced towards the sarcophagus without feeling. Without fear. Without hate. Without triumph. He wondered how Swan could have sensed anything from it, even with hallucinogenic aid. At the same time, he had no doubt that his brother had been right. "This one," he said, standing before the gilded apparition.

Knox brushed past him, staring with a hand at his chin. "The sarcophagus of a court musician," he began without preamble. "Unearthed and brought to London in 1886, the year Robert Louis Stevenson wrote *Jekyll and Hyde*. Of the half dozen families who owned it over the next two years, three were decimated by fire, two by disease, and the last by a plague of accidents and misadventures. The museum purchased it, quite cheaply, in 1888, right around the time of the Whitechapel murders. One of men who lugged it up here broke his foot when it fell. The other went mad quite suddenly and died in an asylum. It's been here ever since."

"No fuckin' kidding," said Swan. He slipped a pry-bar from his jacket. "Let's crack her open."

"Hold it a second," said Bob, striding forward. "Shouldn't we check for alarms or something?"

"Right," Knox agreed. "There has to be more than a pair of security guards in this place. How do we know it's safe to touch that thing?"

"We don't." Randall reached and grasped both sides of the lid, then pulled. The entire front of the sarcophagus came loose with a screech of metal, suddenly heavy in his hands. He tightened his grip, arms tensing, the flat silver eyes an inch from his face. Staggering backward, he squatted down and lowered the lid carefully to the floor. He let it drop the last little bit to avoid crushing his fingers. The wooden floor vibrated with a dull thud. Breathing heavily, he turned back to the exposed interior. His face froze.

A mummified body rested inside, tiny within the wooden shell. Clean strips of linen wound meticulously about her limbs, her waist and bosom. Only the head was exposed. Six silver loops pierced the rim of her left ear. Three silver studs decorated the right. Blond stubble covered her head, except for the blue-black coxcomb sticking up from the center in brushed spikes. Her eyes were gone. Trails of blood oozed from the shriveled gouges, red tears long dry.

Rose vomited where he stood, retching through his fingers. He doubled over, convulsing until his stomach had emptied. "Well," he said, still coughing bile, "at least she didn't get her head cut off."

Without even looking at him, Swan hit Rose a backhanded blow that sent him sprawling.

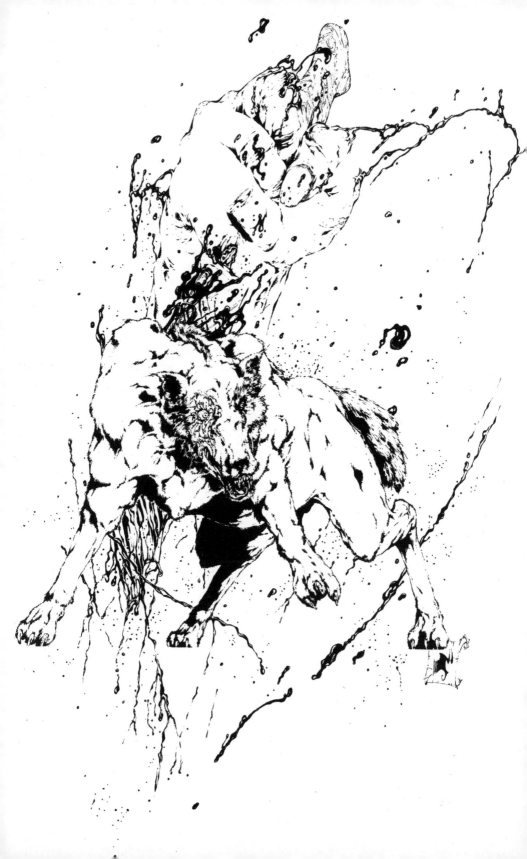

chapter seventeen

"That bitch," Swan said, soft and uninflected. He reached a hand inside the sarcophagus to caress Shannon's ashen cheek, the blond stubble of her hair. "I'll kill her."

"I'm sorry," Knox said, "but we've got to get out of here." He pointed to a spot on Swan's shoulder. A red circle of light no larger than a dime played across the leather sleeve. "Silent alarm." Swan let his hand fall.

"Shit," Randall swore, glancing down the length of the wall. A small knob the approximate shape of a doorbell glowed faintly between a pair of coffins, parallel with the invisible beam.

Knox tugged gently on Swan's arm until he lowered his gaze from Shannon's face. "Leave her. We have to go." Swan swallowed hard, then let the eldest brother lead him away. Knox fired a harsh glance and Randall. "Pick up your friend and move."

Randall helped Bob hoist Rose from the floor. A crimson welt had already appeared, starting under one eye and spreading up the bridge of his nose. Blood leaked from both nostrils, and his legs gave way when they stood him up. He staggered, arms flapping, then found his balance. They retreated through the archway with the urgent speed of soldiers in defeat. The twin statues of Anubis leered at them as they passed.

Knox and Swan took the lead, retracing their path at a run. Randall chased after them, his mind numb. She knew we were coming, he thought. She knew. A glance over his shoulder showed the humans falling behind. Rose ran with a heavy, uneven limp. Bob held back, a pace behind him.

They sprinted down to the second floor, past the snuffboxes and the battle flags, through the hall of weapons. The suits of armor watched their flight with empty eyes. They bunched together at the main balcony. Randall nearly pitched over the railing and down to the marble floor of the foyer as he dodged Knox's abruptly motionless form. He pulled away from the view with a wrench of vertigo. They rounded the railing and descended the main stairs. The forks merged at the landing.

A guard stood at the foot of the stairs, legs akimbo, a knight-stick clutched in both hands. "Halt!" he yelled, his voice firm despite his nervously darting eyes. Randall stumbled to a stop in the middle of the last flight of stairs. He could just see the corpse of the second guard laying in the archway to the left. Not forty yards away, the deep blue sky of night shone through the glass doors of the main entrance. The police, he thought, are on their way.

Swan hit the guard in a blur. He pulled the man off the ground by his shirtfront, then slammed him down into the donation box. The glass exploded. Coins sprayed outward in a wave, spilling across the marble floor with an insect clatter. Grinning like a death mask, Swan leapt up onto the pedestal. He jumped up and down on the man's chest, growling to himself. The dangling arms jerked with each successive blow.

"God damn you!" Rose shouted, trotting bandy-legged down the stairs. "Stop!" He limped over the carpet of scattered coins, grabbing Swan by the hem of his spiked jacket. Randall did not even see the kick land. Rose skidded into the stairs, doubled up around his stomach. He did not get up.

With a final howl, Swan vaulted off the body and sped towards the main entrance. Pivoting gracefully, he sent the flat of his heel hammering into the armored brass lock. The doors flew open. Alarm bells rang. He vanished into the darkness.

"Help me," said Bob, struggling to lift Rose's inert form. Randall descended the remaining stairs. He hunched down and draped one lifeless arm over his shoulders. Knox grabbed the feet. They trundled him across the grey marble floor, broken glass and dead coins scraping beneath their feet, the alarm bells vibrating their skulls.

They got him out the front door. Swan was nowhere to be seen. They carried Rose down the concrete steps and into the vacant courtyard. "Don't stop," Knox cautioned, guiding them towards the underground station at the far corner.

"I won't," Randall answered.

�

Rose came to on the train. Knox probed his chest for fractured ribs while Bob and Randall crowded in on either side. "Nothing broken," Knox said with relief. "Can you breathe okay?"

"Yeah, sure." Rose inhaled deeply. "No problem." He straightened in the molded plastic seat. "I think I need beer."

"Later." Knox held up a finger. "Follow this with both eyes." He moved the hand from side to side, then up and down. "Very good. How's your head feel? Any obvious dents?"

"No new ones." Rose grinned a minor, lopsided version of his classic grin. "Am I free to go now, Officer Friendly?"

"Let me just have a look at that leg." Knox crouched down between seats and pulled off Rose's boot. Two middle-aged women sitting across the aisle stared as though watching television.

Rose turned his attention to the others. "So what do we do now, Captain?"

Randall seated himself in the chair opposite. "Good question." He glanced at his hands, obscurely startled to find them clean. "I've no idea what's going on here anymore. Maybe I never did. The smart move would be to clear out of London immediately, forget about Mother, try and lose ourselves somewhere."

"That's not what I asked."

The ghost of a smile twitched Randall's lips. "I'd like to stay, of course. Lisel has to be in the sleep. If we can find her, we can finish her.

Realistically, I suppose she could be hidden anywhere in the world by now. But I have the feeling she's here."

"Could be," said Bob, chewing his lower lip thoughtfully. "When Rose shot her... How long do you figure she could keep going after a thing like that?"

"Not long," Randall replied. "A head shot would've put me under on the spot. She couldn't have stayed on her feet for more than a few minutes, I imagine."

"That means she had help getting away," Bob concluded, "some sort of automatic contingency plan."

"Wait," said Randall. "I see where you're headed. Whatever her fallback plan was, she wouldn't have had time to alter it too drastically before she came after us in Santa Cruz. Besides, she's arrogant. She was counting on destroying us. When Rose nailed her, I'll bet her people took her straight back to London, if not to the British Museum."

"Right," said Bob. "She's here. All we have do is guess where."

"On the other hand," Rose interjected, "I hear Amsterdam is lovely this time of year." Knox held his knee with one hand, grasped the ankle with the other, and slowly levered the leg straight. Rose stiffened. "You found it," he said, his voice an octave higher.

Knox let the leg relax. "Pulled your Achilles tendon." He stood, handing Rose his boot. "Should heal on its own if you don't traumatize it any further. Soak it in hot water as often as you can manage. And if you're doing anything strenuous..."

"Favor the other leg," Rose finished. "Drink plenty of liquids, get lots of bed rest, always wear a condom, and cover my mouth when I cough." He pulled on his boot. "Tell me, Knox, have you ever been a camp counselor?"

"No. But I was an army medic for a while." He sat down next to Randall. "Penance."

Light flashed into the car. The white tiles of the station flew by the window. Inertia pulled them forward while the train braked, then jerked them back into their seats when it stopped. The pneumatic doors hissed open. The women across the aisle stood abruptly and left the car. A fat man with a cello case took their seats. "Where are we, anyway?" Rose asked, peering out the window at the red station signs.

"We're on the Circle Line," Knox answered. "Been around twice now." The doors hissed closed, and the train began to accelerate. "Bayswater's coming up in a couple of stops, if we want to go back to the boarding house."

Bob arched an eyebrow. "Do we?" The external light vanished as the train reentered the tunnel.

"If only to pick up our stuff," Randall answered. "It might be a good idea to move, though."

"What about Swan?" Knox asked.

"Swan can find us if he really wants to."

"That's what I'm afraid of," Rose muttered.

Randall leaned forward in his seat. "Don't worry about him," he said earnestly. "If Swan shows himself, I'll personally teach him some manners."

"If I'd had my pistol tonight, I would have put a bullet in him for what he did to that guard."

"I know. I'm sorry."

The train sped on through the featureless darkness. After a time Rose turned to Bob, who sat at his side. "How does my face look?" he asked. "I mean, is it bad?"

Bob studied him for a moment. "The bruising should fade. Your nose is a little off center, though."

"Really?" Rose touched his face with tentative fingers, wincing at the light contact. "Do you think you could fix it?"

"Yeah, but it'll hurt like a son of a bitch."

"Oh." Rose scratched at his beard for a moment, considering. "Okay," he said at length. "Go ahead and do it."

Bob pulled a bandana out of his back pocket. He wrapped it around his hand, then gently gripped the bridge of Rose's nose between his shrouded thumb and forefinger. "Now remember," he said, "you asked me to do this."

After the second scream, the man with the cello glared at them in annoyance.

⅋

It had been dark for many hours by the time they returned to Bayswater, and the landlady made a point of locking the door at sunset.

Randall rang the bell. No sound came from within the house, no stirring of movement. Randall put an eye to one pane of the fan-shaped window. The formal entry hall was dark and empty. After a moment, he rang the bell again. Silence.

"You don't suppose," Knox began, "that Swan got here ahead of us and did something?"

"Maybe." Randall suppressed a shudder. "I think we'd better find out." He tried the door. It opened easily. They stepped cautiously inside. Randall locked the door behind them.

Rose found the switch and turned on the light. A narrow table of beveled teak lined one side of the hall, its back flush with the wall while the other edges curved sinuously. Neat stacks of mail sat to one side. A crystal bowl rested on a doily in the center, two burgundy blooms floating in clear water. Coats and jackets hung from pegs on the opposite wall. The stems of several umbrellas protruded from a giant World War II era shell casing parked beside the mat. "Somebody must be home," said Bob. Rose glanced from the umbrellas to the coats, but did not reply.

A brief open area beyond the hall led to the kitchen on the left and the front parlor on the right. Spiral stairs of wrought iron wound up through ceiling. Rows of musty, leather-bound books filled the shelves set into the far wall, giving off the smell of rain. Randall advanced hesitantly. The kitchen was utterly black, lightless and noiseless as interstellar space. But a pale glow illuminated the parlor, flickering like a spent candle. "This way," he said, and moved inside.

Dust floated in the air, thick as mist, swirling on unseen currents. Straight-backed chairs cast prison-bar shadows. An oval couch with wooden arms and a framed backrest hunched down before a low tea table, its sea blue upholstery mapped with continents of mildew. A modern space lamp stood in one corner, dead and dark. Yellowed lace shrouded the furniture, the webs of intricate spiders. Exotic rugs covered the floor in overlapping layers.

A silver tea service sat on a kitchen cart. The wavering light flowed and rippled over the mirrored surfaces. Randall stared, feeling himself drawn inward. He imagined brutal spirits, millennia old, trapped within the beaten metal, calling for release.

"Randall." He flinched at the sound. Knox stood beside him. "Over there." The strange light emanated from the next room, nebulous grey tendrils creeping through the airborne dust. The door itself, opened partway into the parlor, blocked their view of its source.

Randall motioned for the humans. They fell in behind him. As a group, they circled around the desolate furniture. Reaching the far door, Randall pulled it open. Pale light trembled upon his face. The death stench, blood and urine, washed over him.

The landlady lay face down on the floor, arms thrown forward. A large portion of her neck had been torn away. Red, wet strings of flesh dangled from the edges of the wound. Exposed vertebrae gleamed clean and white. Blood soaked her housecoat, streaked her outstretched hands. A dark stain obliterated the pattern of the Oriental rug beneath her. Fuzzy slippers covered her feet, painted toenails protruding from the open fronts.

A portable television rested on the circular seat of an antique piano stool, antennae extended. On the screen, a black and white movie played. Humphrey Bogart, middle-aged and sporting a tuxedo, argued with young Audrey Hepburn. Their lips moved soundlessly. Large blue letters floated in the bottom corner of the image. *MUTE.* The flickering light fell across the landlady's body, turning her pooled blood from red to black at random intervals.

A large man sat in the rocking chair directly across from the TV set, slouched down and sprawled out, the remote control on one knee. Dark hair hung to his shoulders in tangles. Blood smeared his face and hands, matted the dense curls on his bare chest. A roll of fat spilled over the top of his designer jeans. He turned to look at them, his head swiveling lazily. Scars etched the right side of his face, interwoven lines of puckered skin running from forehead to jaw. Though the pull of the wounds distorted the shape of the socket, the eye within was whole. The man grinned. "About time you showed up," he said in a loud baritone. "I was beginning to wonder if maybe you boys got yourselves lost."

Randall stood frozen in the doorway. Knox stumbled into his shoulder. The eldest brother's eyes went wide. "Jesus Christ," he breathed.

"Not even close," Jim drawled. He slumped back against the rocker. "You believe that?" he demanded, addressing Bogart and Hepburn. "I come all this way. I wait here all fucking night. And then they don't even remember who I am." He pulled a crystal decanter of brandy from the floor beside him, put it to his lips and tilted it back. The amber liquid drained into him. He set bottle on his lap and belched. "Shit. What fucking ingratitude."

"We remember you, Jim," said Randall. "We remember you quite well." He made a quick scan of the room. Shelves and cupboards lined the walls, jammed with books and photo albums, faded cigar boxes. There were no windows and no other doors. Randall advanced into the room until he stood above the landlady's body, the soles of his boots in her blood. The others followed him in, blocking the exit. "Was there something you wanted to see us about?"

Jim frowned at the television. He gestured with the remote, flicking his wrist as though cracking a buggy whip. The scene changed abruptly to color, a luxury car speeding along a mountain road. He flicked the remote again. A newscaster read silently at his desk. "Withered bitch doesn't even have cable," he complained. He gave them a disinterested glance. "You guys watch much TV?" he asked. "I fucking love cable. That cartoon channel... I could watch Roger Ramjet for-fucking-ever. Best thing they ever invented, besides whiskey and women." He scratched his stomach with bloody fingers. "Guess nobody invented women. If one guy had come up with the idea, they'd of shot him before it caught on."

"Don't be a prick," said Randall. His hardwood knife was in its boot sheath, an easy motion away. "You must have something on your mind, to go to all this trouble. Why don't you spill it?"

"Right," said Jim. "Down to business." He plucked up the decanter of brandy, emptied it with two huge swallows, then let it drop. It bounced harmlessly on the rug, rolling to a stop just short of the blood. Jim stretched his legs and put one bare foot up on the piano stool, blocking the screen. His nails were thick and yellow, the ends ragged. He pushed with his foot, rocking the stool backward. The television slid off and smashed on the floor, throwing sparks. Jim flung the remote after it. "Message from your mother," he said. "Either you lay off or you're gonna die. Something like that. She put it better, but I can't fucking remember."

"Is that so?" Randall's vision adjusted rapidly to the dimness. He risked a glance at his friends. Knox and Rose flanked him. His brother wore an impassive face, devoid of expression. Randall knew that face, knew that it hid a smoldering wrath. Rose looked more obviously enraged. The welt under his eye had turned purple. His teeth ground together. He's seen too many corpses tonight, Randall thought. Just don't do anything stupid. We may need that pissed off energy before this is over. Bad Bob stood in the doorway, alert but calm. Randall snapped his attention back to Jim. "How is Mother, anyway?"

"She's been better." Jim kicked the stool down onto the remains of the TV.

"Where is she?"

Jim looked at Randall, his grin widening. Pieces of raw, red meat clung to his yellow teeth. "You guys are hopeless. First you don't know who I am. Now you don't know where she is. Shit. Bet you couldn't find your own bungholes without a map."

"Tell us where she is," said Randall, "or you're never leaving this room."

Jim laughed hugely, doubled over and shaking, his raucous baritone echoing off the walls. He pounded one fist against the arm of the rocking chair. "That's a good one," he said, barely able to speak. He sniffed, then wiped away tears, leaving crimson streaks trailing from the corners of his eyes. "You guys are a hoot, I swear."

Randall raised his right foot and jerked the hardwood knife from its sheath. "Tell us."

Jim stood up from the rocking chair, a head taller than any of them. He shrugged his shoulders, loosening them like a prizefighter. "Just try it," he drawled. "You pussies couldn't bruise ripe peaches."

"Son of a bitch," said Knox. He leapt forward, a fist already swinging. Jim grabbed his arm and flung him to one side. Knox slammed into the wall, demolishing a shelf. Books crashed to the floor. A fishbowl shattered, scattering proof of purchase seals.

Jim spun back around, but Randall was already there. Their eyes met for the briefest of instants. Lunging forward, Randall thrust the hardwood blade into Jim's hairy stomach. Black blood sprayed from the puncture. Jim's face crumpled. He gave an animal grunt of pain. Randall jerked the knife upward, tearing towards the lungs. With an incoherent roar, Jim grabbed him by the neck and shoved him backward. The room spun. Randall lost his grip on the knife. His back hit something sharp, driving the air from his chest. His vision swam.

He leapt up the moment his balance returned. Knox crouched in the far corner of the room, poised to spring. Both the humans were down. Rose sprawled across the old woman's body. Bob sat against the doorjamb, holding his head. Jim was gone.

"Shit!" Randall dashed out the door without waiting to see who followed. The parlor was empty, its atmosphere of dust invisible now that the flickering light had been extinguished. He skirted the furniture, then skidded to halt in the entry hall. Red footprints, widely spaced, stained the tile floor. He chased them up the spiral staircase.

"Wait!" Rose rushed into the hall, trailed by the others. The old woman's blood smeared his t-shirt and jeans. "Let's check the kitchen. See if there's anything we can use as weapons."

"No time," called Randall, already halfway up the steps. "We can't let this motherfucker get away."

"If he'd wanted to escape, he would have gone for the door." Rose reasoned. "He's probably waiting at the head of the stairs, ready to jump on the first idiot who runs through."

Randall paused, looking up at the hole in the ceiling. He could see nothing in the blackness beyond, but the death stench stung his nostrils. "You may have a point," he conceded.

There was no light switch on the kitchen wall. They fumbled in the dark, groping further and further into the room, until the dangling cord brushed against Randall's face. He pulled it. The naked bulb blinded them for a moment.

The daisy print wallpaper had begun to peel away near the ceiling. Several generations worth of burn marks and knife scars marred the sun yellow counter tops. An impressive collection of copper-bottom pots and cast-iron skillets hung from an array of hooks. A variety of knives clung to a magnetic rack above the stove. "Nice," said Bob, hefting a tarnished meat cleaver. He passed Rose a carving knife. "Which would you prefer, Knox? Slices or fillets?"

"I'll take this." He pulled a large, flat-headed tenderizer from a drawer. "Thanks all the same."

Randall accepted a blade. He noticed a flashlight recharging in an outlet and took that too.

They mounted the staircase, Randall in the lead, aiming the flashlight beam into the darkened hole. Nothing threatening appeared, only empty hallway and the iron lattice of the guardrail. He advanced cautiously, crouching down as he neared the ceiling and searching in all directions. Nothing. Standing up, he quickly topped the stairs.

Randall played the flashlight along the walls, hunting for the switch. He found it, then saw the fan-shaped stain spattering the doors of the linen cupboard. Fingers numb, he flipped on the light.

Maimed bodies filled the far end of the hall. A blond youth in hiking gear sat dead beneath the cupboard. His head hung to one side. Three parallel slashes opened up his neck, the wounds pulled apart like red gills. Further on, a half-naked man lay face down on his own intestines. The rubbery coils spread out from his abdomen in a rough circle, as though he had swallowed a live grenade. Deep gouges covered his back. A woman sprawled across his legs, her grey jogging suit in tatters. Blood soaked her hair, so that it was impossible to tell what color it had been. There was nothing left of her face. Another pair of bodies lay tangled at the foot of the stairs leading to the top floor. Jim's red footprints disappeared into the carnage.

Randall inhaled the heavy musk of spilled blood. Though his stomach twisted in revulsion, part of him acknowledged the power of the scene before him. I have never accepted what I have become, he thought. Not completely, not with abandon. He looked at the woman without a face. The ravaged mass of tissue gleamed wetly in the harsh light. This is what it looks like, Randall told himself. This is total surrender.

"Oh my God," said Rose, cresting the stairs behind him. He wobbled, stunned, then leaned against the wall for support. "Oh my God," he repeated.

Bob stared grimly at the litter of corpses, his eyes like stones. "This bastard needs to die," he said quietly.

"Not until he tells us where Lisel is," Randall warned. "After that, you can kill him all you want." The hallway ran the length of the second floor, with guest bedrooms to either side. One door in the midst of the slaughter stood open. "In there," said Randall.

Knox frowned. "That's the obvious choice, you realize."

"Jim's an obvious sort of guy." Holding his kitchen knife at the ready, Randall led them forward. He stepped over the legs of the boy with the slit neck, keeping his eyes on the doors. The blood-soaked carpet squelched under his boots. He stopped just short of the next two bodies. The man's intestines spilled across the entire width of the hall. Gritting his teeth, Randall placed one foot firmly in the tangle. He shifted his weight, and felt the fleshy tubing give. The smell of dung steamed up at him. He leapt quickly to firmer footing, only to find himself staring down at the faceless woman. Bile rose in his throat.

"I don't think I can do that," said Rose. He looked steadily at the corpses, his face pale with horror.

"That's okay," said Randall. "You and Bob stay there, cover that end of the hall. Make sure he doesn't escape downstairs if he manages to get past us."

The two humans backed off slightly. Knox walked straight over the mass of entrails without so much as looking at them. "Ready?"

"Always." Weapons up, they entered the guest room.

A naked woman lay upon the double bed, completely savaged. Ragged cuts covered her limbs, her stomach and breasts, her face. Her entire body was sticky with blood. Vacant eyes swung towards them as they entered, and one hand moved a little.

"She's alive." Knox dropped his tenderizer and rushed to the bed. He snatched up the woman's wrist, feeling her pulse.

Randall aimed the flashlight into the darkened corners of the room. He stepped on something uneven. Glancing down, he saw his hardwood knife resting on the floor. Something snarled in the blackness. Randall whipped up the flashlight just in time to see the luminous blue eyes, the muzzle full of jagged fangs. Then the terrible weight fell upon him.

The monster's jaws snapped at his face. Randall kept one arm up as a guard. With the other he stabbed at the shaggy chest, jabbing the kitchen knife into unresisting flesh over and over again. The beast did not seem to care. Its front paws tore at Randall's chest while its hind claws raked his legs. The creature spit and snarled, desperate to get around the warding arm, ripping at its prone victim all the while. A thick scar ran down one side of the canine face, hairless and white, puckering the socket of one bright eye.

Randall shifted his attack, thrusting his knife at the creature's head. He nicked the muzzle, then thrust again. The blade bit into the soft animal nose. Hot fluid spurted onto Randall's face. The beast yelped. With a vicious snap, the creature caught Randall's knife hand in its teeth.

The jaws clamped down, razor fangs biting deep. Randall hissed in pain. The creature jerked his arm from side to side, nearly wrenching it from the socket. Randall tried to grab the knife with his free hand, but dropped it to the floor. Above him, the blue eyes flashed.

A pair of nondescript workman's boots appeared to either side of Randall's head. The butt of a brass table-lamp crashed down on the creature's skull, not once, but four times in quick succession. Randall looked upward. Knox stood over him, his face livid with rage, his lips pulled back in a fearful snarl. He raised the lamp over his shoulder, and clubbed the beast again.

The creature stared stupidly for a moment, its restless claws now still. All at once it tensed. Digging into Randall's body for traction, the beast sprang straight at Knox. The lamp hit the floor, the light bulb bursting with a pop.

Randall surged upright. Knox lay across the double bed, his limbs in a hopeless tangle. The naked woman huddled at one corner of the mattress, as far away from him as possible.

With a bark, the creature sprang from the shadow of the bed. Randall ducked to one side. But instead of tackling him, the beast bolted through the open door. "Jesus Christ!" Bob shouted, down the hall. Someone screamed. Randall snatched his hardwood knife from the floor and ran out.

The gigantic wolf stood atop Rose, claws tearing, its jaws working at one sleeve of his leather jacket. Bad Bob chopped at the bristling back with his cleaver. Rose screamed again, beating futilely at the creature's head with an empty fist.

Randall sprinted across the litter of corpses without seeing them, hatred burning in his lungs. He knocked Bob aside. Curling one hand into the wolf's tangled mane, he drove the hardwood blade straight through one blazing blue eye.

The creature stiffened, shuddered. Its legs folded, and it fell to one side.

Randall pulled out the knife. The animal twitched. Thick fluid smeared the blade to the handle. The white scar puckered the socket around the punctured eye. His fury receded, leaving only a cold hollow.

chapter **eighteen**

"Are you sure this is absolutely necessary?"

Pinching his nose, Randall poured paint thinner onto the corpses in the hall. "No," he replied. "But I'd just as soon not leave behind a half dozen potential flesh-eating monsters with valid international passports." He emptied the last of the can onto the hiker with the slashed neck. "Besides, it's not as if any of these poor bastards is eligible for an open casket."

"True enough." Rose coughed painfully, then backed away from the rising fumes. "What about the woman? You going to throw her on the fire too?"

Randall tossed the can in among the bodies. The dregs dripped onto the carpet, dissolving tiny patches of dried blood. "Wasn't planning on it. I may be a pragmatist, but I'm not a murderer."

"That's a matter of opinion."

Randall winced. "Believe it or not, Renfield, there's a difference between killing and murder." He tapped his temple. "Up here. You can kill a man and still be sane. In war. In self-defense. Out of some higher necessity. What Jim did to these people... it's beyond purpose, psychotic. I could never do anything like this."

"Sure." Rose gave him a bitter look. "Compared to Jim, you're the God damn flying nun. So what? I know what you are, what you can do. Don't think I've forgotten Santa Cruz. I saw you, drenched in that girl's blood."

"Lisa Robinson was a mistake," Randall said firmly. "I didn't mean to kill her. I lost my control. It..." He stopped speaking abruptly. "Point taken." He looked beyond Rose to the body of the wolf. "Hand me that kerosene, would you? I want to make sure there's nothing left of this son of a bitch but cinders."

He uncapped the cylindrical canister and began dowsing the monstrous corpse. The transparent oil soaked into the matted fur, darkening it from grey to black. Randall up-ended the container over the creature's head. "Take it easy," said Rose. "If that's really Jim, the alcohol in his bloodstream should keep him burning for hours."

"Sorry." Randall poured a wide line of kerosene from the wolf to its victims, then doubled back to the spiral stairs. "You better go down ahead of me."

"Yeah." Walking stiffly, his clothes torn and stained, Rose descended the stairs.

Randall stood on the top step for a moment, looking at the wolf. It stared back, one eyed, teeth bared in a final silent snarl. Randall pulled a box of kitchen matches from a trench coat pocket, jogged one out, and struck it. Watching the flame burn toward his fingers, he tried to think of something appropriate to say. Nothing came to mind. "Fuck it." He dropped the match to the floor. The kerosene exploded. Blue flame filled the hall from floor to ceiling. It vanished an instant later, leaving splashes of fire clinging to the walls. The bodies burned fiercely, giving off a sweet black smoke. The wolf's hoary coat curled into ash. "See you in hell, Jimbo."

Knox and Rose crouched at the foot of the stairs, stuffing clothes into a canvas bag. Bob leaned against the front door, toying with the remains of a smoke detector. The woman they had found sat on the floor, a sweatshirt and slacks jammed onto her body, hands clutching her face. Blood had already begun to soak through her new clothing in places.

"You take care of the landlady?" Randall asked.

"Burning merrily," Knox assured him.

"Good. I got a little too enthusiastic with the paint thinner upstairs. We'd better split before the ceiling caves in on us." He paused at the foot of the stairs. "Bob, you find any aerosol for me?"

"Nothing industrial." He tossed Randall a can of butter flavored cooking spray. "That do?"

"Guess so." Randall checked the can to make sure it had a flammability warning. "You guys take off. I'll meet you outside." Knox stood, slinging the canvas bag over his shoulder. Rose pulled the catatonic woman to her feet and led her to the door.

When they had gone, Randall headed for the kitchen. He set the remaining kerosene atop the stove, then dug into his pockets for a match. Cranking the gas up high, he lit the oven. Flame leapt out at him, snuffing the match and singeing his fingers. He rolled the can of cooking spray onto the bottom rack, slammed the oven door, and fled.

The others stood waiting for him at the corner. He ran past them, eyes rolled back in mock fright. They rushed to catch up, laughing a little. Several blocks away they heard a muffled bang.

"Slow down," said Knox. "When the fire brigade shows up, we don't want to be spotted running from the scene."

Rose fell behind, breathing raggedly. Some of his slashes had begun to bleed again. The woman clung heavily to his arm, her pale hands gripping his sleeve. Randall pried her away as gently as he could, handing her off to Bob. His own wounds ached terribly. The scratches on his chest were minor, purely superficial. But at least two tendons in each leg had been severed. Randall could feel them, the frayed ends pulled back towards their anchor points like snapped rubber bands. Combined with the gross muscular damage, they made walking rather difficult. He kept up, but he would pay for it later. The sleep called to him, a cold longing in his bones.

"I want out," said Rose.

Randall looked at his friend with tired puzzlement. "What?"

"I want out of this," he repeated. "When you've taken care of Lisel, I'm gone, history." His eyes looked clear and somber above the scarlet welt, the anger and the humor washed out of them, perhaps forever.

Blood covered his clothes, his own and that of others. "I've had enough of this shit. I quit."

"It's more complicated than that," Randall told him. "Even if we do take care of Mother, you're going to be needing our help for a while. Our protection."

Rose shook his head. "I can handle Swan, if that's what you're worried about. I shoot straight, and I'm a light sleeper."

"That's not what I meant." Randall slowed his step until the others were out of earshot. "How much do you know about werewolves?"

Rose stared at him for a moment, obviously puzzled. "Not a lot," he said at last. "To tell the truth, I was expecting Jim to mutate into Warren Zevon and whisper 'Rosebud.' Or something like that."

"No such luck," said Randall. "Just goes to show, we can't really be sure what we're dealing with. According to folklore, anyone bitten by a werewolf is infected. The victims it kills either stay dead or don't, depending on whose mythology you buy. But most of the variations agree anyone who survives the attack starts sprouting palm hair by the next full moon. You see what I'm driving at?"

Wide eyed, Rose pushed up the sleeve of his leather jacket. Twin rows of puncture wounds, not particularly deep, ran diagonally across his arm. "Could just be bruising," he said, unconvinced.

"Sure. And the legends could be wrong. Lots of them are." Randall cast about for a moment then pointed out the moon, which was just past new. "On the other hand, you might need a flea collar two weeks from now. At any rate, you can see why I want you to stick around."

"And here I thought you were captivated by my sparkling personality." Rose considered the wounds on his arm, then pulled his sleeve back down. "Jesus. What a thing to spring on a person. Couldn't you have told me in some upscale restaurant, lingering over coffee? 'Great meal. I particularly enjoyed the squid pâté. By the way, Rose, you're a werewolf. Pass the Sweet and Low.' I think I would have taken it better that way."

"There's nothing definite about this," Randall said, trying to sound reassuring. "For all we know there may be some natural control on the lycanthrope population, just as there is with my people. If it spreads as easily as the legends say, why isn't the world overrun by now?"

"Maybe it has been," Rose speculated. "Maybe they're all in disguise. As lawyers." He scratched at his beard. "It would certainly explain a few things. Hey, what about the woman? What about you?"

"I'm not too worried about myself," Randall answered. "I'm immune to disease. Haven't had so much as a cold since my elevation. Besides, nothing seems to have happened to Swan, and he got bitten weeks ago." He gestured at the woman, who trailed behind Bob like a boat in tow. "I'm more concerned about her. If anybody's going to catch it, she will. I'd like to keep an eye on her, but I don't think we can handle the excess baggage right now. And it's only a matter of time before somebody starts searching for her. I figure the best we can do is fix it so she'll be confined for a while."

"Sounds okay," Rose agreed. "How were you planning on pulling that off?"

Randall spread his hands. "I'm open to suggestions."

Rose thought for a moment, then snapped his fingers. "Hey, Knox," he called, "is the tube station still open?"

The others paused to let them catch up. Knox pulled the amputated face of a cheap wristwatch from his pants pocket. "Not for much longer."

"In that case, we'd better hurry."

Ↄↄ

They put her on a subway car not fifteen minutes before the line shut down. The security guard minding the turnstiles gave them a suspicious look when they returned without her, not having used their own sixty pence tickets. Whatever he thought about them, he kept it to himself. Randall dropped the woman's passport and identification cards into the first letterbox they found. With any luck, she would be in a holding cell or a padded room until she remembered how to speak.

In the public restroom, they cleaned up and changed clothes. Rose picked a pair of old chino pants and a blue cable sweater from the bag of pilfered garments, depositing his bloody rags in the trash bin. Randall traded his jeans and Castroville t-shirt for an ill-fitting pair of slacks and a rumpled Oxford. His trench coat had sustained several long tears, but he decided to retain it. Bob filled one of the sinks and scrubbed his face and hands while Knox sifted through the possessions of the boarding house dead. A coin-purse lurking in a vest pocket contained a wad of high denomination German marks, as well as nearly a hundred pounds in crisp British notes. One pair of pants concealed a long letter, handwritten in flowing French.

After wandering the streets for a quarter of an hour, Randall flagged down a vacant taxi and asked the driver to take them to the nearest major hotel. He drove a considerable distance, skirting the perimeter of Hyde Park and moving eastward into Westminster, finally bringing them to a Hilton not far from the opera house. Randall tipped the man well, appreciating his silence during the ride and hoping it might extend to any later inquiries.

A fair number of travelers filled the hotel lobby, lining up at the front desk. Most of the people looked exhausted, eyes bleary, weighed down by children and suitcases. Except for the absence of luggage, Randall supposed his group fit right in. They checked into adjoining rooms, one for the humans and one for the brothers. An obnoxiously bright-eyed bellboy led them to their doors, luggage or no. Randall dropped a random scatter of change into his expectant hand.

The room was small for its price. Randall lay diagonally across the bed and his feet still stuck off the edge. He let his body relax as much as he dared. The sleep dragged at his mind, a lullaby whisper. Knox sat before the combination desk and dresser, laboriously reading the French letter. Randall watched his brother's reflection in the attached mirror as he mouthed the foreign syllables. For over an hour Knox pondered the handful of pages. Finally he sat back, rubbing his eyes behind his reading glasses. He folded the letter, and placed it in a drawer. "So what did it say?" Randall asked, for something to discuss. He could feel his body trying to desert him.

"About what you'd expect," Knox answered. "Declarations of love. Memories of bliss. Plans and proposals. Promises of faith. Lots of exuberant adjectives. Rather depressing under the circumstances. Are you sure you don't want to sleep? I'll watch you."

"My legs are a mess. I'd be out for a week, and we can't afford to wait." Randall boosted himself into a sitting position. His feet itched, but he could not make his legs move. Hauling on his pants, he pulled his knees up until he could reach his boots. He leaned forward to pull them off and his legs slid back down. Knox observed him in silence. "How about it?" said Randall. "You going to give me a hand or sit there like Buddha all evening?"

"Okay, but I'm not touching your socks." Knox abandoned his desk, whisked off Randall's boots and stood them next to the door. "For a man who has lived more than two hundred years, you are exceptionally impatient."

"I'll learn to meditate in the morning." Randall hauled his legs up again, then scratched furiously at the soles of his feet. "Assuming it doesn't take up too much of my time."

"Cute." Rummaging through his pack, Knox retrieved his copy of *Finnegan's Wake*. He returned to his seat. "You ought to try reading for a year or two. Just find a nice library and start with A. You'd be surprised how much you can learn before piles set in."

"I tried that once, in Santa Cruz. Some idiot in a cherry red convertible talked me into a game of billiards."

"My mistake." Knox glanced up from his pages. "You really should sleep. A week here won't set us back any further than circumstances already have."

Randall laughed. "A week here will put us in the poor house. Do you know how much this place costs a night?"

"So I'll rob a bank."

"I thought you were going to guard my slumber."

"We'll just prop you up in the getaway car."

"Now who's being cute?" Randall let himself sink back against the mattress. The majority of his nerves had gone dead. His body seemed to float, suspended above the floor. He stared at the ceiling until he imagined it had begun to recede very slowly. "Do you think I'm a murderer?" he asked.

"We're all murderers," Knox replied, a disembodied voice. "It's an occupational hazard."

Randall listened attentively, but his brother said nothing more. Gradually he began to hear sounds within the silence. The oscillating hum of cars on the street below. Conversations in adjacent rooms, reduced to nonsense by filtering walls. The miscellaneous knocks and groans of a sleepy building. Pages turning. Randall's body faded away. He watched the plaster ceiling ebb and flow as slowly as a glacier, a pinpoint of awareness in an unexplained reality. If he closed his eyes, he felt certain that he would vanish altogether. Finally only sight and sound remained, void of meaning.

Some time later, there came a sharp knock at the door. Knox pushed his chair back, yawning audibly, then passed through Randall's field of vision. "Who's there?" he asked.

"Room service," said an unfamiliar male voice.

Knox did not open the door. "I didn't order anything," he said suspiciously. There was no reply.

After a moment Randall heard the locks turn and hinges squeak. He struggled to sit up. His nerves lit all at once, wounds throbbing in time to his heartbeat. Swarming blackness dissolved his vision, fading as his body stabilized. He breathed in hoarse, oxygen-starved gulps.

Knox shut the door and sat down on the edge of the bed, bearing a plastic tray. A chrome heat-cover concealed the contents of a single plate. There was no napkin or flatware. Knox arched one pale eyebrow. "Dare we?"

"May as well," said Randall. "It's a little small to be an atom bomb." Knox lifted the cover. A live sparrow lay atop a small white envelope, both wings broken. The bird blinked in the sudden light. It tried to fly, bent wings flapping uselessly, then collapsed. Randall took the sparrow in one hand, feeling it shiver. He grasped its head gently between his thumb and forefinger, then snapped its neck. It spasmed once, dry feet brushing against his palm. He placed the body on the tray. Inside the envelope were four tickets to the Regent's Park outdoor theater, front row. "I'll be damned," said Randall. "She's awake."

"That's impossible," said Knox. "She couldn't have healed so quickly. Maybe Swan sent us this stuff."

Randall shook his head. "This isn't his style. If Swan wanted to talk to us, he'd kick down the door." He scrutinized the tickets, then brandished them with a grin. "Macbeth."

"I suppose you consider that conclusive evidence." Knox removed his glasses and rubbed wearily at his eyes. "Mind if I borrow that knife of yours?"

"What for?"

With gentle hands, Knox picked up the mutilated sparrow. "No sense letting it go to waste."

ॐ

Randall half expected Lisel to appear on stage in the persona of Lady Macbeth, skillfully goading her husband into regicide. But she was not among the cast, or even the audience, so far as he could tell. From his front row seat, he scanned the entire arc of the amphitheater. None of the absorbed, attentive faces looked at all familiar. The production itself was superb. Once he gave up searching the crowd, Randall succumbed to the dark spell of the drama. Macbeth's descent into brutality was horrifyingly credible, even if the theatrical violence was not. Less than six feet from the stage, Randall felt like a voyeur covertly witnessing the destruction of his neighbor.

During the intermission, he happened to examine his program. Paper-clipped to the playbill was an unruled three-by-five card inscribed with large, archaically perfect handwriting. It read *Queen Mary's gardens, central arbor, after the performance.* For a brief moment Randall imagined himself prowling the hedges, knife in hand, only to find some love-struck teenage girl in full orthodontic headgear. He stood, and slipped the card into his pocket. "I think I'm going to get a glass of wine," he announced. "Anybody care to join me?"

"You're buying, I'm drinking," said Rose. They skirted the stage and left through a side exit. "Promise me something, Randall. If I turn into a schnauzer, fill my bowl with beer."

"So long as you promise not to piss in my boots."

"You drive a hard bargain, mister."

The refreshment stand looked much like any other, a long trailer of corrugated panels with multiple service windows and faded awnings. In deference to the theater crowd, it sold cheesecake and spiced cider rather than sausages and soda. His hands warming around a styrofoam cup of mulled wine, Randall circulated through the crush of playgoers. The sun had set just before the play began, and the sky hung deep blue and starless overhead. A thumbnail moon dripped pearly rays, drizzling the top of a slow moving cloudbank. "Projectors," Randall murmured to himself.

"What was that?" Rose took a healthy swig from his own cup, then gasped in pain. "Christ, I think I cauterized my tongue."

"Does that mean you'll stop heckling the Weird Sisters?"

"I'll mull it over."

They returned to their seats after the first call. Knox glanced up as they wove through the crowd. "See anything?" he asked anxiously.

"Read this." Randall showed him the note. "You didn't happen to get a good look at the usher who seated us?"

Knox scanned the card then handed it back. "Afraid not," he admitted. Bob shook his head in the negative.

"At any rate," said Randall, "it's pretty clear she's not around here." He took one last look about the theater, then sat. "I suppose it's safe to enjoy the rest of the show."

"Enjoy," Bob repeated. "Interesting choice of verb."

The second half took hold of Randall and set his nerves on edge. Murder followed upon murder with the inescapable logic of a madman in retreat. The lighting shifted as the scenes progressed, yellow sharpening to orange deepening to red. By the time Macduff brandished the tyrant's severed head, a crimson radiance washed the stage like fire. All prophecies fulfilled, the curtain fell upon a scene of total devastation. Randall sat stunned, deaf to the applause. Foreboding lodged in his mind.

They filed out through a gate in the wooden fence enclosing the amphitheater, onto a wide lawn. Regent's Park had technically closed for the evening. The majority of the crowd ambled down the path towards parked cars or bicycles chained to lampposts. Some few lingered in dim tree shadows, chatting quietly. "So what did you think of the play?" Knox asked.

Bob answered first. "I think old Shakespeare was trying his best to spook us."

"I think it worked," said Randall. Indeed, he felt extremely uneasy. The night landscape would not fit neatly into his mind. Individually, each object looked familiar enough. The trees, their trunks all but hidden by shaggy tufts of leaves. The manicured lawn, drifts of grass clippings browning in the hollows. Knuckled roots protruding from hard dirt paths. Randall named them silently to himself. Still, the feeling of strangeness remained. "So much for catharsis," he said aloud.

A high hedge separated the Queen's garden from the rest of the park's inner circle. They passed beneath an arched trellis thick with trailing ivy. A field of roses swayed in the cooling breeze, woven through with mazed pathways. Moonlight glazed the naked blooms, voluptuous petals seducing the hues of midnight. Ruby flowers bled burgundy dewdrops. Pale blossoms glowed with phantom incandescence, banshee wigs on brows of indigo. The shadows of thorns wavered, exposing the secret centers of neighboring blooms, their innermost buttons of pungent nectar. The feminine aroma suffused the air like drug smoke.

"Anybody making clever comments about my name," said Rose, "gets an elbow in the face."

"You realize, of course," Knox replied, "that some people might regard that as a challenge."

Rose stuck out his elbows and flapped them menacingly. "Some people might find their noses pinned to the backs of their skulls."

"Some people aren't impressed." Knox selected a path at random and set off through the jungle of flowers. Waist-high hedges ran to either side, continuous walls of sculpted foliage, the individual plants tangled intimately together. Even when the color and species of bloom changed there was no definite border. One blended into the next like paints on a careless pallete.

Their scent, strong as a shattered bottle of perfume, made Randall dizzy. He tried not to inhale too deeply. All the same, his lungs felt infected. The aroma consumed his attention like an unexpected caress. To distract himself, he observed single blossoms as they passed. They looked almost alive, drifting on the breeze, the distended organs of some vegetable intelligence. He had the unnerving impression of heads turning, eyes drinking his image. The flowers seemed to pulsate, fleshy petals dilating, compound vaginas anticipating consummation.

Randall walked as quickly as he could, following the unexpected twists and turns of their chosen pathway. His wounds throbbed, a warm, humid ache that invaded him completely. Somehow his legs continued to function. The parallel hedges curved around the perimeter of a still pond. Feverish green algae scummed the surface, dotted with pale pustules of fungus. The reek of corruption mingled with the blatant sensuality of the pollen. Randall swallowed with an effort, the wine heavy in his stomach.

The hedges terminated at a wall of dark greenery, a wide wooden lattice laced with flowering vines. A low portal offered the only passage. They ducked through. Randall stopped short, dangling roots exploring his hair. They had arrived.

A trellis ring enclosed the arbor, shot through with a variety of blooms. Wedge-shaped rose beds surrounded a central fountain, paths radiating away like wheel spokes. Ornate benches marked the compass points, partially secluded by stands of tree roses. Each plant had been exquisitely pruned, foliage coaxed into perfect spheres. Randall's sense of purpose returned with a thrill of blood. The pain, the vague disorientation the garden had engendered, vanished as though burned from his body.

Lisel sat in the bench directly across the circle, hands at her sides, ankles crossed. She wore Chinese slippers, loose trousers and a turtleneck, each the exact same shade of black. A simple clip held her golden hair back, away from her face. Randall stared. A knob of scar tissue no larger than a cigarette burn hovered above her right eyebrow. "Is that you, Mother?" he asked in a clear voice. "For some reason, I was expecting the Queen of Hearts."

She laughed, a rich indulgent sound. "How nice. You've developed a sense of humor since last we met. You were always too serious for your own benefit. But given enough time, I suppose anyone can improve themselves." She pursed her lips in a stylized expression of parental concern. "I hope you haven't neglected your other pursuits."

"Not at all." Randall raised his arms, encompassing his companions. "We've done a lot together." He advanced casually, like a man navigating an office party, around the circle of roses. The others followed him as if by whim or coincidence. "We've beaten on a few barmen, burned down a couple of buildings, killed the odd person or two." He made himself smile. "We even went to a museum."

One corner of Lisel's mouth wrinkled in annoyance. Her icy blue eyes conveyed oceans of sour resentment. "Honestly, children, you had no cause to come calling on me at home. After all, a lady needs her beauty sleep."

Randall stopped a few feet from her bench. He made a show of looking her over, paying particular attention to what remained of the entry wound. "You seem to be doing fine without it."

She inclined her head as though accepting a compliment. "Many changes accompany full maturity. The ability to heal on your feet is one of the more useful embellishments, as I'm sure you'll discover eventually."

"Some day, in the fullness of time, hypothetically speaking." Randall folded his arms across his chest in a deliberate gesture of discontent. "What do you expect us to do? Wait patiently until you die of boredom?"

"Not necessarily." Lisel shifted in her seat, appearing suddenly uncomfortable. She averted her eyes with the petulant reluctance of someone conceding to an unwelcome truth. Randall tensed, instantly suspicious. "That is," she continued, "what I've invited you here to discuss."

"How sweet," Knox said with a palpable sneer. Randall glanced at him in surprise. For some reason, he had not expected the others to participate. Now the eldest brother came forward, wearing his best scowl of scholarly condescension. "Just what do you think you can offer?" he inquired. "We advance one generation at a time, over the bodies of our benefactors. For us to mature you have to die, and no amount of melodramatic body language is going to change that."

Fury flashed in the frigid depths of Lisel's eyes. "Shut your hole," she said with a rasp, "and listen." Knox stood mute, clearly taken aback. After a moment of silence, Lisel relaxed. She draped her arms across the back of the bench, stretching sensually. "I'm getting tired of this cat and mouse nonsense," she said, once again eyeing Randall. "I hunt you, you hunt me. Periodically we maim each other. Then we rest up for a while, only to repeat the whole process again. And where has all this wasted effort gotten us?"

"Is that a rhetorical question?" asked Rose, looking dubiously around the moonlit arbor.

"Of course." Lisel batted her golden lashes at him. "Such atrocious manners. I see you're still not properly housebroken."

Rose flinched as though struck. "Fuck you!"

Lisel nodded politely, then returned her attention to Randall. "To be brief, I have decided to answer your challenge. Your claim is, after all, legitimate. And besides, I'm sick of seeing your face every time I turn around. I propose one final duel between us, blade to blade, to the death. No tricks." She fixed Knox with a chill look. "And no interference. If I win, I expect the rest of you to leave me in peace for no less than a hundred years, in return for which I will refrain from tearing out your respective spines for an equal period. If you win…" She spread her hands eloquently. "I don't think I need make any promises." Kicking one leg up over the arm of the bench, she leaned back, smiling mysteriously.

"Those are my terms," she said. "Do you accept?"

Randall snorted. "Of course not." He savored the shadow of doubt that flickered across Lisel's face. "If you've grown senile enough to meet the four of us alone, I'm certainly not going to surrender the advantage." Randall slipped the hardwood knife from its boot sheath. The death of the wolf had stained the blade black. He leveled the weapon at Lisel. "Ready, gentlemen?"

"You better fucking believe it." Swan walked nimbly around the lip of the fountain, his bare feet as pale as the marble rim. He wore nothing but the slacks Bob had loaned him, the legs torn off at the knees, and the stolen leather jacket. His tattoos glowed indigo in the moonlight. The Celtic knots bunched and relaxed as he moved. The dragon on his chest flexed like a living thing. An abused grocery bag dangled from one hand.

"Well, if it isn't Mommy's little angel." Lisel reclined in the bench, apparently unworried. She favored Swan with a look of feigned affection. "I thought I'd tasted your death's blood, my child."

Swan shrugged. "Rumors of my demise, and all that shit." He stepped lightly to the ground. "Sorry I didn't come back earlier," he told Randall, "but you wouldn't believe how hard it is to find one of these in England." Reaching into the bag, he pulled out an aged breech-loading shotgun, the barrels sawed off just short of the stock.

Lisel leapt to her feet, a movement of sheer panic that lacked all grace or deliberation. Swan raised the shotgun with both hands and fired.

Thunder echoed through the arbor. Lisel vanished in a spray of flame. When the hot smoke cleared, she lay slumped against the bench. Blood pumped from the crater in her chest. Seared tissue hung from shattered ribs. She drew a bubbling breath, useless hands crawling along the ironwork. Fear dissolved the brittle ice of her eyes.

Swan spat into the fountain. He sauntered towards Lisel, then placed the truncated barrels against her forehead. She flinched away from the heat. "Stupid bitch," he said, and pulled the trigger. When the echoes died away, he cracked open the breech and dumped the cartridges out to hiss on the damp lawn.

chapter nineteen

Knox fished the cherry out of his soda and held it out at arm's length. It dangled between his pinched fingers like a miniature Christmas ornament. "Nearly a thousand restaurants in London proper and you bring us to this place."

Rose smiled insanely. "You don't like it? What's not to like?" He gestured at the wall behind their booth. "Over here we have one of the Beatles first gold records, fragments of a white on white Fender Stratocaster personally smashed and incinerated by Jimi Hendrix, and the complete set of Johnny Rotten's mug shots." He paused to gulp down his own drink, something unnaturally green and boiling with carbonation. "I understand they have one of Elvis's corsets in the men's room. That's a real coup, you know. Normally they don't get American memorabilia. Are you going to eat that?"

"No." Knox dropped the cherry onto the spotless white table top. The inverted reflections of neon beer signs blinked from the glossy surface. "I don't suppose you know who used to own that?" He jabbed a finger at the classic Corvette Stingray suspended upside-down from the ceiling.

Rose shrugged. "Isaac Newton." He popped the cherry into his mouth, stem and all. "Watch this." His cheeks puffed out and his tongue worked inside his mouth, squirming between his lips and teeth. He breathed through his nose, squinting as though something had come loose inside his skull.

"If it's constipation," said Randall, "I've seen it before."

Rose pursed his lips, extruding the pink stem with a neat square knot tied precisely in the middle. He plucked the stem and swallowed the cherry.

"That's great," said Swan. "You should put that on your fucking resumé, man. 'Ex-convict werewolf looking for a fresh start. Gives good head.'"

"I am not a werewolf," Rose said adamantly. "Besides, I can't do ten-key worth shit." He twiddled his fingers.

"Maybe if you used your tongue..."

Their waitress glided up on antique skates key-clamped to a pair of red Converse high tops. She executed a half turn to kill her momentum, metallic wheels rasping across the tile floor. Her skirt gathered about her knees then reversed its spin and flared out again. The overpadded shoulders of her pink on black blouse jutted out in dangerous looking triangles. She pulled a pencil from the bun in her hair, simultaneously cracking her bubble-gum. "So," she inquired in an accent somewhere between Brighton and the Bronx, "you guys decided yet?"

Rose gazed up at her wistfully. "Your name wouldn't happen to be Nicole, would it?"

"Of course not." She tapped her tag with inch long nails, each one painted a different color. "It's Zoe. I'm the waitress."

"That's a relief," said Knox. "From your mode of dress, I supposed you were an Imperial concubine to Ming the Merciless."

Zoe gave him a blank look. "There's a half-hour wait outside already, Mac. You going to order, or what?"

"Don't listen to him," said Rose. "He's been dead for over three centuries." He held up the remains of his frothing green beverage. "I'll have another one of these, whatever it is, a double cheeseburger with too many onions, and a plate of chili fries. My friends here are moral vegetarians and only eat animals that lived full and active lives before expiring of old age. I'd like you to bring them each the strongest mixed drink you can think of. Maybe it'll loosen them up a little."

"Actually," said Bob, "I'd like a burger and a beer."

Zoe paused momentarily in her transcription. "Even if foul play is involved?"

"So long as it's beef, you can bludgeon it yourself for all I care."

"Anyone else care to contradict Mister Mouth?" She made eye contact all around, seemingly immune to Rose's pout.

"That drink sounds fine," said Randall. "I'm in the mood to get severely hammered." Knox assented to the same with a nod.

"Coffee for me," said Swan. "Black." Zoe tucked her pen back into her hairdo and skated off towards the polished chrome soda fountain.

"She wants my body," Rose declared. "Trust me, I can tell."

"Yeah, right." Swan turned his coffee cup right side up on his saucer. "You know women inside and out."

"Especially out." Rose downed the last of his drink. "Say, Randall, could you lend me a couple of drachmas for the jukebox?"

"And here I thought you were footing the bill, for once."

"Lisel was right. You have developed a sense of humor."

Randall dug into his pockets, dumping a fistful of coins onto the table. Rose scooped them into his empty glass, then bounced up from the booth. "This places is so cool," he said to no one in particular. "I wonder if they have the Time Warp."

"Well," said Knox, "Our friend seems to be recovering his usual temperament."

"Call it denial," Bob replied. "Wormwood is excellent at that. When he got out of prison, he insisted that he had been ice-fishing for eighteen months up in Alaska. Talked about it all the time. Made up stories about flying swordfish. If Toad-Eater hadn't been on the inside with him, we might've started to believe him eventually. Right now, I'll bet you he's scared shitless."

Across the restaurant, Rose hovered indecisively before the mammoth jukebox. Rainbows of neon arced over its face like a casino marquee. Electric pink lava bubbled in recessed cylinders. Rose fed the machine his coins and punched in his selections. A moment later, music blared over the P.A. He made his way to the men's room, jumping to the left and stepping to the right as the song directed. "Of course," said Randall. "How could I possibly have missed it?"

Zoe coasted up with their drinks held high on a platter. She filled Swan's coffee cup, poured Bob's beer for him as though it were fine wine, then set two pint glasses brimming with an opaque orange liquid before Knox and Randall. Reaching back into her hairdo once again, she extracted a handful of drinking straws and flung them at the booth. Smiling cheerfully, she pushed off from the table and was gone. Knox retrieved a straw and stuck it into his drink. It stayed upright, like a signpost with half its length buried in firm soil. "In British restaurants," he said, "the gratuity is customarily added into your bill."

"That would explain it," said Bob.

Randall eyed his drink. It looked suspiciously like orange soda mixed with milk. He raised his glass and took a healthy swig. It tasted like sherbet on his tongue, but seared his throat all the way down. "Not bad," he said aloud. "Two or three of these should put me in a coma."

Bob sipped meditatively at his beer. "So," he said eventually, "what's it like?"

Randall frowned. "Sort of an Orange Julius laced with lighter fluid. Want a taste?"

"Not the drink." Bob fended it off with an exasperated wave. "Maturity. Elevation. Whatever it is you guys call it. You got what you wanted. How does it feel?"

Randall inventoried his wounds. His legs felt like nerveless meat hanging from his body. The scratches on his chest itched as though infected. "It's funny," he said. "I don't feel any better at all. Sort of like birthdays, or new years. You're supposed to feel changed, but nothing's different. It's just another day. Right after she died, I kept thinking there must be something left to do, some ritual to perform. I expected to be electrified. Instead, I feel just as fucked up as ever." He took a long pull on his drink.

"You know," said Knox, "that's a real possibility." He ran a hand through his hair. "Maybe there is something else we need to do, something we're unaware of."

Swan shook his head. "I don't buy it. Sure, we're working with next to zero information here, but even Mother admitted the bottom line. She dies, we get the power. That's just the way it is, man." He looked down at his coffee. "Then again, I don't feel any different either."

"So where does that leave us?" asked Bob.

Swan grinned. "Well now, I can think of one sure-fire way to find out if we've graduated." He licked his teeth.

"Swell. Just don't ask me to volunteer."

Rose skipped up and slid into his seat. "You guys just have to see that bathroom," he said. "Not only do they have the King's corset, they've got the throne he expired on. Can you believe it?" When no one answered, he glanced around the table. "Why are you all looking at me like that?"

ℜ

Swan returned to the hotel room, a smile to rival Rose's stretched across his face, his limbs buzzing with suppressed energy. Randall lay inert on the bed, his body a fading memory. "Did it work?" He spoke with difficulty.

"God damn right it worked." Swan flowed back and forth before the bed, moving in a rapid dance that Randall gradually realized was fast-forward Tai Chi. His body trailed a wake of hot, agitated air each time it passed. The tattoo dragon flexed and writhed.

"You sure?" Randall forced himself to sit upright, his muscles screaming like bent metal. "I mean, are you absolutely positive."

Swan paused, and pulled his Japanese punch dagger from a sheath at the small of his back. He splayed one hand on the dark surface of the writing desk. Without so much as a grunt of pain, he rammed the blade through his upturned palm, driving it deep into the wood. He shifted his grip, then jerked it free again. Slick crimson stained the lower third of the blade. Swan raised his hand, turning it for Randall to see. It was completely whole.

"Fucking hell," Randall breathed. "Did you even feel that?"

"Nope." Swan swung back into his accelerated routine, his lean form moving in ritualized patterns. The knife blade arced through the warm air, cutting silver trails through Randall's vision. "Christ," said Swan, "I need to do something to burn off this buzz. I feel like a God damn electrical filament."

"I feel it, too." Randall looked down at his own hands and did not recognize them. Fingers as scarred and lifeless as wind-cut wood bent slowly at the knots of his knuckles. There was no feeling in them, as though they had already cracked apart, flaked into dust. He looked back at Swan, the liquid ease of his movements something he could no longer understand. "How many did you take?"

"Just the one." Swan pulled something out of a jacket pocket. "Want an Italian passport? You could probably pass for Sicilian." He tossed it on the bed. "I don't need it. Think I'll be hanging out here for a while."

Randall watched as Swan cleaned his knife on the bed sheet, then pivoted back into the form. "You're not coming back with us?"

"Nah. London's my scene. Cali was always your turf. You and Knox." The knife drew quick circles through the air, the flow of Tai Chi melting into the tense grace of a Regency fencing stance. "Besides, man, somebody's got to stay and clean up all of Mother's little helpers. We found her bolt hole, sure, but not her real pad. And I ought to lay the news on the local families. They get a little edgy when shit like this goes down. Thought I might go back for Shannon, too. Bury her someplace real."

"Sounds good," Randall answered. But he wasn't really listening. It's over, he told himself. I never quite believed it would end. Strange, but now that it's done I don't know what to think. Maybe that's what an ending is. Jesus, I'm tired. He allowed himself to lay back on the bed, dead muscles going slack. Then a new thought struck him. "Where's Knox? He left with you. Or did I imagine that?"

"Had to ditch him." Swan's fluid pacing slowed for a moment. He would not meet Randall's eyes.

"Why? What happened?"

The knife blade burned with renewed fervor, flashing through the basic sword strikes in a sinuous blur of motion. Swan advanced and retreated, waging a duel that only he could see. "Knox went a little apeshit. I thought it might happen. Abstinence'll do that to you. When you've been dry so fucking long, like Knox, your control goes. You get a taste, hell, even a little taste, and you can't make yourself stop." Swan ceased moving abruptly. He bowed to the window, then sheathed his knife at his back. "Anyway, it wasn't too pretty."

"What did he do, exactly?"

Swan shrugged uncomfortably. "Read the morning paper."

"Shit," said Randall. "That bad?"

"Yeah." Swan ducked down out of view, then came back up with Randall's new flight bag. "Mind if I snake this? The Remington's kind of conspicuous." Without waiting for an answer, he pulled open a dresser drawer and stuffed the shotgun into the bag along with a random assortment of clothes.

"You cutting out now?" Randall asked. He felt as though he should say something, but was uncertain how to talk to Swan. Words meant so little to him. Instead, he watched the young immortal light a cigarette, his tattooed body burning with an animal beauty, even standing still. "Thanks for coming back," he said at last.

"The bitch deserved it," Swan answered, smoke drifting from his mouth.

"Yeah," Randall agreed. "But I'm not sure how it would have gone if you hadn't shown up."

"That's the trouble with you assholes. Even when you cheat you still play by the rules." Swan hefted the bag, the shotgun clanking dully, and headed for the door.

When he had gone, Randall hauled himself to his feet. A vision of Lisa Robinson wavered like heat haze before him, her face pale above the rent pulp of her throat. He could smell the warm scent of her hair beneath the stench of blood. "No time for that." Randall rubbed at his eyes until her image smeared, dissolved. "Business first." He knocked softly on the adjoining door, which led to the humans' room.

ℛ

"You realize you're asking me to bet my ass here." Rose sat on the edge of his bed. He took a hit of Southern Comfort. An hour ago the bottle had been full. Now there was barely a third remaining. "I mean, if you're wrong about this there's no take two." He extended the bottle with an unsteady hand. "Is there?"

Randall knocked back a large dose of alcohol. "You know what?" he said. "I hate Southern Comfort. Always have. Tastes like fucking Listerine." He folded his arms across the back of the chair and rested his chin atop them. The bottle dangled from his numb fingers, virtually forgotten.

"Stop trying to change the subject." Rose's face crumpled into an exaggerated frown of disapproval. "The fact is, you want to chew a hole in my neck and see if it takes."

"I was not trying to change the subject," Randall said indignantly. "I have merely ceased trying to persuade you. After all, it's your call." He gave a solemn nod. "Pass me the bottle, would you?"

"Give me that." Rose plucked the liquor from Randall's nerveless fingers. "I think you've had enough. This hundred proof shit is dangerous." He took a big swallow, then set it carefully on the floor. "Remember your precious brain cells."

"Brain cells? What?" Randall giggled. "Oh, I remember that

conversation." The giggle escalated into a fit of hoarse laughter. "Now I know," he wheezed out, "why they call it shot gunning." He raised his hands in the classic rifle aiming gesture. "Bang!" The simulated recoil sent him rocking back into the combination dresser desk. He scrambled not to slide off his seat, snickering.

"That's not funny, Randall. I mean really. That's not funny at all." Rose caressed the wound that ran under his eye and across the bridge of his nose. The welt had faded, becoming an ugly brown bruise.

Randall's laughing fit tapered off into a cough. "I'm sorry," he said with drunken simplicity. "You're not mad, are you?"

A hint of Rose's maniac smile tugged at the corners of his mouth. "Depends. You know that some words have two meanings." He groped for the bottle, put it to his lips and tilted it way up. The level of liquid inside dropped an inch. He belched, then wiped his mouth on the back of his hand. "Keep talking."

"What for?" Randall accepted the bottle and took a modest hit. By now, the taste only bothered him a little. "I just told you I'm not going to twist your arm over this. I don't have it in me."

"Some salesman you are." Rose got to his feet, swaying heavily. He lurched across the room, nearly colliding with the bathroom door. Twisting the knob, he stumbled inside. Randall heard clumsy snaps and zippers. "I don't want to wind up like Jim," Rose continued over the fire-hose roar of urine hitting the bowl. "I'd honestly rather snuff it first. That's the only reason I'm even listening to you. But if you want me to guinea pig for you, you're going to have to convince me that I'm getting the long end of the stick." The waterfall continued for over a minute before stuttering to a stop. Rose appeared in the doorway, his t-shirt snagged in his fly. "So how about it? Can I become one of you without turning into a rabid, blood-sucking freak? No offense."

Randall spread his hands helplessly, thinking of Knox. "To be honest, I don't even know if it'll work. Assuming I've got the power to elevate you, those bites of yours might mess things up. For all I know, you could become the world's first vamp-wolf." He chuckled at the word. "Sorry." Lifting the bottle, he took a drink to steady himself. "But if it does work, and if you've got the willpower, you can survive without human blood." He shrugged loosely. "I'm afraid that's the best I can offer."

Rose took a deep breath, then let it out in a slow sigh. "Okay," he said. "Bite me."

"Huh?" Randall had to clamp down hard on the giggles. Even so, one or two escaped.

"I mean, let's do it." Rose seemed a good deal more sober than he should be. His entire body had tensed as though awaiting a blow.

Randall held out the Southern Comfort. "Want to finish the bottle?"

Rose shook his head. "Maybe later."

"Sure." Randall stood cautiously, his legs numb from foot to thigh. It took an act of will to make them move at all. Worse yet, there was a perceptible delay between the order and the execution. Randall felt as though he were operating construction equipment by remote control. His sense of placement had deserted him entirely. Even his hands were never quite where he expected them to be. "We'd better do this in the bathroom," he reasoned. "No sense fucking up the carpeting."

Rose ushered him inside. "Glad to see your priorities are in order."

Switching on the light, Randall happened to glance at the toilet. The water in the bowl was bright green. He decided not to ask. Sidestepping Rose, he hoisted his legs over the edge of the bathtub. His boots thumped hollowly on the molded fiberglass. He set the bottle of alcohol on a ledge beside the hotel soap.

Rose clambered into the tub and slid the shower door closed. He smiled uneasily. "Why do I keep expecting Anthony Perkins to dash into the room?"

Adjusting his balance, Randall maneuvered his arms until they rested on his friend's shoulders. "I hope to hell this works," he said.

"Me, too." Rose looked away. "You say anything more sentimental than that, and I swear to God I'll knee you in the nuts."

"Let's leave God out of this." Randall clenched his fists around handfuls of Rose's jacket. "Ready?"

"No." His smile bloomed. Not his maniacal grin, but something altogether new. For an instant, Rose looked absolutely serene. "But do it anyway."

Randall lunged forward with all the speed his drunken disorientation would allow. His lips slid onto the taut skin of Rose's neck, forming a wet seal. Without giving himself any time to hesitate, he took a single rending bite from the sweat-slick flesh. Rose yelped and tried to pull away. Randall held him firm. Jugular blood burst into his mouth, and the red lust leapt to meet it.

Rose howled in pain, the sound echoing hollowly in the confined space. His fists beat against Randall's back. Furious hands clawed and hammered while his legs pushed desperately away from the terrible embrace.

Randall scarcely noticed. Hot blood pulsed down his throat, lighting a fire deep in the center of his chest. The alien heat expanded with each new surge, until the sensation seemed larger than the barriers of his body. White lava flowed in his veins, seeping outward towards his limbs. Soon every capillary burned like a lit fuse, points of agony crawling through his incandescent flesh. Still the sphere of fire continued to grow. The power intensified as it expanded, and Randall realized that he had heretofore touched only the outer fringes. Soon, he floated in the deep core.

His own blood boiled. The taint of alcohol evaporated as though it had never existed. Even the red lust, a force it had taken him decades to subjugate, withered meekly before the all-consuming fire. The heat filled his mind, burning new pathways through the coral corridors of his brain. A single thought came to him clearly through the inferno. Lisel. Cold, brittle Lisel. How had she endured this scourging flame? It did not seem possible. A final explosion sent Randall back to himself with a physical jolt.

The fringe of Rose's beard tickled his cheek. Randall took his lips away and lowered his friend to the bottom of the tub. The bite looked like a tear in sackcloth, dry and pale, not a drop of red to be seen. Christ, thought Randall. Where could all that blood have gone? He certainly did not feel gorged. In fact, he felt terribly hungry.

Condensation fogged the shower door. Randall's clothes hung limp and wrinkled from his limbs, all the shape steamed out of them. The air in the bathroom tasted thick. He flexed his hands, suddenly supple, feeling each elegant tendon ripple. His legs felt equally whole and powerful. Glancing down, Randall noticed the Southern Comfort sitting on the soap ledge. The glass felt warm to the touch. He took a good hit and swirled the biting liquid around his mouth, enjoying the aftertaste of blood. Throwing his head back, he drained the bottle in three large swallows. The alcohol seared a path straight to the pit of his stomach.

The power was his. Smiling grimly, he squeezed the empty bottle until it shattered in his hand.

ക്ക

Knox did not return that morning, and Rose did not awaken. He lay in the dry bathtub, a bloodless corpse reeking of alcohol. His booted feet sat near the drain, cramped and crooked in the small space. Randall knelt at the foot of the tub and refolded his legs into a more comfortable position.

Bad Bob knocked on the doorframe. "How long until we know for sure?"

"Beats me." Randall looked at his friend's face, the white skin under the bristling beard, the motionless eyes beneath closed lids. "I came out of it in less than an hour, sore as hell and starving. But what with those bites of Jim's I don't know what's going on inside him." Randall stood. "Shit, Bob, he could be dead. Really dead."

"Yeah." Bob sagged against the wall, exhausted in spite of a night's sleep. "Well, how long should we stay, do you think? How long until we give up?"

"He should be awake now. It still might happen, but I don't know when." Randall closed the shower door. "We could put him someplace safe, I suppose. At any rate, we ought to at least wait here until Knox comes back."

"I don't think Knox will be coming back." Bob held aloft the morning edition of the *Sun*. "I saw this in the lobby." Inch high capitals underlined the masthead. *ELEVEN KILLED IN CAMDEN PUB.* Below was a police composite sketch of the suspect. It looked very little like Knox. It looked very little like a human being.

"Shit." Randall snatched the paper from Bob's hand and flung it to the floor. The sketch stared up at him. "Piss and blood." He pounded a fist into the wall, feeling nothing. "What the bloody fuckin' hell are we supposed to do now?"

"Pour me a drink," said a hoarse voice from the tub, "and we'll take it from there."

chapter **twenty**

Randall Springfield stepped into the ocean. "Jesus," he yelped, and immediately sprang back onto the hard-packed sand.

"Get burned?" Rose inquired, sitting some distance from shore on a large, dry rock.

"No," said Randall, startled to find a foot at the end of his leg. "Water's just cold, I guess. Not a sensation I'm used to."

"What about me?" Rose sniffed at an armpit. "I'm getting a bit ripe over here. None of the stewardesses would talk to me on the plane."

"That's just your personality," said Bob. The biker chieftain waded in an exposed tide pool, jeans rolled up to his knees.

"When I turn into a slobbering dog-creature remind me to bite you. Hard." Rose contemplated the state of his underarms a moment longer. "Seriously though, Jim splashed around without singeing any. Maybe I can, too."

"Sure," said Randall. A breaking wave tumbled its way to the wet tidemark, collapsed and retreated, sucking shell fragments and polished gravel from the strand. "Soak your head in that and we'll find out."

The three men were alone on the isolated beach, accessible only by a cautious walk across a rotting trellis bridge, followed by a short rappel down a sandstone cliff. A maze of submerged rocks made landing a boat impossible. The convex sweep of the surrounding cliffs cut off nearly all of the horizon. Spiral caves, too narrow for human passage, funneled in the sounds of volleyball and mariachi music from La Jolla Shores, a quarter mile to the north. Broken bottles, decaying condoms, and the occasional piece of discarded swimwear covered the upper reaches of the shore like mulch. There was no vegetation to speak of, just the furry green algae coating the tidal boulders and the storm-sculpted stump of a dead tree, hung with the bones of birds. "Been here before?" Rose had asked when he saw it.

Randall advanced into the water. An instant chill shot through his legs, feeling strangely similar to a bad scald. He could sense each bone in both feet as an individual ache. Blue veins stood out from his skin. Randall followed a loose string of submerged stones out to a larger rock, its green face just slightly above the waterline. The slick algae squelched and slid between his toes. Frigid rings circled his thighs, the soaking cuffs of his rolled up jeans.

"Some messiah you are," Rose called from the shore. "Your knees are wet."

Randall turned cautiously to glare at his friend. "Just pray I don't baptize your ass right here."

"Go ahead and try it. Next thing you know, some go-go dancer's walking off with your head in a bag."

"I hate it when that happens." A wave broke over the green rock, washing down its sloped face. Randall bent carefully to dip his hands in the water. He brushed damp fingers against his cheeks, tasted the salt on his tongue. "Two hundred years," he said to himself. "Long enough, I suppose." He stood silently on the rock, swaying with the heave and pull of the rising tide. Hot facets of reflected sunlight rose and sank in the calm water beyond the cliffs. Foam collected at the base of the rock, uncoiling and reforming with each beat of the waves. For a moment it seemed as though he looked down upon a darkened land from a great height. Randall stepped back from the edge, suddenly dizzy.

"We ought to get moving," said Bob, clambering out of his tide pool. "You been transfigured yet, or what?"

Before Randall could answer a breaker powered over the rock, the frigid rush up to his shins. His toes curled, gripping vainly at the algae's greasy mane. The wave rolled back, sucking at his heels. His footing gave, and Randall pitched sideways into deep water.

He opened his eyes on world of tumbling weeds and barnacled stone. Low, muted noises pushed at his ears. He swung his head, sensing no change in the quality of light, the density of wrinkled vines. Do not inhale, a voice in his mind instructed. Kicking feet searched for purchase, found nothing, then something that felt soft and alive. He pushed violently away and struck his head. Nausea sent the air coughing from his lungs. Brine burned its way up his nose. He spun frantically, swallowing water, wide eyes hunting for a scrap of sky.

Something clamped onto his leg. He spun sickeningly. Strong hands clasped his shoulders, then darted under his arms to lock across his chest. His head broached the surface. Randall sneezed brine, then clenched his eyes and mouth shut as another wave broke over him. Bad

Bob hauled him onto the green rock, held him as he coughed and sputtered. The two men sat in an awkward embrace, waves crashing against their sides, while Randall breathed again.

Rose sat at the edge of the waterline, a burned foot clutched in both hands, laughing.

℀

The old man behind the register of the Ocotillo general store looked exactly the same. He wore the same plaid flannel shirt and weathered baseball cap. The same roadmap of veins showed through his hands and neck. The lines etched into his face looked just as deep. "Put this on number three," said Randall, passing him a wrinkled twenty.

The old man turned and looked out the window. Bob stood by the pump, ready to fuel the Barracuda. "She take all of this?" the old man asked.

"At least." Randall watched the old man ring up the sale. He worked the register with all of his attention, patient fingers tracing the keypad in search of the correct numbers. I have lived longer than this man, Randall told himself. Twice, perhaps three times as long. Why do I think of him as old? Because he is used up, worn down? Or because I am not? "If you could live forever," Randall asked aloud, "would you want to?"

The clerk raised his head, regarding him solemnly. "Gracious, no," he said. "I've seen more than plenty already. Things don't change all that much, anyhow."

Rose sidled up to the counter with an armload of beer. A bag of chips dangled from his mouth. He set the cans down with a heavy clang, then let the bag drop. "Thought I'd try these new salt and vinegar chips. I hear they're absolutely disgusting." He pried a beer from the pile and popped it open. "You wouldn't mind footing the bill, would you, seeing as how you're bound for the great beyond and everything?"

Randall passed the clerk another twenty. "Guess you were right."

℀

The abandoned house sat just outside of town in a wide sand lot choked with thumbnail cactus and splintered lumber. Four vacant windows faced the two lane highway leading out toward the desert preserve. A pair of mattresses, eaten down to the coils by burrowing rats, lay baking in the afternoon heat.

Inside, the floor and walls had been stripped to the bare concrete. The kitchen still contained a rusted out sink and decrepit gas stove. Rose's beer sat inside a doorless, World War II era Frigidaire. The remains of a sofa sat below the window in the main room, its springs woven through with spiders' nests. A cracked porcelain toilet leaned in the corner. Graffiti covered the concrete, mostly names, interspersed with threats and promises. In the bedroom, a splash of white paint ran down one wall and onto the floor. In the irregular blank space someone had scrawled *STOP WRITING IN HERE!* in thick red capitals.

Rose sat on a dirty foam-rubber pad nursing a beer. His leather jacket hung from a nail in the window frame. Sweat stood out on his face. "I wonder how many sunburnt, acne scarred desert boys pulled down their first pair of panties in this room."

Randall crouched with his back to the wall, facing the window and the highway beyond. "I thought nobody was hip enough to fuck in Ocotillo."

Rose took a final swallow, crumpled his can, and tossed it onto a growing pile. "Now that you mention it, I don't see too many used mambas or french diddlers hereabouts. Maybe they don't believe in birth control."

"Hell," said Bad Bob, coming in from the kitchen. He tossed each of the men a beer then popped one open for himself. "Couldn't we wait in the saloon? The decor might not be quite up to these standards, but they probably have A.C."

"You can cut out if you like," Randall answered. "I want to be where I can see the highway."

Bob grinned, then lowered himself carefully to the floor. He stretched his legs out and leaned back against the doorframe. "Nervous?"

"Yeah." Randall contemplated his beer as though it puzzled him immensely. "Funny, huh?" He set the can aside, unopened. "You really think they'll show?"

"Sure," said Bob. "Most of the boys who ran the Magic Kingdom raid said they'd be here. And Silverfish has been spreading the word ever since we left for London. You'll have plenty of volunteers."

"They probably think I'm some kind of nut case." Randall slipped the hardwood knife from his boot. The blood of Jim Sullivan's wolf incarnation had stained the blade permanently black. He polished it with the hem of his shirt. "Only you and Toad-Eater know any different."

"They'll believe me if they'll believe anybody." Bob took a hit from his beer. "If nobody shows we'll just head back to L.A. and you can set yourself on fire again."

Rose reached up and pulled a cigarette pack from his jacket, then jogged out a twisted, hand-rolled joint. "Speaking of open flame," he said, "do either of you sweat-lodge types have a light?"

Bob passed him his heavy silver lighter. "You been hoarding that for your resurrection?"

"Nah." Rose puffed the joint into life and took a solid hit. Smoke seeped gradually out his nose. "I scored it off Pa Kettle while you two were fucking with the car. Can't imagine how he grows the shit out here." He took another hit and handed it off to Randall.

The joint went around, shrinking steadily. Smoke curled in the bar of white sun passing though the window only to vanish in the shade. A beetle crawled across the floor to taste the ash. "So Wormwood," asked Bob, after a lengthy toke, "what are going to do with the rest of forever?"

"I've got it all planned out." Rose tossed another can onto his pile of empties. "First I'm gonna go to Hollywood, hire myself out as a stunt man. You know, jump off buildings, catch bullets in my teeth and shit. It'll be great. All the directors'll want me, cause I won't need safety equipment. Save 'em all kinds of hassle. Or maybe I'll bodyguard for juicy starlets, I don't know. Anyway, once I make enough money, I thought I'd buy a black BMW and tour the country fighting evil. Beat up on land developers and crooked aldermen. Make flame throwers out of egg timers and bubble gum, that sort of thing." Bob coughed, laughing around the stub of the joint. Rose lit a second. "Sound cool?"

"Sounds great," answered Randall. "But what are you really going to do?"

Rose shrugged. "Drink. Chase skirts. Suck blood. Hold up liquor stores." He blew a cloud of smoke at the ceiling. "I am who I am, you know?"

"Indeed." Randall inspected his knife. The blade shone from polishing, but the dark stain remained. He tucked it back into his boot. "What about you, Bob?"

The graying biker flicked the dead stub of the joint into the corner. "Not sure. To tell the truth, I wasn't positive we'd ever make it to this stage of the game. Maybe I'll sell my dealership, buy some land up north someplace, hang out by myself for a while. There's a lot of things you put aside when you figure you're short on time. Like when I was kid I wanted to play jazz clarinet. Never put the time in to learn how. Always seemed like there was something better to do just then. Maybe I'll learn now. If I don't like it, I haven't lost anything."

"It feels that way at first," Randall agreed. "But somehow, the things you put off never seem to get done. You change. Situations drift. People die. You miss times, opportunities. It isn't much different, really." He accepted the second joint. "It's just a life, like any other."

"Somber," said Rose, and giggled.

They were interrupted by a low hum from outside, which increased steadily in volume. A motorcycle flashed past the window, pipes booming. Randall stood. Another pair of Harleys sped out of sight along highway. The sound of approaching engines continued to grow. Randall dropped the joint at Rose's feet and headed for the door.

It looked more like a motorized attack than a caravan. The huge cycles clustered in formations of twos and threes, wingmen behind a leader, spaced out across both lanes of tarmac. Black panzer helmets flashed in the sun, erect spikes stabbing at the sky. Wave upon wave they came, appearing over the horizon a few seconds apart, in a ragged line that thickened as it passed. Randall stood in the swirling dust of the abandoned yard. He had counted nearly a hundred already, and still the formations tightened, grew closer and closer together. The cycles roared by for twenty minutes, some pausing to circle the house, throwing great clouds of sand into the air before rejoining the pack. One man sprayed the Barracuda with beer. Randall recognized Toad-Eater on his 1300 cc monster bike. Silverfish raised a hand in salute while Corrie clung to her waist. They tore around the house until the line thinned out, then rode away at its tail.

As the sand settled, the three men watched the last of the cycles disappear into the desert. "How many?" asked Bob.

"I counted two-hundred and thirteen," said Randall. "I'm not sure I got them all."

"Wow," said Rose, the joint dangling from his lips. "Is this even the same fucking planet we lit up on?"

Randall took the car keys from his pocket. "I don't think I care."

❦

It took Randall three days to transform all who had come. Bad Bob submitted first, and no one else dared to volunteer until he had arisen. The biker chieftain lay inert within the ridge fort of the Dolomite mine for two hours. During that time, Randall ran among the dunes of the canyon floor, venting the blazing energy the blood had given him. He returned when cheers sounded from the encampment above.

Randall worked as fast as possible, taking as many lives as he could stand to ingest at once and leaving the bodies at the top of the ridge. While they changed he ran mad circles around the camp, pursued by a pack of Harleys, pelted with bottles and empty cans. By night he leapt through the fires of dry sage and scrub brush that burned continuously in the darkness. Soon another group of men and women would ascend to the ridge fort, while the newly awakened dispersed among the hills in search of blood.

By the second day live game became scarce. Some of the bikers began to attack each other, while another group took to prying snakes out of their burrows. Randall paused in his furious dashes through the camp, ending fights and explaining the rules of immortal life as he knew them. And despite the shortage of blood, none of the transformed left the desert. They hungered while Randall gorged. Time blurred for him, until he could no longer remember how much he had fed, how long he had run. Randall stabbed himself with his blackened knife, burned himself with coals. The pain sharpened his focus on the moment. The rapid healing of his wounds helped to bleed off the intolerable heat that filled his body.

The blood began to sicken him. The fuel it gave to the fire inside tasted black on his tongue. He felt torn up from within, seared through by powers too great for the frame of his flesh to hold. Randall knew he had fed too much, that each fresh surge of life was now destroying him somehow. Soon, very soon, he felt certain that he would shatter like super-heated glass, melt like an overtaxed fuse. He did not expect to live to finish his work. But there came a time when no living men appeared to replace those fallen at his feet. Randall collapsed, crawled from the ridge fort into the sun, and vomited a stream of blood from mouth and nose that ran all the way to the canyon floor.

The last man awoke at noon on the third day, a heavyset stranger in standard biker garb. Randall followed him down the ridge. Flies swarmed up from a meandering line of darkened sand. The new immortals sat around the remains of fires, drinking and joking, tinkering with their machines. They rose as Randall passed and walked with him in a growing entourage. The camp broke up behind him as he went.

They found Rose sitting alone, stirring the ashes of a sage fire with a stick. His snub-nose .38 rested on his knee. "You've finished?" he asked without looking up.

"Yes." Randall kicked at the ring of scorched rocks, rolling their blackened sides into the sand with his boots. "Promise me you'll clean up when you've finished here. I hate to leave a mess."

"No problem." Rose unlatched the cylinder of his gun. The brass butts of new cartridges gleamed from the chambers. He snapped the weapon shut. "Sure you want me to do this?"

A sea of anxious faces surrounded them, more immortals than Randall had ever met in two centuries of living. Far more. Perhaps the largest number of his kind ever gathered together at once. The sheer number of his unfamiliar children thrilled and frightened him. "I can hardly back out now. I don't want to. I don't think they'd let me."

"Probably not." Rose smiled wryly. "No sense putting this off then, I suppose." He stood, the gun in his hand. The crowd behind Randall parted quickly to either side. The two friends regarded one another calmly across the shallow pit of ashes. "So what's it like?" Rose asked. "Death, I mean."

"You should know," Randall answered. "You've been there, too." He unsheathed his hardwood knife and held it out, handle first.

Rose accepted the blade, tucking it into his belt. "I don't remember."

"Neither do I." Randall turned and paced a short distance away. "You'll have to remind me." He removed his battered trench coat and tossed it to the crowd. A dark haired woman caught it and put it on, snarling at a man who held the sleeve. Randall turned out his pockets. A ring of keys fell to the sand, along with a small wad of British pound notes. "You'll have to leave me my boots," he said. "I'm not going to hell barefoot."

Rose thumbed back the hammer of his .38, the weapon held slack at his side. "Any last words?"

Randall thought for a moment, then began to laugh. "I can't think of a fucking thing," he said, "except goodbye."

"Guess that'll have to do." Rose raised the pistol, gripping it with both hands, and pulled the trigger.

The shot hit Randall right between the eyes.

When the body had fallen, Rose stepped up and emptied the revolver into its chest. He unlatched the cylinder, ejected the warm casings, and slipped them into the pocket of his leather jacket.

A man Rose did not know came out of the crowd with a Colt .45 automatic. He fired a round into the body, collected the shell, then holstered the gun at his hip and mounted a motorcycle. He kicked the engine into life and rode off down the wash toward the highway.

The fierce woman wearing Randall's coat appeared with a derringer. She left a single slug in the corpse and walked away.

One by one the bikers departed, each making their own wound in the body of their benefactor. Those without guns stabbed him with bowie knives or switchblades. Those without knives settled for a booted kick. When at last only Bob's clan remained, Randall's body had become a loose pile of torn, bleeding flesh.

They laid him on the bench seat of the Barracuda, siphoned the gas from the tank, and spread it over the car. Bob snapped on his silver lighter and tossed it over the windshield. The car burned with an intense heat. The red paint curled and disintegrated, the upholstery crackled. Thick brown smoke flowed out from under the hood. The headlights burst. The tires sagged. They stayed until the fire died out, and nothing but metal remained.

When the bones had cooled enough to touch, they buried them at the top of the ridge. All except the skull, which Rose placed on an arm of the rock chair, with the view of the canyon below.

They departed in darkness, Bad Bob in a sidecar, Rose on the back of Toad-Eater's mammoth Harley. Unable to link his arms around the man's waist, he clung to the tail of his coat. The blacktop flowed under them, taking them out of the wasteland.

epilogue

Rose checked into the motel alone, even though Bad Bob and Toad-Eater had ridden with him. The longhaired desk clerk did not seem to notice the two bikers loitering out front, or maybe he just didn't care. Rose took the key on its orange plastic ring, and the three men rode their motorcycles to the back of the building.

The room looked like every other motel he had ever seen. Worn carpet. Sagging bed. Thick, indestructible drapes. Television bolted to the wall. Rose dropped his pack, fished out his revolver and handed it to Bob. "Remember," he said, "if you hear me howling and snarling, don't open the door."

Toad-Eater took a hammer and a pair of boards from the side-pouches of his bike. "I don't think we'll forget."

"Good luck, Lon Chaney." Bob passed Rose a case of Tecate. "See you in the morning."

Rose took the beer. "This is all I get? I mean really, dawn is a good nine hours from now."

Toad-Eater slapped him on the shoulder. "Guess you'll just have to suffer." He gently pushed Rose inside, and closed the door.

Rose listened to them hammer, sealing him in. When the noise ceased, he lifted the drapes and looked outside. They sat on the concrete curb, their backs to the window. Rose let the drapes fall. He sat down on the bed and opened a beer, waiting for the moon to rise.

Acknowledgments

Okay, yeah, I wrote the words, but without the help of a lot of other people, they'd still just be a bunch of pages going brown in an old Assorted Teas box.

Before its current publication, **Wasting the Dawn** appeared as a series of chapbook/zines. Thanks to all the people who helped to produce the self-published version: Matt Micone, my wife Rebecca Smith, Eleonor England, Marla Mealey, Clay Tschudy, Tracy Sheppard, Shannon Grove, Brenda Cook, and Kate Kane. Special thanks to Tim Kane, who was, is, and always will be Rose.

A number of people reviewed the original incarnation of **Wasting the Dawn** in their own DIY publications. Thanks to: Heidi Preuss of *Requiem*, Eric Held of *The Vampire Information Exchange Newsletter*, Tim Emswiler of *Weird Times*, Juile Hoverson of *Serendipity's Circle*, and Catherine Krusberg of *The Vampire's Crypt*. Thanks also to Symon Brando of *Substance D* and Rod Marsden of *Prohibited Matter* for trading ad space halfway around the planet.

Big thanks to the retailers brave enough to sell this book before it had a barcode: Mysterious Galaxy of San Diego, Dark Delicacies of Burbank, Mark Ziesing Books up in Shingletown, and (of course) Comickaze in San Diego.

For the present edition, thanks to Ted Adams of IDW for taking this book to a larger audience than I had ever hoped to reach. A lot of gratitude and not a little amazement goes to Breed for his incredible interiors. When I look at his drawings, I can actually see what I wrote. Thanks also to Ben Templesmith for applying his considerable talents to the jacket. Finally, enormous thanks to Robert Scott for putting his time, energy, and money into this project when I could not afford to use my own. This one's for you, man.

David Hurwitz